T0354287

THE CASE FOR THE SECOND COMING AND NEW JERUSALEM

AMATERASU AND KALKI

iUniverse, Inc.
New York   Bloomington

The Case for the Second Coming and New Jerusalem

iUniverse books may be ordered through booksellers or by contacting:

iUniverse
1663 Liberty Drive
Bloomington, IN 47403
www.iuniverse.com
1-800-Authors (1-800-288-4677)

Because of the dynamic nature of the Internet, any Web addresses or links contained in this book may have changed since publication and may no longer be valid. The views expressed in this work are solely those of the author and do not necessarily reflect the views of the publisher, and the publisher hereby disclaims any responsibility for them.

ISBN: 978-1-4502-3466-5 (pbk)
ISBN: 978-1-4502-3467-2 (ebook)

Printed in the United States of America

iUniverse rev. date: 5/26/10

For Lilian and the Indigos

KALKI acknowledgements:

Over the years some people have championed my work, befriended me, housed me, fed me, had sex with me, entertained me, given me molecules that made me feel very good and smart, and even employed me. I am eternally grateful to the following people and entities:

Sir Marty, Otis and Verna, Dovus, Counting Water, Nicole D, Oliver, Dillon, Victoria J and Audrey G, Cousins Dale, Mike and Larry, Brother William, Sisters Patti and Teresa, Scott from StoneCat, Anya H., Tim from FunkBone, The Office Jesus Seth, T. Strednak, J. Brockner, C. Brandli, M. Parlin, G. Tavares, Root Bros, M. Korbel, Paintball/Kung-Fu Jonathan, Niece Jessica, Danny D and Seth from Fine Line, Susie Seitan, J. and B. Wech, Frank and Em from The Point, Gary "Stoma", Limner, Eli from the FL Pit, Jake, RoadRunner and Brit from Hudson St. '09, M. "Starky", and AJ – F**K Welbutrin!

RIP B. Reed, see you on the other side of the rainbow vortex.

A humble nod to the REAL Christian folks at Loaves-n-Fishes (proof beggars can be choosers and there is a free lunch), Catholic Charities (Thanks for helping with the back rent that time), and The Salvation Army.

These websites have been very cool: Resonance Project, Sacred Cow, Divine Cosmos, ZPenergy, Edison Nation, IUniverse.

The bands that have enhanced my life throughout the years in chronological order: WASP, Skinny Puppy, Ministry, Slayer, KMFDM, Fear Factory, Helmet, TOOL, Dimmu Borgir, Strapping Young Lad, Behemoth, Eluveitie, Arcturus, Aborym, The Berzerker.

The only girlfriends I ever had, Melisande and Annarose (I'm still honored you chose me). And a Special Thanks to my three myspace muses Redhead Becca, Rhiannon from Poland and Marina from NYC, your willingness to indulge me has healed my inner dork. My Celebrity Muse from the tender age of 13 - Milla J from Kiev, you actually got me through the worst years of my life. Most of all I must bow before Amaterasu whose heart and skills made this book possible.

AMATERASU acknowledgements:

First and foremost I acknowledge my father, who taught me the art of calculating probabilities. Also Robert Heinlein, Steven Barnes, Isaac Asimov, Robert Forward, among many great science fiction authors. Mary Catherine of the library, the good people at the Red Cross Homeless Shelter, Bill Hicks, and DMT. Gary McKinnon and all brave whistleblowers. Those in my family who kept the faith, and friends who helped me as they could. Marty for his medicine and Magic, keeping me sane. AboveTopSecret.com and all the discerning posters, Stephen Colbert, Dean Kamen, and Ian, who led me in good directions. And my inspiration and my light, Kalki.

Contents

INTRODUCTION

Amaterasu and Kalki are pseudonyms but also the preferred embodiment of our left hand path where we take on archetypal deities. The DSM (catalog of psychological pathology) does not have "christ complex;" the closest that psychology can come to us is eccentric (wacky but functional) and delusional (having exceptional goals). Amaterasu is an old school science fiction geek, Aquarius, born in '57. Kalki is a Gen-X "free energy messiah," Pisces, born in '75.

Our respective works are first and foremost masturbatory and self-referential. We really are seeking *our bliss* here...and we will not stop seeking until it is found. One place it won't be found is in the End Times section of your Christian book store.

The authors of popular eschatological books of late, both fictional and speculative, have profited from the inherent "fear porn" associated with antichrist and earthquake, and the self-righteousness associated with The Rapture.

This book is the only book that addresses The Second Coming and New Jerusalem; the

POSITIVE aspects of our transition. In regards to the utopian idealism and means of getting there, a critical question you must ask throughout is: **"Who could possibly oppose this?"** That also applies to some revisionism of physics theory/religion.

Amaterasu's story does not factor in any of what I offer in terms of the galactic cross event in 2012. This is important to make distinct. Revelation portrays New Jerusalem as some kind of heavenly crystalline construct that envelopes the earth allowing for a golden age of superpowers...OK, astro-quantum physics.

Let's say that's all bunk, that there will be no cosmic vetting or dimensional bifurcation of good souls from bad souls. If that's the case then humanity will have to unify under some new, and more importantly, *necessary* social structure and infrastructure. We must attack the future assuming that what I'm offering metaphysically is just another fairytale; we must evolve on our own because we can.

At first I was opposed to her secular vision of the future, even refusing to read her book because it did not star me... But then I finally read it and it moved me like I have not been moved since my Star Wars days. It was never her purpose in our Soul Trip to promote me but the future I can create. I'm all nuts and bolts, the means. It's her feminine touch that tempers my yang and gives it purpose. Honestly, and maybe this is my ego talking but, as cool as Judgment Day could be, I'd rather get through this without help from God, Aliens or simple celestial movement. I feel like humanity would be denied a chance to prove itself as a sane species – on the whole. Then again...perhaps it's had its chance.

Amaterasu's story is important because it comes from her heart, like most profound works, personal or otherwise, it incubated a long time then just appeared and spilled out like something wanting to be born. Years of science fiction reading have been distilled here, always asking *what if!* Her distinctly feminine sensuality (could it really be a golden age without food and sex?) contrasts with her Aquarian pragmatism; because of this she drives home the point that we can't separate human behavior and technology. As the book <u>SWITCH</u> teaches, it's a *situation* problem, not a *people* problem.

We listen to the "Bob and Tom" radio program sometimes in the morning, and there's a song we heard which goes, "Where the fuck is my jet pack?" This sums up our lives. I want to live in her world more than anything, and I know how to create it, which helps. I had lost sight of this "Abundance Paradigm" among the nuts and bolts, but now WE have a crystal clear vision of what benevolent use of advanced technology (either from me, history, aliens, black budget programs, accumulative academia or other mad scientists) can allow for – absolute freedom. The only reason you would think this future too fantastic to happen is because you have been immersed in its opposite for so long. Scarcity and entropy are synonymous and are the dominant paradigm. Why Satan should be upset that his time is ending, is beyond me. Surely he knew that is what would happen with entropy as the model.

There are certain aspects of Amaterasu's work I disagree with. I do not believe we need to get rid of currency but if we could, kewl. We need to integrate Capitalism, Socialism, and Communism openly and put that on a negentropic foundation. Throw in E-Govt and you have a living, adaptive socio-economic structure that is as Darwinian as it is Marxist – the sun shines on all, some will burn, others bask.

She wants to forgive the bad guys and that's a powerful thing but…I feel that only people that want to be forgiven should be. I also feel that forgiveness of this scale is between the bad guy and his creator – not my place to judge the continuity of an oversoul, just the stupid form it currently holds. If it were up to me I'd turn 99% of humanity into fertilizer, but that's just the wrath talking.

Amaterasu is the Shinto Sun Goddess – may her abundant light emblazon your mind and enchant your life.

THE ABUNDANCE PARADIGM

by Amaterasu

Introduction

To my reader, fellow Individual of Sentience,

I am finding it hard to reconcile what I see of people around me with what I see in the world.

Around me there are people who just want to get business done, to be left alone or to get together and shift consciousness.

Some groups shift consciousnesses in the spiritual vibration of shared dogma, others within the love and trust of the people they're with. Some choose the common vibration of a drug. Bars are a prime example, as are groups of friends passing around a joint.

And yet there are a relative few who are choosing to suggest that war is a solution. War on Drugs as much as War on Iraq. War is only a "solution" if there is money to be made. And though a Human heart would go to all costs to find a solution that did not justify a war, a Lizard heart would try to find a profit in war.

What I tried to do in my book is present why the differences between those I see day to day exist as they do, compared to people who choose to profit from war.

Some of what I present will sound "out there," I assure you, but I used these aspects to convey to you, my cherished reader, what we on our planet are now – and JUST now – in our history, capable of doing if we just... got the word out, and did it.

1

The Terra Papers, Gary McKinnon, the effort to "sanitize" the internet, and all other such specifics I bring up *are* on the internet, and I saw that they could explain things very well around me, and also saw the opportunity to build a solution around what I had with those data to consider.

The truth of these sources is yours to judge. Type them into search engines and you will find them – Gary is video, and the Papers are at freedomdomain.com. All I'm saying is that it does make sense. And I think we can make abundance happen, the truth of some things notwithstanding.

As for the efforts to take over the internet, read internet news and you will see stories about it in a number of places, with details you can look up.

The level of robotics is where we are at. Yes, now. The "locust-brained" robot exists. (That in quotes, because it is measured data from the impulses recorded from a locust and then used in the programming. NOT a real locust brain! [grin]) And I recently watched an awesomely nimble robot that righted itself, as it moved around, even after being kicked and nearly losing it. Just like a critter.

So I conclude that we have arrived.

The assertion that this planet has plenty comes from the fact that if each individual was given ¼ acre of land in Australia, there would still be a good chunk of Australia left over. And I thought, well, sure, not every ¼ acre is good to support a human off of – though a great many are – but then there's the whole rest of the world.

Combine this with energy from the plenum, and abundance shows its basic nature in the Universe.

So if you find things in my story hard to accept, understand that what I show you can be ours whether the "odd" things are true or not.

All I might ask of you, my dear reader, is to immerse yourself in the first two chapters, enjoying the scenery – put yourself in the experience – and brace yourself for The Diary in Chapter Three.

Then ask yourself when you are done reading what it is you would do if all transportation and tools were at your disposal, within informed willingness. Play an instrument? Play games? Sail on the seas? Make a comic book? Climb the Andes? Program a robot (open source, mais oui)? Box in a ring? None of these? All of them?

And then, if you understand the value of my book, allow it to touch many others.

Thank you for reading.

Amaterasu

.

Chapter 1

I finally crested that soft-gray world of half-sleep, stretching my every sinew under the luxury of silk satin. With eyes parted slightly, I looked around my terrace-garden room, breathing in the scent of lilacs and orchids and rich loam, listening to the song of the larks that made the zen-jungle of my house their home.

I had had the choice of whatever I wanted, of course, in devising my perfect house. I could have chosen anything – from a rustic cabin on Earth's surface up to a palace on the Moon or Mars. My choice had been this aerie which floated above the solid land of the planet's crust, with view of whatever beauty I chose to visit.

Built as a circle, the roof domed over the space in a crescent shape, leaving the center as a terrace to the outside world. Under the roofed portion, there were no walls, except at the perimeter, defining my studio, Lee's study and photo developing lab, and guest rooms. Under the main part, partitions stood, confining my bedroom, my bathroom, the kitchen, and dining room, with the living room open on the side facing the terrace. All the rooms were partitioned within my manicured garden-jungle, which had paved pathways running throughout, and sculptures in an Egyptian motif tucked here and there.

The windows and the terrace around the edge of my house were confined by an energy field, unseen but detectable to the touch. The field extended, completing invisibly the dome above.

I pushed away the sheet and sat, breathing deeply in satisfaction. Though I could have chosen to be cleansed, dressed and groomed by my robot valet, one of my many 'botties, there was something almost decadent in reaching for my robe and strolling to my cleansing fall – the waterfall and pool which holds hot water – to bathe myself. Stroking the cloth, so filled with sudsy sweetness, over my arms, legs and torso, I washed away what sweat and grime there was. I reveled in the application of cleansing cream, suited precisely for the skin I was born to, rubbing it, scrubbing it, into my face.

Floating in the pool, I rinsed myself, and then poured a generous amount of shampoo into my palm. The waist-length damp locks sudsed up as I applied the foamy liquid, and a sweet patchouli scent joined the earth-blossom richness of the surrounding flowers. I moved under the fall, which steamed as it fell, and rinsed the lion's mane I call my hair.

Stepping forth from my bath, I grasped the ultra-plush towel which sat ready on a shelf nearby, and smoothed it over my damp skin.

Rather than use the insta-dryer, which would, I knew, dry and brush (and even coif should I request it) my hair, I picked up the abalone brush I had found in that queer little ancients shop in Belize – I had seen it and asked if the owner would part with it. He had smiled and suggested a small painting by the Infamous Isadore Illumente (my humble self) would be perfect payment. I offered him his choice of the paintings I had done and were still mine to give, calling forth my holoport – my "holographic portfolio," for any distant historians – and, the shop keeper having chosen one (one of my darker ones called Struggling under Scarcity), the brush was mine.

Slipping back into my robe, I made my way to the terrace through my private jungle. The trees opened onto the wide, semicircular deck that seemed to drop off at the edge. A gentle breeze was detectable as I crossed the deck to the end of the stonework pavement and looked down. Below I could see the waters of the Colorado River winding through the walls of the greatest canyon on our planet. The walls, in fact, were higher than I was, though not by much.

Leaning against the force that kept me (and anything else) from falling over that edge, I began to brush out the kinks and snarls from my matted hair, taming the mane, allowing the abalone brush to separate the strands and facilitate drying. A long while I stood there against that invisible rail, feeling the sun and the breeze frolic in turn against my face and arms, teasing at the slit in my robe, carrying away the damp patchouli waters infusing my hair.

Looking out over the wide rift, looking mostly east, seeing the late morning sun splash the canyon into sparkles and shadows, I drank in the warming air. (I allow unfettered Earth air through my house whenever the weather is not inclement.) I saw a house floating along the river below, quite a bit lower down, moving downstream, and a short while later another

6

whizzed past silently overhead in a southwesterly direction. I breathed and brushed and blended with the sublime.

After my hair was fully dry, I turned from the Grand Canyon view, idly contemplating, as I walked back to the stone-paved path through the jungle, where it would be that I would choose to wake up the next morning, and thinking it would be nice to revisit that hidden canyon off the beach in Northern California called Fern Canyon. Of course, my domicile would not fit in that narrow opening, but I could surely lower the ramp to the beach and take a stroll there with Lee, avoiding the little stream that runs through the rock-littered white sand that lay between the sheer, dark dampness of the walls barely seen in glimpses through the thick fern growth that grew up and up and up the tall walls that allowed just a very little sky above.

Yes, I thought, that is where I want to go.

Reaching the mirrored alcove, I cast an eye over my appearance. Deciding I would like to have my hair put up, I sent the thought out, and the little 'bottie slipped silently into the alcove with me. Taking my imagery as its design, it busied itself lifting my tresses here, sweeping them there, and pinning them just so with the dazzling pearl-and-gold pieces given to me by Auntie Suzy.

Auntie Suzy is a jewelry designer. That is her bliss. She has made an estimated 500 thousand bits of jewelry, and though many have been traded away for things she wanted, most she took full pleasure in gifting to her friends and to those who expressed deep affinity for a given piece.

I sent a thought to the wardie – the wardrobe 'bottie – to create my garb for the day. The wardie used my images and produced (ala the replicator in the kitchen) the rugged khaki pants, replete with pockets, and the lavender blouse I had in mind. Taking pleasure in the dressing ritual, I sent a message to the valet 'bottie to stay put. I really don't know why I keep it around – I seldom need the speed it offers, and rarely use it.

The last bit of my attire was my Witness Necklace, of which I had several to match my outfits, all of which were artisan crafted. I selected a striking purple one from the collection and slipped it around my neck, settling the camera piece on my right shoulder, and closing the clasp. I always wore a Witness Necklace in public – most everybody chooses to do so, of course.

I reflected on the advantages the development of the Datacube technology offered (the technology which allowed plenty of storage to record every moment of one's life, and keep Calendar and other records of important data, such as who had created that lovely table I had seen at Programmer Art's place when Lee and I were there for Art's secondary skill, culinary requests from the replicator. Somehow Art had the knack of combining ingredients into gustatorial feats of magic).

Every individual could record their perspective in their personal Datacube, and no one had the right to the data recorded but the individual Itself.

Datacubes, of course, are unassailable. Amelia Ringer, bless her, I say, was instrumental in ensuring this for each one of us. She fought to make sure that it was understood in society that each individual owned their own perspective, outright and ultimately. She argued that if there is a dispute over any issue, anyone may release any part of the data they, themselves, have collected, and also cannot be forced to suppress what they know.

Amazingly, with that dual dam of data flow, where one cannot be forced to release one's data, yet could also not be forced to keep silent, incidents of dispute dropped as the practice of wearing some form of Personal Witness took hold, either overtly (as I wear) or covertly, as many chose in the beginnings of Datacube use. Most now wear their recording devices blatantly as a courtesy to inform others that their perspective is being recorded.

I choose to record what I do out and about; it is our right – or really, our protection – and I have captured some hilarious moments that I have shared at parties, making it all worthwhile. And besides, when I connect to the camera I can look through its lens, seeing where it points – even behind me – without turning around. Most people choose to wear Witness devices, and one presumed always that there were recording devices going everywhere in public.

My Datacube not only recorded my perspective, it gave my instructions to the various 'botties, and in general was the heart of my house. On top of that, I could communicate with it from anywhere on the planet.

Dressed for the day, I ask for my Calendar – a scheduler, it is really, for whether it was Monday or Saturday only made a difference in whether some art or activity was scheduled for that day, and not in things like whether there was something one HAD to do – like go to work or pay taxes. Though I remember quite well my plans for the day, there have been times I thought I did – remembered the plans – only to discover I had forgotten something, so I made it a habit to check just in case.

As the Calendar formed its holographic self where I expected it, in air over my lap, I leaned back into my favorite couch. It was an Old Thing, my couch – something that came from before the labor was done by 'botties, by someone's hand and attention – and thus to have found it was a stroke of luck for me. Most everyone I knew who cared about Old Things had at least one or two.

My sole Old Thing was my couch. It was deep maroon, a sort of Cleopatra's lounge affair. The brocade upholstery had held up well; it too was Old. The addition of some spun gold lace at strategic points hid well the fraying spots, and I could proudly say there was no stain that I could see. I had done the sewing-on of the accent gold myself, for I love to do that sort of thing now and then. The wardie created the exquisite lace to my concept, and the result pleased me.

It sat in the living room, against the partition furthest from the terrace, with palms standing in back of it on either side. Pots with gardenia growing clung to the partition, in between which ran a small trickle of splashing water which fell down a staircase of protrusions from the wall that the partition provided, resulting in a quiet slip down the wall punctuated by a soft giggle of particularly exuberant fluid.

The Calendar displayed my expectations: the theatre guild was showing the latest of Ogden Pierce's plays, but I wasn't in the mood. Maybe next week… There was the bazaar, as usual this time of the cycle, and I thought it was a good possibility I might go. But really, today was not the day I looked at. It was tomorrow's single item that tickled my eyes. Tomorrow Lee would be home.

Lee was my love, and through all the years we had known one another, Lee always came back to me. He loved to go on photographic shoots in the wilds of the planet that seemed to move below me as the house made its way gracefully through the air, heading for the northern coast of California. I had a number of my favorite of Lee's photographs in my gallery here, in the spaces below my house; we intersperse our respective art there, and offer much of it for view should anyone ask. Much of our work was often used by those whose bliss was to publish nature journals or educational material, in Lee's case, or offered in holoart groups on the web, in both our cases.

Lee had no house, though if he wanted one, he could surely have had one. He liked my house and was content to call my house his home. I, in turn, adored it in him that he was so happy to call my house his home.

After thought, I decided that I would spend only a little time at the bazaar, and come home to my own bliss – painting.

I got up and made my way out of my sanctuary, down the jungle-path hall to the J.D. The Jump Door was encircled with Egyptian themed symbols and icons. Sculptor Jed had offered to decorate the portal and, I must say, I found it to be a perfect addition to the garden that surrounded it. With intent in mind, with the place I was headed to, I stepped through the portal.

I looked around and took in wares, spread out on the steps and tables that were formed in a long river below me in the open free mall. This was a place that more often was a maze that lovers and children wandered through or played games in, but this cycle day, it was filled with the work of artisans. I stood at the top of the winding path, looking at all the New Things. All the things, created from love, by the proud Merchants languishing in repose, or seated in conversation with a prospective taker. Or perhaps animated, and inviting a look from those who passed by.

I had chosen the entrance at the top of the mall, liking the down-hill slope of the stroll through the seats and tables and alcoves used to display work and choose owners. There was much to see, laid out: jewelry and furniture and hand-sewn clothing, sculptures and paintings and decorations of all kinds. I thought it might be soon that I would bring my paintings here again to offer in their original to exchange and gift.

Around me swirled many a shopper, showing delight over this thing or that, with Merchants drawing them in for conversation and gifting. Now and again a Merchant expressed doubt that the shopper was the right one to receive their special creation. The shoppers would sometimes state their case for their appreciation and perhaps the Merchant would change his or her mind. Often the shopper would reconsider their desires and agree with the Merchant, moving on.

After some minutes perusing, my eye was caught by a fountain, which seemed to combine water and somehow light in ways that the light caught the water, cupping it with no discernable bowl yet holding it still, and then tossed it in arcs and streams and sprays to again be caught or showered downward in gemstone hues.

Seeing my gaze, hearing perhaps my gasp of delight, the Merchant approached me.

"Do you see something that appeals?" she asked.

I smiled. "Yes, I do indeed! That fountain is lovely!"

The Merchant smiled in return. "Who might I be having the pleasure to give this work to?" she eagerly inquired.

"I call myself Izzy," I replied, "but I am called by others, 'Infamous Isadore Illumente.'" I cast my eyes downward, a bit modest of the name. It was given to me when I was a wild and crazy teen, and though I wouldn't say I had done anything really infamous, the title stuck and I chose it as my Web Name. "And you, what name do you have, Artist-Merchant?"

"I'm Fleur d'Eau to many, but I call myself Flo." Flo's smile brightened. "'Izzy,' you say? Then Izzy I shall call you! Come here and sit, Izzy. Let's talk a bit." She reached for my hand and I was led to a curved seat along the mall's edge on the other side of the fountain.

Together we sat, and I learned that Flo was a water-and-energy sculptor, she had two children who usually were there to help her find the right recipient of her work (and who offered a piece or two of their own, now and then) named Sam, who was 13, and Dee, who was 8 – Sam had found a name as SoundMan Sam Hobson, as his bliss was music, and often he was asked to play at celebrations. Dee was still dallying with things, finding her bliss. At the moment, though, they had both chosen to see what was out there in the bazaar and had gone off, promising not to be long.

Flo's partner Jacob, the father of Sam and Dee, was exploring the solar system and would be back in six months. Flo and the kids missed him a lot.

Flo learned that I had not yet chosen children, but that I had Lee in my life, and we might some day choose children. We talked about the play by Pierce, and soon discovered we both had seen many of the same works. I suggested that we might meet up at Pierce's play, with any of our friends and family who wanted to come along – Flo said it would be just her and her daughter, as Sam was not very interested in plays unless they were musicals – on the third day of the cycle next. I had brought up my Calendar and, seeing the spot open, I had suggested it. Flo, checking hers, agreed, happy that her time was free then too.

I made the note, offering to pick up the tickets for the four of us, and smiled back as she looked up from making note as well.

"Flo, I thank you for your lovely work. There is a place in my garden that will set it off perfectly."

Flo smiled. "The way your whole being lit up when you saw it, I just knew I had made it for you." She took my hand and leaned in to me. "Thank you for appreciating it."

I squeezed her hand, smiling back, and said nothing.

"Well, where shall I send this?" Flo asked as she stood.

Joining her in standing I gave her the picture-key through the co-ord 'bottie she gestured to, thinking the code image quickly and concisely. A moment later the lovely fountain was picked up by the Movers, a couple of the all around lift'n'tote 'botties, and they headed towards the nearest J.D.

I smiled and continued along the path after a final exchange of thanks. Little else stood out at all, and none I felt the need to have in my life. As I walked the first few paces, I gave placement orders to my house for the fountain, envisioning it standing where I thought would best suit both the garden and the fountain, and knew that all would be where I saw it in my mind when I got home.

I passed a band playing music with happy abandon, while many stopped to dance or listen. Perhaps SoundMan Sam had taken up with others to create this sound and one of the players I heard was him.

A short while later I tired of looking and listening, being hungry now, and yearning to paint – something, anything… Whatever came out on the canvas.

Seeing a J.D. handy, I held the vision of my memory key strongly in my mind – the image of a special moment in my life, that told my home J.D. that it was me – and stepped into my house. I had given that key to my Datacube when I first had my home constructed, and it could recognize my image no matter if I was sober or (seldom) intoxicated. I never feared that someone would want to "break in," as they called it in the Old Days. Whatever for? Sure, someone might covet my Old couch, I suppose, or one of my original paintings. But if someone wanted my Old couch badly enough to implore me for it, I would willingly let it go to them, for it must mean more to them than to me. And if anyone asks for my paintings, I am honored.

Asking for the fruits of another's Love labors is the most common method of trade, though many times the Laborer offers Its creations and they are usually taken gracefully.

I breathed deeply the scent of my garden, my jungle, then stepped along the path to the kitchen. I knew I could have a meal, in perfect prime and preparation, laid before me, but I found cooking a pleasure and usually did not rely fully on the replicator and serving 'botties.

I wanted something simple… To the replicator I asked, with visions of shell and yolk and clearness, for three eggs. And then a handful of truffles, some butter freshly churned, scallion and garlic, cream and cheese. I pulled the copper bowl from its place in my cupboards, and my whisk as well. Breaking the eggs, I whipped, the shells being tossed into the M.W.D. – the Molecular Waste Disposal, sort of a reverse replicator.

Setting aside the eggs, I chopped the truffles, the scallion, the garlic. Returning to the eggs, I added cream and whipped. And whipped a bit more.

Next a skillet came out of my cupboards, and onto the heat it went. Butter was melted and the chopped morsels leaped to a sizzle as I added them, stirring them, coating them in creamery goodness. As brownness set in to the scallions and garlic, I scooped out a spoonful to set aside, and turned once more to the eggs, and whipped again, then poured them into the truffles and scallion and garlic.

The heat I turned down, and a lid I laid upon the top.

While the eggs slowly hardened, I grated the cheese – a mellow swiss – and then peeked at the eggs. They were rising, like a flat soufflé, and I sprinkled most of the cheese over the fluffy surface, returning the lid to its place.

For a moment there was nothing to do, so I sent an image of my table in the dining area, set but lacking a plate, to my Datacube, my house, and knew the proper 'botties would be sent to do the bidding. Then I peeked again at my omelet to see the cheese well melted.

I pulled the skillet off the heat, removing the lid, and pulling a plate from my cupboards. I slid the omelet out of the skillet and onto the plate, neatly folding it as I did so. Cheese oozed from the edges invitingly. I sprinkled the creation with the last of the cheese, and then slapped the spoonful of truffle reserve upon the very top. My mouth was watering.

I lifted the plate, calling assurances to the 'botties that cared, that the kitchen could now be cleaned, and then moved into my sunny spot with a crystal-topped table, which was set for one, sans plate. I placed the plate in its appointed spot and sat. Again, I breathed deeply, and looked at last in the direction of the fountain, given in delight by Flo. It stood in a shady spot, all the better to draw attention to the light as it played with the water.

The scent of the truffles mingled with the rich aroma of the jungle that grew in my house. And I began my repast.

After breakfast, I made my way to my studio. There stood my easel, with a canvas in pristine white propped in place, waiting for my creativity to spill forth. A palate rested on a small table next to the easel, with tubes of paint, rags, cleaners, brushes, and spreaders in easy reach. So focused I was on the object of my creative outlet, I hardly noticed the rest of my sunny room: the hardwood floors in a pale ash, the wide windows that looked out on the sky and the horizon, the seats beneath the windows, the shelves and drawers containing books – mostly for reference – and other supplies.

I wrapped a smock around me and sat upon the stool, which placed me in front of the canvas and in arm's reach of the palate and supplies. In my mind's eye I saw a young girl, smiling, glowing with innocent pleasure as she lifted a tolerant cat above her in her hands. With this picture burning in my head, I laid the first strokes of paint, and as the hours – which seemed to me mere minutes – passed, the girl and the cat she loved formed before me in paint and bliss.

Chapter 2

I began the day much as I had the day before, but that I did not consult my Calendar. I knew I had left it blank but for Lee's return. I expected him in the late morning – his email had said that he would be at a J.D. by then, down in Ithaca, New York. And then he would be here.

I busied myself looking for things to straighten up, clean, or otherwise put to rights, but of course the house 'botties had ensured that nothing was amiss, and so the moving of pillows and shifting of bric-a-brac were arbitrary, and merely offered my hands something to do.

As I was exercising what patience I could muster, the house announced that Lil, my best friend, was calling. By all means, I responded in my head, bring her in. Lil's holographic self appeared in the room with me, and I smiled widely.

Lil was the first to speak. "Izzy! Is he home yet?" She knew that Lee was expected home, but also knew the time would depend on when he managed to get to a J.D. from the wilds of the surface.

"Not yet, Lil," I replied. "But I just know it will be soon. What's up?"

"Well," Lil eagerly responded, "I was thinking we could get together, the four of us, and maybe spend time at the Pyramids sometime today. I mean, after you and Lee…reacquaint yourselves…" Lil grinned and winked.

I laughed. "That sounds wonderful! Which Pyramids did you have in mind?" I thought she might have the Asian or the Mayan pyramids in mind, but I rather knew she meant the Egyptian ones.

Sure enough, Lil said, "The ones in Egypt." She rolled her eyes and shook her head with a smile that betrayed the mock disgust in me as being a friendly jab.

"Well, I wasn't sure. There ARE many others to choose from," I said with equal mock archness.

Lil nodded, grinning, and moved on. "So what is Lee taking pictures of this trip?"

"He mentioned something about 'poverty ruins,' but he often finds something to distract himself from the stated goal, so I am never sure until he returns and shows me."

Lil giggled. "So you have more to look forward to than just Lee, eh?" Her hologram raised a teasing brow in my direction. I laughed and assured her that I would let her know when Lee and I were done with our reacquaintance, and we could iron out the specifics of time and J.D. location then. After agreeing, Lil's hologram vanished, and I was left again to plump and adjust pillows, and poke around my displays of things for a more aesthetic arrangement.

Half an hour later Lee walked into my house. With sounds of delight we were in each other's arms, kissing and entwining our arms and legs.

Lee is tall, 6'1", with dark chocolate skin. His eyes are blue – strikingly so – and his build is slender. He is a counterpoint to my fair skin and dark eyes. And though we both have black hair, mine is long and straight to his tight, short curls.

After our enduring embrace, Lee pulled back and said, "I found something this time I think you would be interested in." Though he tried to deliver this in a nonchalant way, I could sense the excitement he was concealing.

"What is it?" I asked, responding to the excitement, rather than the forced nonchalance, rubbing my hands together in anticipation.

"Here," he offered, as he reached into his pack, which he had laid upon the sofa, and drew out a plastic-wrapped bundle. It was rectangular and flat, and rather small.

Taking the prize from his hands, I turned it over, but the opposite side gave no further clues. I saw that the outer plastic was an Old-style zipper-closed bag, and through its rumpled clearness, I could see another plastic covering inside. Looking up at Lee, I beamed a smile, and then cracked the zipper, pulling out what felt like a book within the thin brown plastic bag – an Old shopping bag, a very minor Old item; like the zipper bag, it was rather ubiquitous, so many having been made back in the overall scarcity Humans once struggled within.

I glanced again at Lee to see the excitement and anticipation break forth on his features, and then I opened the brown plastic. Inside was what appeared indeed to be a book, with a dark blue binding. It was Old, that was certain, and as I looked the cover over, I could just make out a single word on the cover: Diary.

"A diary?" I asked. "Whose? And where did you find it?"

Lee replied, with clear thrill to be telling me this, "It seems to be the diary of Amelia Ringer."

I widened my eyes in amazement. "THE Amelia Ringer?" Lee nodded eagerly, clearly enjoying my pleasure. "So where WAS it? How did you find it???" I entreated.

"Well, I was doing a shoot of the poverty ruins where she lived – I didn't tell you because it was going to be a surprise – and hoped to capture information about her for you. I guess I hit the jackpot." I nodded vigorously, as Lee continued, "Anyway, the house is well into decay at this point. And when I was moving across the floor of her bedroom, a couple of the boards gave way – nearly broke my ankle, I tell you! – and I saw the bag poking out from under the rotting wood. Seems the hidden space in the floor was where she hid her diary."

I looked down at the book I held, imagining Amelia lifting the corner of a concealing rug, perhaps, and opening the small, hidden panel to tuck her diary safely away from prying eyes. "Awesome," was all I could say.

Then gingerly I opened the cover and revealed a yellowed bookplate stuck to the first sheet of paper. An image of a girl, in an Old-style pale blue dress with puffy sleeves, petticoat peeking, as she reclined on her stomach in green grass and read a red book, with her legs bent at the knee and crossed at the ankle above her back, graced the top of the bookplate. Below this blond-haired young girl were printed the words, 'This Book Belongs To,' and below that, on a line provided, was written in a gentle script, 'Amelia Ringer.' My heart skipped a beat.

Again I looked at Lee. "What a find! This we shall have to offer to the Museum…but not until I read it, first!" Lee grinned and I grinned too.

I gently returned the book to the bags, zipping the outer one closed. "Well, this can wait a short while. I arranged with Lil to go to the Pyramids – in Egypt – tonight…if that is of interest to you…" Lee gave a good-natured nod. "And after I properly welcome you home, of course. That being what I want to do now." I gave him an impish look, and he drew my meaning precisely. As he reached for my hand, I set the diary of Amelia Ringer on a nearby table, and together we made our way to my bed.

Later, as we bathed away the heat of our passion beneath the waters of my fall, I asked, "Did you read any of the diary?"

Lee poured water over my shoulder and breasts, taking a moment to reply. "Actually, I just glanced over the pages. I thought it would be most enjoyable to read the entries together." I smiled and nodded earnestly. Lee knew of my…great interest in Amelia's history – ok, that was an understatement, my interest. And so I felt a warm streak of appreciation that he wanted to share my delight in his find, his gift to me.

"I better call up Lil and let her know we will be ready soon," I commented as I reluctantly pulled myself from the waters of the bathing pool and let the fall pour its rinsing cleanness over my body. Lee remained reclined but I knew he would soon follow.

Deciding to opt for expedience, I sent the proper images to the wardie and 'botties to dress me in rugged wear, appropriate for hiking around, as well as a plain, bound hairstyle to keep my tresses from catching and tangling. An equally plain and rugged Personal Witness piece was to be placed on my shoulder. Moments later I was tended to with the clothes and items I had requested and the style of dressed hair I wanted, and then I was ready to call Lil.

I asked the holophone to connect me, and after a short wait, Lil appeared as she had before. I knew that at her end, I was standing in her house as she was standing here in mine.

"Hey, Izzy! Ready for the adventure?" Lil's happy tone filled the room.

I nodded with enthusiasm. "We are indeed! Who all is going at your end? Still just you and Nassim? Or did you round up others since we last spoke?"

"Still just the four of us," Lil replied. "I wanted this to be more of a sharing and less of a party, eh?"

Nodding, I agreed. "Yeah, too many and the time with Lee would be limited. Thanks, Lil."

"Not a problem, kid," she said kindly. "I know it's been a while since you two have been together, and I didn't want to clutter your time too much."

"Well, shall we use the J.D. near the Sphinx? Start there and then head for the Pyramids? In, say, half an hour?" I wanted to make sure Lee had time to dress as he preferred, which is to say, without the 'botties.

"Sounds like a plan, kid. See you there and then!" Lil waved.

"Oh, and wait till I tell you what Lee found on this trip!" I added before she could leave. She hesitated, a brow lifted in inquiry. "Well, you'll hear all about it soon."

"Brat!" Lil exclaimed teasingly.

"Yep," I agreed, with a wink. "See you soon, Lil." And I left the connection. Her hologram winked out.

Shortly, Lee came in, dressed as ruggedly as I was, yet carrying the look with a debonair grace, as he managed to carry in most anything he wore – or didn't wear.

"Ten minutes till we have to be there," I announced. Lee nodded once and then pulled me into his arms to kiss me for most of that time. Finally I broke from his kisses and said, "Sphinx J.D." He nodded again, and we went to the J.D. He motioned for me to go first, and I stepped through the J.D. into Egypt.

I quickly moved off the landing there, making room for the next arrival, which was Lee, and we looked around for Lil and Nassim.

"Guess we're first," I remarked. Lee wrapped an arm around my shoulder as we took in the morning light, as well as the general bustle in the area. Though it had been well after nightfall where we had been, here the sun peeked brightly from the eastern horizon. Several people we did not know, but exchanged smiles with, walked through the static-curtain of the J.D. and moved off in their own directions. And then Lil walked through. She smiled brightly and came towards us, hugging first me and then Lee. We turned to watch the J.D. together.

Another stranger, smiling to us as she passed by, came through, and then Nassim stepped out. Whereas Lil was tall and fair, with blond hair that loosely curled, Nassim was shorter – nearly as short as myself – and had close-cropped, brown hair and olive complexion. He, too, came and bear-hugged both Lee and me, as we exchanged the greetings of friends.

Together we headed towards the Sphinx, looking in awe at the remains of the stone creature and marveling at how wrongly an age we Humans had been told this very ancient work was and, despite the evidence, we had blithely accepted. As we walked, Lil could contain herself no longer.

"So, Lee… Izzy said you found something interesting on this last trip of yours. I gathered it was something out of the ordinary. What could a photographer find of interest except interesting things to take pictures of?"

I watched as Lee looked first at me with a flash of mock reproval – I knew it was mock, because I knew he was looking forward to announcing his find – and then turn to Lil to answer. He launched into the story of what he was photographing, what happened with the floorboards, what he saw and picked up out of the hollow beneath, and ending with a description of what it was and who wrote it.

Like me, Lil asked, "THE Amelia Ringer?" Nassim mouthed the question silently, in near sync with Lil's voiced question, his eyes widening even as the implications hit him.

"The Amelia Ringer," Lee confirmed, without the stressed word.

I added, "Yes. THE Amelia Ringer! I held the diary in my hands and read the bookplate! Isn't that awesome?!?"

"Well, what does it say…I mean, anything new to add to her story?" Nassim asked.

"We don't know yet," I jumped in ahead of Lee as he opened his mouth to respond. "We're going to read it together."

Lil sighed, smiling. "You two are just too romantic!"

"I promise we'll keep you two posted," I offered eagerly.

"You'd better," Lil said, and Nassim's body language echoed. "Or else!" Lil added with a wry grin. I laughed and Lee smiled widely.

We took the tour of the Sphinx and walked over to the Great Pyramid, quite a trek, really, and I was glad to have the shoes I had chosen. After touring this wonder as well, we agreed we were all hungry. Lil smiled her mischievous smile and mentioned that Chef Allouba – THE Chef Allouba – had offered his personal table to us, the table he saved for short notice friends, in his Moroccan Bistro. She had taken the liberty to contact him and make the reservations.

Lee and I were delighted. I love Moroccan food as does he, and we had never had the honor to sit at Chef Allouba's table. But I had heard that Chef Allouba was the best. He used actual Earth food, even though the replicated food had just as much essence energy, nutritional value, taste and looks as real Earth ingredients, but it was his purist nature coming to play that he chose to keep it all from nature. It was part of his artist's pallet, just as my paints were of mine.

Together we looked for the nearest J.D. as Lil mentally sent the Chef's Invitation, via the house-web system, so that we all could wind up in the same place, and the J.D. on the other side would welcome us. Finding one nearby, we took our turns passing through the portal.

Chef Allouba's place was marvelous, built high on a mountain, with a view as wonderful as any from the heights my own house might attain. Gold curtains segmented areas with cushioned benches around large circular brass tables. Done in muted magenta and goldenrod, with upholstery in ornate design reflecting these colors, as well as teal and yellow, the place was rich in character. Old Things of Moroccan make accented the walls here and there, and oil lamp chandeliers hung down above the tables from the very high ceiling, giving intimate lighting and an authentic incense from the scented oil in the lamps.

Chef Allouba, who I recognized from holograms I had seen on the web, greeted us soon after we arrived.

"Lil, darling. It is a pleasure to meet you in the flesh," the Chef announced as he moved to embrace her in greeting. "And you must be the reunited lovebirds!" Chef had turned to Lee and me with merry and welcoming eyes, as we smiled in return and touched shoulders in a subtle subconscious display of conjoined spirit. First me and then Lee received his embrace, and then he turned to Nassim. "Ah, Nassim. So glad you could join me once again!" And again, his warm embrace came, this time for Nassim.

After a few words of thanks from all of us for opening his home to us, the Chef led us to our table, through a path between curtained alcoves, fountains, and inviting aromas, where we settled in. "I must be off to my bliss, making food for you to enjoy. Here is Sarah who will serve you," Chef Allouba said as a pretty woman stepped into our alcove, dressed in traditional Moroccan garb. "She is a very special lady and I am lucky she came to my service." As Sarah smiled, Chef Allouba departed.

Sarah had brought with her a stand supporting an ornate, enameled bowl atop. She set it before us and ducked out, returning with a tall silver ewer and a tray of finger towels. Nassim reached his hands out over the bowl and Sarah poured rose water from high up in a stream over Nassim's hands. He rubbed and cleansed his hands and then reached for a towel, wiping the moisture away.

Taking Nassim's cue, I held my hands out and felt the warm, sweet waters splash enjoyably onto my hands and through my fingers. Having ablated, I too took a towel and watched as Lee and then Lil did the same.

As she was pouring the aromatic water, I asked Sarah how she came to offer her services to Chef Allouba in this capacity. It is unusual to have serving staff in human form. Most places use 'botties for service. Sarah smiled and explained that she loves facilitating such experiences, and besides, she admitted, she got the best Moroccan food on Earth! All the time! I laughed, and we all thanked her warmly for her service.

As we chatted and laughed, happy in one another's company, Chef Allouba began sending, via Sarah, dish after dish of fragrant, pungent, sweet and tart and savory delights for us to eat. Lamb and couscous, mint and pears, figs and apples, came in dish after dish, set upon the table, and eaten by all of us with our fingers. All was very traditional, and very delightful.

Sarah also poured glasses of a sweet wine, an aromatic tea, a strong coffee as the meal progressed and as each of us might want.

In the middle of the meal, belly dancers and a troupe of musicians made their way into our little space, and we gleefully applauded, commenting on the delicate design of the outfits the dancers wore, and laughing in our joy and camaraderie. The enjoyment the performers were experiencing was evident. They were in their bliss.

As the performers smiled and left to entertain other guests, with thanks for our appreciation and attention, I brought up my Calendar above my lap and asked Lil, "Hey, what are you doing here?" as I pointed to a day a couple of days ahead. "We're going to the fireworks show in San Francisco and I was hoping you could come over."

Lil brought up her Calendar and wrinkled her nose. "Sorry, Izzy. I have plans to be with Rajid Gupta for his class in jewelry-making – I couldn't believe he had an opening and I got in! – and Nassim will be giving a lecture in London on his theories in particle physics. Wish we had the time free, though. I LOVE fireworks!"

"Maybe next year," I suggested as I shrugged and shut off my Calendar. "It's really spectacular. And gets more so every year!" I grinned.

"Next year for sure!" Lil promised.

When the last crispy, cinnamoned piece of the dessert was being consumed, Chef Allouba returned, seating himself with us. Sarah, too, joined us, as 'botties quietly snuck in and cleared away the dishes that remained, the crumbs and the spills, and also offering steaming towels to clean again our hands.

"So, I presume the meal was satisfactory, my friends?" the Chef inquired through his wide and welcoming smile.

"More than merely satisfactory!" I exclaimed. "Thank you so much, both of you…ALL of you," I said, waving my arm to include the performers, though they were gone from our alcove now.

Sarah showed her pleasure at the exuberant compliment, and replied, "Thank you. You were a joy to offer service to. Truly, I enjoyed myself immensely to see your enjoyment."

Nassim spoke, "A wonderful experience as always, Joe." That must be Chef Allouba's personal name, I thought. I did not realize that Nassim was so close to Chef Allouba, but that explains why his wife had no trouble setting this meal up. I had initially thought we might check the Web for places serving their fair in Cairo to keep the Egyptian theme going, but I thought this was better.

We chatted a while with Chef "Joe" Allouba and with Sarah (she insisted that that is the only name she has). Then the Chef took his leave to chat with others he had welcomed to enjoy his cuisine. Sarah led us back to the J.D. and we decided that it had been a long and enjoyable while. Lee was tired in particular, having spent the morning hiking back to a J.D. from the poverty ruins, and hiking the plaza at Giza. We decided we would call one another soon and meanwhile we would rest. Oh, and read the diary to report on, of course.

With final thanks to Sarah, and to be relayed to The Chef and the performers, we returned to our respective homes.

Chapter 3

The following morning I made breakfast, and, with the help of a 'bottie, I served it to Lee in bed, climbing in next to him and tucking the silk of the sheets around me. I loved to see his pleasure taken from my efforts, and if he had had none, I would not have bothered. But he savored each bite, and thanked me more than once. When the 'bottie had cleared things away, we made love again, with passion as great as when he first returned.

As we lay there in the gentle warmth of the afterglow, kissing each other's noses, eyelids, and shoulders, I asked, "Is it time to read the diary?"

Lee smiled lazily, looking into my eyes. Finally he released me from his arms and stretched, then said, "Yeah. I think so."

I called a 'bottie to bring the book and moments later it arrived. We propped our backs up with pillows and I carefully removed the diary from its plastic covers, setting it between us. With respect and a gentle hand, I opened the diary to the first page, and we began to read:

October 7, 2008

I begin this diary today because it occurred to me that someday my efforts in this world might be of interest. Why? Because I find myself with Big Ideas (ok, that's how I think of them, at any rate; I see where they could lead us on this planet, and it sure looks awesome to me) and a notion of how to set them into play. And if I succeed, some might want to see what happened from my own perspective.

I found this book, blank pages and all, in the hall at Loaves and Fishes – Ithaca's version of "soup kitchen." There it was sitting on the back table for any who wanted it to take. And I wanted it, so I took it. Sometimes something of surprising quality shows up on that table, and I thank in my heart those who provide these things to those like me who are struggling.

Let me explain my life situation as it is now. I am broke and homeless. The Red Cross is making sure I have a place to sleep, and I go to Loaves and Fishes five days a week for the meal they serve, as well as the donated items they lay out on the back table. The community there is awesome, and though I do not share the dogma of many, I share the spirit fully.

This is a far cry from where I once was. Once I was making $60,000 a year working for a military contractor as a civilian. But when 9/11 happened, the contracts for what I was doing – graphics for interactive software to teach recruits how to operate military devices and machinery – those contracts dried up. And when they dried up, and I found myself out on the post-9/11 job market... Which is to say, I discovered that there were no jobs to be had. No one was hiring, and things in my life deteriorated from there. And here destitute I sit with what sure seems like Big Ideas.

Let me tell you about my Big Ideas...

It has occurred to me that we sit at a point in our history, for the first time in our history, where we can cast off human slavery to machinery. We now have what it will take to mechanize all the mind-numbing work, the heavy labor, the dirty and undesirable work. But there are problems, obstacles to this goal.

It is true that Nikola Tesla devised a way to pull free energy from the vacuum – which is really a plenum, an opposite of a vacuum where energy seethes in abundance. They (and there is a They who would control us) have kept this energy from us. And the reason it was hidden away, the reason so many human advances have been hidden away, is because if we had the power and the cures and the life extensions and all the other solutions that have been suppressed and hidden...They would have no power over us.

They could not bleed us of our money – for energy to run our cars and our appliances, our heat and our cooling, for "medicines" that leave us with more issues than we started with, and in turn we spend all the more to "treat" the added problems, for stop-gap measures such as skin creams and potions and other "rejuvenation" scams.

They would have no power over us.

So we have the technology to build the machinery to do what needs to be done, and there is energy to make it happen. And this is unique in our history.

There are multitudes of ways to bring harmony and health to each and every one of us. But most people don't know about these things, believing in the scarcity and lack of development that we are told to believe in. Most will not believe that free energy is a reality, and won't until it breaks the surface of popular awareness. As long as it is kept secret, we as a whole can be kept…powerless.

But yet… There is the Internet. The Internet is our hope, and They know this. Already They are seeing us use it to spread information…and They are very scared of what this might mean. They are trying to take control of the information flow, removing net neutrality.

So something has to be done – SOON!

I looked at Lee. "Good thing something was done," I remarked. "Otherwise we would not be where we are today."

Lee nodded. "A very good thing indeed!" We both knew that plans had been in the works to kill off most Humans, enslaving the remainder through mind control, mind wipes, and propaganda. The vision had been to kill most of us, through disease, starvation, "natural" disasters designed by evil, power-hungry beings and executed through HAARP and other facilities – and then to take the few "pleasing" humans underground while the Earth healed, to emerge when the planet had become livable again.

Of course, that did not happen – because of Amelia and her Ideas. We read on.

December 28, 2008

Well, I didn't really think this would be a daily thing. Besides, writing about the mundanities of my life doesn't interest me, nor is it likely to interest any reader. Suffice it to say that I found a job – doing production work at one of the local papers – and got an apartment. Roaches and fleas infest the place, and the kitchen sink is filthy. The previous tenant, I am told, was a crack dealer and who knows what else. So who knows what they did in that sink. But it is a home I can afford and is better than sleeping on the streets in New England's winter.

Anyway, I write here now because I wrote an article about what we could do, what humanity could do now, with the level of technology we have. In the article I described a world where robots tended our fields and gardens... I wrote of land, even what to us might seem marginal land because of its location, plowed by robots, planted by robots, and tended by robots. Machines, maybe a hive of a thousand, double the size of a tarantula, for each acre, removing any need to use human labor as they plow, plant, water, weed, and remove insects from the parts of the plants we eat. Programs that prune as needed, water as needed, and then, of course, harvest when ready. There would be larger specialty robots – those that carry the harvest bounty in large loads out of the fields to a storage or immediate use distribution. With this degree of attention, virtually all of the crop would be marketable.

And then the robots would mulch the remainder, preparing the fertilizer for the next crop.

Designed to rotate crops in the most efficient way such that the soil is never depleted and it needs no petro-help, the robots would fill our fields with organic, healthy crops. Robots would clean and gently transport our food-stuffs to us. Other robots could prepare our foods if we didn't feel like doing this ourselves.

Combined with free energy, this would be possible now.

29

I also brought up the concept of organic livestock farming, where the cows are herded through sections of field day by day, eating their natural diet, with chickens following three days later when the grubs in the cow patties have reached a perfection for healthy chickens to eat. Roost the chickens over a mulch pit, where their manure adds to the fertile elements. Build a level of mulch, adding bits of corn, mix with sawdust and other organics, and allow pigs to root for the fermented corn when it has ripened, thereby turning the mulch.

Very organic, natural processes guided in gentle touch by robots.

Now, the ancient task of shepherd, steward of the land, could be mechanized. We, for the first time in our history, have the technology and resources to do this!

Robots could tend all of this, and we could have organic meats, milk and eggs for all. If the resources we have – from internet emergence of Social Special Interest (which often is a reflection of what we would do if we could afford it (whatever "it" is) or more to the point, if it were afforded to us) to what land we have on this planet – if our resources were managed with thought to the natural processes by which they operate, and we had lots of shepherds, life would be effectively heaven.

So I asked, why isn't this being done?

I might conclude that there is intent counter to the freeing of humanity unto a heavenly end.

Anyway, I posted my article on several websites. I am grateful I have an old laptop. Though the screen has issues, I can prop it just so to see what I am doing, even though it is awkward typing, and roaming the Web when I can connect. But it gets it done.

I hope my words are taken to heart – that the people out there I post to will see that benevolent-intent is key. To accomplish benevolent-intent, open source on all things programmed should be embraced, encouraged by using only open source code on personal appliances, be they the toaster or the toilet-scrubbing 'bottie – I call them 'botties, those things that take care of things.

Products programmed in open source, code that anyone can look at and those that could read the code could watchdog ala eBay on a public website. The quality programs would gain reputation, and the aim would be for perfection, rather than some product that will generate future sales.

In fact, this would be what would happen all around. That quality would gain reputation as ratings were posted on the free, neutral Web.

In this scarcity paradigm that we are choosing to live in – though there is plenty for all; it just is very badly managed – we find it hard to envision ways the bounty of the earth can be all of ours, and what it would mean if it came to pass with humanity in control.

The tech point we have arrived at in Human History is affecting all humans: a new, totally novel point we are at. This fact places a gais on us as humanity to make a choice. All of us are at a point where we could choose to give the tasks that need intensive labor or concentration to machines (and to any humans that *want* to do them). And it turns out that all tasks that no one REALLY wants to do can be done with what we have now. Or we could choose to allow our race to be commanded as slaves by Them, the Elite, the Lizard Hearted.

One key, and I keep coming back to it, is free energy. After watching the – BBC, it might have been – broadcast of the Gary McKinnon interview on the internet, and the heavily edited excitement he had at the discovery of free energy in his made-public romp inside US black ops computers, I wonder why there aren't many who are gleefully passing on to their loved ones how we have the tools to end human slavery. I wonder why this hasn't been brought to the point of tipping – to the tipping point – where we are mandating it!

Looking at the world, and knowing that free energy is in the hands of some, what more can I conclude but that there are some who would suppress the knowledge. Gary, last I heard, was being extradited from Britain to the US for trial… Been a while, and I wonder what became of him. But, for now at least, he's still there on the internet being interviewed.

On the margin was jotted,

Must remember to look him up on the Web when I get on next at the library!

We read on, giving a soft grunt to let the other know the page could be turned – Lee was usually the first to grunt, though I was soon behind him, as we snuggled together, enjoying the love we had.

If some can grasp what a point we are at, where an application of ethics to the resources of the planet as a whole might determine whether we go down one of two very divergent paths as a race, where one path leads to being controlled by an Elite few and the other to freedom and abundance, maybe they will take up the call as well and we will choose wisely.

I sighed. Reading this, I reflected on the choices that were made and how grateful we humans were.

Looking up at Lee, I asked, "Break time?" He smiled and nodded. "Then come with me and look. I have something to show you."

Chapter 4

We paused briefly to dress; I chose a warm, fine wool drape – so fine a wool that it felt of fine velvet rather than fine wool – that fell to my knees in soft folds of red cascade. To this I added a belt of intricate Mayan symbols, wrought in gold and mounted closely on a titanium structure reminiscent of a snake's skin – a gift from Noni, who was now doing more than site-seeing, digging in the Central American Pyramids. On my feet I pulled boots, with deep treads and shin high lacing. The boots were red, too.

Lee wore boots (as I had suggested), jeans just the right amount of snug, and a gray wool jacket with hood pulled over his head and the zipper allowing just the right amount of his chest in view.

Taking his hand I led him out to the terrace and we looked at the white sands, liberally dotted with large black stones, of a beach that ran north and south. We were looking inland from a point about 20 feet above the crashing surf that rolled in its ever-steady yet chaotic way into the stones and over the sands of the beach. From where we stood, the 15 foot high, dark cliffs that hedged the beach about 50 feet inland could be peeked over, showing a lush forest of short growth with trees liberally interspersed. The feature most prominent was the gash in the wall of the cliffs.

In front of us the white sand continued into a canyon with sheer cliff on either side, about 15 feet wide, with ferns covering the sides of the walls of what gave mostly the impression of a winding hallway into a temple. Finding out where that canyon led was a very inviting prospect. Lee turned to me and smiled widely but said nothing.

The house had already extended a ramp down to the beach for us, opening the energy field and sending a tube of energy around the ramp to the sands below. I took Lee's hand to lead him into Fern Canyon.

When we reached the beach, I scanned for other people who might have chosen to visit this place at this time, but the gray, cloud-covered skies showed no one else around. I drew the crisp salt air, quite cool and damp, into my lungs, listening to the waves stroke rock and caress sand. Then we aimed for the path that led into to the cliffs, which now loomed well above our heads.

Sand crunched under foot but did not echo down the hall, so lush and buffered the walls were with ferns. The stream that splashed gently on its way to the sea amidst the sand pathway ran, crystal clear, sometimes on the left and sometimes on the right, requiring that Lee and I hop over its small width from time to time. The dripping of moisture through the ferns was as muted chimes and the laughter of the stream seemed to dance within its lattice. The path kept going, deeper and deeper, into the cliffs.

We had made the trek in silence, sharing our wonder and delight in smiles, gentle touches, and assists over the stream from time to time. Now Lee spoke, "The path is getting narrower, little by little." I looked and confirmed that the walls of fern-laden cliffs were indeed closer together.

"I wonder how far we can go," I mused.

Lee looked ahead, an expression of happy determination slid across his face and, through a smile, he said, "We will find out!"

I nodded eagerly. "Yes, I think so!" We took each other's hands and continued further into the crevice.

A short while later, the walls had closed in to where we could barely walk between them. Ahead we could see only a narrow crack with ferns choking any further progress.

"Looks like the end," I stated with a bit of disappointment that we hadn't come to a temple as the path had initially promised in its almost manufactured appearance.

Lee nodded. "Still, what an awesome place, this canyon."

"I'm glad you like it," I smiled. "I was here as a child and it occurred to me that you would appreciate it as I had."

We moved back down the canyon and found a wide spot a short way retracing our steps. The stream was running close to one wall and a large bed of sand lay in the curve of the canyon walls. We sat upon the damp carpet, leaning against one another and breathing the sweet, wet, green air. After a while, our cuddling transformed into caresses and kisses. We made love to the sounds of dripping and tumbling waters, the sand sticking to our skin.

We lay there a while, appreciating the coolness of the canyon and the presence of each other's body. After a bit we stood and wiped sand from the other. Finally we gave up on removing all sand, and dressed as best we could with the granules still clinging. We ambled back down the canyon to the house, where we bathed away the last of the grit and made love again in the warm waters that washed us.

I lazily called to the house to make its way down the coast heading towards San Francisco, and though I could feel no movement, I knew that the house had pulled the ramp away from the shores of Fern Canyon and had lifted further into the sky, moving southward.

Lee and I slipped out of the warm water and wrapped ourselves in robes, strolling through the jungle to admire the fountain that Flo had created. I called to have a 'bottie bring the diary and we snuggled again together to read while the fountain played joyously to our right.

> January 8, 2009
>
> I posted my article on several forums and have been getting some interesting comments and questions. The one that I found most interesting was the question about why I am so adamant about bringing about the abundance of the planet. I explained that it is a matter of ethics. As long as humans are kept in the scarcity paradigm – a paradigm built around money to define who is most "deserving" of the goods of the world, but in actuality makes slaves of all but the few to whom the money has aggregated – as long as we accept this system, we will be slaves, with many dying of starvation, thirst and exposure, illness and neglect.
>
> As long as we are controlled, leached of our money by corporations, we will not see the cures that are deliberately hidden and suppressed so that money can be made off our suffering, selling the patentable chemicals that further sicken us and increase what we buy to treat the illnesses induced by the first round of drugs.

It is an ethical choice to do all we can to bring abundance forth.

Another comment I received was when I pointed out that in an abundance paradigm, there will be no money needed. I was accused of being a Communist! I had to explain that Communism is a scarcity paradigm. It is predicated on the idea that there is a finite amount of resources which are divided up equally – each gets a "share." In an abundance paradigm, one may take all one needs or wants, as there is plenty for all. This does not make Communism, but rather eliminates all money-based economies. Capitalism, Socialism, and all such systems, based on money accounting for what any individual might have to trade, become moot in an abundance paradigm.

So many people are convinced that abundance "won't work!" What about greed, some ask. And again, I have to point out that in abundance, greed too becomes moot. If one can have all one wants and needs, regardless of how much that is, greed is meaningless.

Value will be placed on arts and skills – richness will be measured in character rather than a bank account.

What about violent crimes? I point out that with a free internet allowing people to congregate with those of like mind, as well as the ability to do as one wishes when one wishes, few will choose to spend time with those they do not like. Most crime is motivated by frustration – frustration over having too little money or power over one's own life. Even rape is a crime of power, allowing the rapist the feeling of power over another.

When one has complete power over one's life, crime will vanish as people begin to choose what they will do with their time, and who they will spend their time with. Love will flourish, while hatred will lose its teeth. With no groups "above" others, with all living richly, the seeds of hatred will disappear as people spend their time such that all thought of those they might hate in a scarcity paradigm seldom if ever come to mind.

Chapter 5

January 25, 2009

I encounter questions about "sexually deviancy" and especially as it relates to children. I point out that reputation will be everything relative to those whose bliss comes out in loving and nurturing our children. Parents always have the right to give a family to their child, but for any unwanted children, in a system where they are no burden, those who would love them would come forth.

And as a society it would be understood that one should always record one's perspective while with a child, and as soon as a child understands the personal power of documenting one's own perspective, then they, too, can begin their documentation.

This will virtually eliminate any bad behavior in the social context. Anyone can share their evidence, and reputations will be built. The children will be raised in love.

As for sexual deviancy – whatever that is – amongst adults… Well, I think that the ethical approach is that what adults do in a sexual capacity between agreeing parties is no one's affair but those choosing the way they want to spend their time.

It will come to pass, in abundance, where no creative bliss is denied, that sex for procreation will be a choice made by all who are ready for giving love and guidance to a child. An unwanted child will pretty much cease to be.

February 28, 2009

So many things get better if there is no money – which is the necessary evil in a scarcity paradigm. Once you take away the money motivation, by way of abundance, cures are brought forth instead of something to patent that requires repeated purchase.

Again, putting forth our resources into bringing forth abundance shows its ethical nature.

Products will gain durability reputations, an ethical quality – no more planned obsolescence. Honesty will be valued, when there is no money to be bribed with. Things will be valued for who made/gave them and for what they bring to our lives.

People don't seem to grasp how ethical it is choosing abundance, choosing a free internet, choosing our sovereign right to our perspective, choosing our destiny in the direction of abundance. We should be financing research, that all might watch (fully public), to build robots to do the things not enough people want to do (many which no one wants to do). To look for and build for things we just hate to do.

Some tell me that we aren't there yet, robotics is still crude, but I watched a robot programmed, based on a locust's reaction to the Universe, and it was able to detect and avoid obstacles. It will be mainstream soon – if it's not suppressed. And this beginning will blossom out rapidly, as the robot's "awareness" of the Universe is fine-tuned to points where work can be the function of the worker ants we build.

And given that the tech curve, plotted out by a group of statisticians back in the 90's, shows a geometric progression in tech over the last 5,000ish years, where movement on the line began noticeably upward in the 1800's, and jumped incredibly in the 1900's... That tech curve was projected to go infinite in 2012. So if we have locust-equipped robots today, a few months from now we're likely to see significant refinement.

I wonder what infinite tech will look like...

In the meantime, we, as a race must make a choice.

Some have asked me about the possibility of machines gaining consciousness. I explain that everything we create has a level of consciousness, and we might as well ask an ant if it's happy as a machine, for that would be the highest necessary level of consciousness to provide us with abundance. And it would be unethical to try for much higher consciousness, just as it would be unethical to bring a child into the Universe unloved.

And what would be the point? Just to prove it could be done? Who cares? I might presume so. But in abundance, why would we want to complicate our lives with those ethics?

I am enjoying the questions I am getting online. Some of them are well directed. It is allowing me to look at many angles and consider what it would look like in abundance. I keep coming up with Heaven.

Amelia had been right. We see Heaven now daily. Every individual can now choose the style of life they wished to live – in the community of those who share their preference, or as hermits, even. In abundance, it is a choice. Most groups maintained a presence on the Web, and could be found and read up on. People had a tendency to flock together by interests, though with the J.D.'s, family ties were kept by most. I tend towards hermitism, with Lee as my other half. But there are people who make house rounds – everybody is going to open parties or throwing open parties or both. In fact, lots of parties, from subdued intelligencia rationally playing with the puzzle pieces of life to the frat bash style, parties are ubiquitous.

Entertainment of others by hosting parties has become an art.

But what flourished most was Love.

It's hard to imagine seeing the vision of what could be and not having everyone else saying, "Well, duh." It's hard to imagine the blinders the scarcity paradigm wrapped around the minds of those who lived within it.

Then again… There had been those who deliberately amped up "scarcity awareness." They amped up fear. They plotted and planned and folded information to show as little as possible of what was really going on, in politics, in tech, in cures, in spiritual growth, in ethics. Selected ignorance was the fare of the day, and many of these who had resources also plotted ways to take over the Human race, bring it back to a more "manageable" number, keep it in slavehood.

Amelia called them Lizard Hearted. Most everyone now knows who the Lizard Hearted were, and that Amelia called them that. It's on record.

The Lizard Hearted were also developed on Earth, but lacked the DNA of galactic royalty – which Humans all have – and the ability to love. Many of the leaders of Earth had been Lizard Hearted, preferring to toy with the humans they led, making plans to assert power, derived from the scarcity paradigm through the accumulation of the money that kept them in control.

It's rather amazing how much of the truth of our history was available in the infosphere even back in Amelia's time. Most people that encountered it did not believe it, however, preferring the picture that the Lizard Hearted painted, calling the truth "myths." The Terra Papers, written by Robert Morning Sky and taken from the Hopi teachings that were given to them by an ET in 1947 – the Papers were online. They described well the history of Earth – but few who read them actually believed them.

But as Amelia rose in the awareness of the infosphere, as more and more contemplated what she had to say, the Ideas she had…more and more secrets began to break the surface, like so many bubbles from an underground hot spring, as humans saw that there was no need to do their masters' bidding, nothing was (or would be) held over their heads. More and more people aligned themselves with the efforts to build abundance for the human race, and in short order, the truth came out and Humans claimed their collective throne of the planet and solar system of Eridu.

Amelia's diary continued…

> March 15, 2009
>
> OMG! I was asked to appear on The Colbert Report! I was posting about the abundance paradigm, and the

path to get there, what to expect and all – posting all that on the Colbert Nation forum, and it seems that Stephen Colbert himself became intrigued! He offered me the Colbert Bump!

I will be flown to NYC – still unclear when exactly – to prepare for and appear on his show! I am so excited!

"Ah, yes!" Lee exclaimed. "That was what really got the ball rolling."

I nodded, "Yep. That episode is a classic. Bless Stephen for having the sight to see what it all meant!"

One question I get a lot about the abundance paradigm is, "What about lazy people?" I ask, What about them? If their bliss is to be a couch potato, and since their work is not needed and they are no drain on the system, just leave them be! Get on with your own life. But I also point out that most people are lazy out of boredom, being unable to afford to do what they really want to do (race cars, climb mountains, create stained glass art, teach children, scuba dive in Barbados, play video games, create video games, go to amusement parks, design amusement park rides, start a band, research for cures, understand particle physics, coordinate affairs, attend affairs, write useful programs, improve programs – whatever a person might take their bliss from).

So "laziness" will be a temporary condition for nearly all. When there is abundance, there is also no such thing as laziness.

Others object, "But that costs money! How will we get the money?"

I ask them how much R&D 700 billion dollars might afford. Given that in this country we are "bailing out" the Lizard Hearted at incredible sums, why don't we instead bail out humanity from the heretofore unassailable scarcity, poverty, hunger and humiliation we have been resourcefully kept within?

Why not spend the money to rid our world of money, instead of setting ourselves up for hyperinflation, and thereby economic collapse. For that is what we are doing.

Right now in history we can finally rid ourselves of all barriers to realizing each individual's potential. Why don't we do what it takes?

I smiled. Yes, Amelia was right. And thanks to Stephen Colbert, her message hit the tipping point. We made the right choice, and the rest is history.

I reached up and ran my fingers through Lee's hair. "Tomorrow is the annual show in San Francisco. The house is headed that way so that we can have a good vantage for what the Fireworks Boys have in store for us tomorrow night." The Fireworks Boys was one of the best fireworks enthusiast groups around, though they included "girls" too.

"Great," Lee responded. "It's been a while since I've seen fireworks – at least four months!"

I called to the house, asking for a meal of fresh, small Brussels sprouts, lasagna with Portabella mushrooms, crusty, buttery garlic bread, and a freshly baked raspberry tart with lots of whipped cream for dessert. I suggested to Lee that we head to the dining area for our dinner, and after a quick query about the menu – which he approved of – we headed that way.

Chapter 6

The Lizard Hearted, thwarted by the shift to the abundance paradigm when humanity realized what was within Its power, that It could level the playing field of Godhood in the Universe and demand to be respected for Its royal DNA as an equal Entity of Ethical Individuals…

A large portion of the Lizard Hearted saw that it was to their advantage in the long run. They would no longer fight to control us, because they couldn't win – our Spirits demanded liberty – and they, too would be afforded all abundance, as they currently enjoyed, but now they no longer needed to expend so much time scheming to take over. They, too, learned the advantages of abundance, with the right to maintain witness of their own lives, if they wished to. And these Lizard Hearted worked with the Human Hearted, releasing information and otherwise assisting in the abundance revolution.

Many, many – both Human Hearted and Lizard Hearted – saw the advantages of having evidence of their experience. Conventions of respect led to coexistence. And those conventions built up with the introduction, fevered public development, and acceptance of Datacube.

Datacube, which was a concept that Amelia proposed, and the community of Humanity proceeded to open-source program and develop, was a personal data storage device. It had enough storage to record an entire life and was used to Witness the personal experience. Because the world of a few Elite could watch the bulk of humanity, up close and personal, it became vital that we have evidence of any intrusion by Them into our own lives.

Of course, the Elite were a large share of Them…the Lizard Hearted.

What Amelia had in mind, given that we, every human individual, have a right, unalienable, to our experience, and we had the technology to create something that had storage capacities and unbreakable personal code – a personal retina scanner, she thought, though the final choice was a mental image key – with content unalterable, was a way we could all document our own stories. This would allow disputes to be settled, and accusations to be proven.

Every Individual had a Witness.

Amelia also knew that the Internet was vital to Human freedom; it is the heart of the flow of information. She was alarmed at moves in her country, and around the world, to censor its data. Taking away the personal right to testify, on the record, for all to see, would put the power of the evidence in the hands of too few.

If some decide what's on the Internet, she saw, ideas will spread or not as some few saw fit. And that could not be a good thing for freedom – of expression, of witness, of genius.

Her ideas – Ideas, as she would write – were what lead us to Heaven on Earth.

The first few years were tough for many as we got rid of any GMO in the fields and the stubborn-of-paradigm, but the revamp of the farming system into organic sections cultivated by our shepherds, our farming 'botties, and with computed distribution and crop rotation, using all those "Bailout Dollars," what resulted was a "Year and a Day" of struggles – and then abundance. We laugh gratefully now that we bailed ourselves to abundance.

The free energy finally broke out of suppression via a simple device designed and eventually built by a man calling himself the Anti/Christ. Though ways of extracting the energy seething in the plenum had been hidden in Black Ops, A/C's design, based on a crop circle it turns out, was by far the most elegant and simple to construct.

Crop circles were communications to Us, the Human Hearted, designed to circumvent the governments (Lizard Hearted, for the most part) to communicate with all of Us. There was a faction of ET's that believed in the Love we carry and that wanted Us to ascend to our throne, and the circles were the least likely to be suppressed.

With the building of A/C's device, as shown on YouTube, others took up the challenge of replicating his work and soon found that they had a winner. And word spread like wildfire as more and more were saying, Oh my god, it works.

Yep, the rest was history and here we are.

We have groups of adults choosing to live in community, with stray loners – but that's their business – with an ever watchful eye motivated by love and not money on our children. We were afforded the option to live with whatever level of technology we wanted. And now there are groups that live planet side, some even farming. Some stay there, others move elsewhere when they tire of it. Others find places to set a sky house, where they may live abundantly in the wilderness, for decades at a time.

Cures and good intention flooded the Works of Humanity as money was no longer in the equation, and this alleviated suffering – at least on any material level, and very seldom at the hands of another.

People who want to do things may do them, creative endeavors of positive Love, or at least Neutral Love levels, never negative levels as in making another unhappy deliberately. That's pretty much the rule.

It is key to increase Love by encouraging the individual to find Its bliss, with the understanding that taking bliss from UnLove is unacceptable. And the biggest sign of UnLove was unhappiness. Sometimes there is UnLove, but no one is taking bliss from the fact, such as when one person does not want to spend as much time with the other as the other wants, but attitudes and expectations towards one another shifted to where we expected very little in commitment of others' time, instead being honored and grateful for the time we were afforded by those we love.

Educating our children is focused on each child finding Its bliss – in fact, we encourage children to try things, development-appropriate, that interest them. Sex is discussed early on. We explain that sex is a choice, and that if they're not interested it's OK. When a child is interested, we let them know that it is their choice to make, but point out the advantages of foregoing it in favor of learning during formative years. If they choose to become sexually active, we have but one rule: no progeny until the age of 25. Should children be brought forth in any capacity, we watch the child and advocate if the child cannot advocate for Itself.

Individuals tended to change "careers" many times in life, as learning became their bliss. Historians of deeply honest motive arose, garnering respect and accepted authority as their data were examined and found to be unassailable – without the money motive, history could be viewed with no evidence withheld. One's reputation, one's honor, became the evidence of one's wealth. Richness is measured in character, not money or things.

For some, the plans of the Lizard Hearted, in fact, the very existence of the Lizard Hearted, were difficult to accept as real, but as the bulk of the Entities, both of Human heart and Lizard, saw advantages to open communications and the truth was opened to all eyes, acceptance won out.

And we were thankful that there were so many, divided even at the top, that fought with Us. Once Amelia made it clear to so many, neither side having really considered what abundance would mean (too many shying away from it assuming that greed would be its demise ala Communism), the Idea sold to large segments on both sides.

And as, first as a country and then as a species, we embraced freedom, the world let go of individual control, and what emerged was heaven.

There were some that feared the influence of freedom as it pertained to drugs. But few chose drugs that damaged the body – though that was still a choice – as honest education flowed about the long-term effects on the body as well as the mind. We no longer pursued adults making such choices, but merely ensured that any children were safe, and fully educated. Such choices now are never made in ways that endanger others. With that out of the way, it is the Individual's right to experience Its time in any mental frame It so chooses, the use of any drug included.

Marijuana is very prevalent – I even have a section on my terrace dedicated to growing it. Once money was removed from the equation, and "drug companies" existed as companies of people interested in finding drugs that were truly helpful, and as truth flowed unspun, the facts about marijuana came forth in the general view: facts such as an oil from its flower that cured cancer and its excellent function as a stress reliever (along with its incredibly long list of other medical uses). As was seen in California with Medical Marijuana flowing freely through the society at large, society went on functioning as before. In fact, in California there were slightly less crime, accidents, domestic violence and such, and the things that needed to get done got done. Of course now things that no one wants to get done can be done by our 'botties.

Religious groups congregate, sometimes in communities on the planet and with varying levels of technology, sometimes in sky communities. Many Humans are less religious these days but, like me, are very spiritual. Virtually all of us now choose to spend time with people we like, having houses somewhere in the sky and using the J.D.'s to move within the circles of people we like spending time with…doing that which we choose to do because we like it.

As a whole, we are free to choose what level of technology we care to live with, and as a whole we ensure our children are safe. It's the Datacube Laws that ensure that we can prove OUR side of any story…without having anyone able to force us to relinquish our recorded snippets of our lives (or the whole show) involuntarily. The right to one's perspective is absolute. The fact that we choose when we are recording, that we cannot be forced to use any technology, that the record is ours to control…make for a very different life than was experienced in scarcity.

Life's mellowed out greatly since the Old Days. We never see people more than once if we don't like them, unless we are suffering them at the behest of love – one's mother- or father-in-law, for example. There are no pressures to make money, but lots to find one's bliss and run with it.

This is what we teach our children. To take what they need to do what they love doing to the best of their ability. They are taught that the tools they need to do what they love to do will be there whether those tools are needed for an hour, a day, a week, a lifetime.

There was hard effort to move money to invest in abundance, when people finally grasped what abundance, and Witness Laws, and pretty much being with the people we love to be with as we create our lives between us, meant. The bailing out of the Lizard Hearted, to leave the Human Hearted bereft and controlled, was suddenly seen as absurd. Better to promote abundance than to leave most of the planet to die.

Love has sprung up, and though we saw the last few Individuals not quite handling the grasping of the abundance that the Universe <u>really does</u> have to give, not just us but all of those that might be dealing with Humans wanted to join in.

And interestingly, a number have.

"One more entry, and then we can go out and watch the approach to the city?" I asked Lee. He kissed my forehead, and then grinned, grunted and nudged me with his head.

March 17, 2009

People ask me about resources, such as metals, and other building blocks. I point out that back in the 1970's we transmuted lead to gold... Granted at the time we transmuted just a small amount – a few atoms – but we proved it could be done. We only transmuted so small an amount because, with the energy in the equation, it cost around a million dollars an ounce.

But with free energy, we could develop the means to transmute matter on a wholesale level. We could make anything we are in short supply of. Who knows. Maybe this will lead to a Star Trek replicator! (Infinite tech...?)

With 'botties doing all the stuff we want done but don't want to do ourselves, with all the materials we need, such suffering as we see now will vanish.

"'bottie" is never capitalized. I write that because, with all the fear I see that "the robots might TURN on us!," I have to think that we must never think of our machines as Completely Aware and yet, we must make it known that if they ever should come to us with a petition, we will capitalize and recognize them.

But the level of consciousness at which we will be creating will be of a hive nature, with function and instructions, and yes, we can expect emergence from our hive, but, with instruction sets written with a Love motive and not a profit motive, the results will be beneficial to the hive, as well as Humanity.

Things will run smoothly as symbiosis develops within the Entity/machine relationship, and Love will increase. Humans, after all, are loving. It's the Lizard Hearted that try to convince us that, based on what they do and manipulate us to do, we are not loving. And as long as we believe we are not loving, we will not embrace a system that allows Love to flourish.

If we could spend all our time with the ones we love, doing the things we love to do, with no need to worry about how we would get the tools – whatever we want is there for us to request or not – we will increase Love.

It is true that Humans are rarely bad at what they love to do. This means that if we could apply our creative essence to its optimum, with everyone contributing as they love to do, We, as a race in this Universe, would shine.

And it is amazing the list of creative things Humans love to do.

The Arts would blossom; dancers, alone or in troupes, would offer performances, and those that loved the scene that the performances drew would flock. Shakespearean actors, sculptors, comic book creators (often in teams that loved to work together), painters, interior designers, fashion designers even…

Science, too, would be unfettered by scarcity and profit motive. Through a free, unfettered Internet, honest projects would be publicly worked on, and those whose bliss was solving problems, be they mathematical or administrative, or in medicine, life extension, programming, particle physics, astronomy, history, robotics, space travel, and so on, would work on the problems, individually or in groups. Inventors would push the envelope.

Recreation would burgeon. From camping with any level of "tech support" one wanted, to awesome antigrav sky coasters (Gary McKinnon found antigrav amongst the things Black Ops has, along with the free energy, so I KNOW we could make them today if the tech was released). Games would be played on the Internet and in person. Games would be invented… People would party. But few would spend all their time partying. Most, with nothing blocking them from their creative bliss, would use the parties as a break from the focused-creative process, co-creating the party scene for a while.

Services will increase, as those of us whose bliss is being of service can choose to be.

As long as information is readily available for anyone who wants it (with the one exception of one's personal perspective), with no one group deciding what is "acceptable," along with free communication – the Internet unfettered, in other words – abundance will become heaven.

Open source everything. The more open we are, the more we can watchdog, promoting good products over malicious intent. The fact that the bulk of malicious intent is driven by scarcity – a need for money or a feeling of powerlessness – means that, in abundance, malicious intent (reduction of Love) will be rare, as reputations build. Rating of "service," whatever service that might be, will be available online, and reputations will build in all areas, from what robots are best to what babysitters… to artists, scientists, activities, locations, etc.

Yes, I think it will be heaven – IF people can cast off the scarcity paradigm enough to see what abundance – and the unique point at which we sit in history, technologically – would bring. And I am working to educate them…

Stephen will help, I do not doubt. I will owe him much thanks for any effort he puts forth to bring this into being. It's so exciting! His team called today and said they would have me on May 5th, and they will fly me out the weekend before to spend time discussing how best to impart the information and still be funny. I think I can do that!

Lee and I sat there, thinking about what the Ideas led to, then Lee got up, with me closely following. Together we strolled out to the terrace, casting our attention to the coastline, ¼ mile below us, floating northward and pulling the skyline of San Francisco ever closer to us. It was dark already and light spilled abundantly from the city buildings in the distance, most of which had taken on the role of "museum," but many of which still housed people including many of the Fireworks Boys.

Other lights shone in places below to the east on the coastline, communities of performers, scientists, researchers, chess players, amusement parks, and such, along with many who just chose to plant their home on the ground. Wind blew in gentle breaths, and the clean, crisp air felt invigorating, kindling a warm and happy sense of shared time between Lee and me. We kissed deeply, and then turned back to watch the darkness of the waters below us counterpointed by the starfield of lights onshore that drifted slowly past.

Later, as we pulled into the city and found a good view of the Golden Gate Bridge, looking inland, we checked the Web for places to share a meal, finding Hai Ling's after several apologies from Gourmets that had no room that evening. Ling served Chinese and Thai, and was quite highly rated. When we called, Ling's Calendar confirmed that Ling had a table at 10 PM, so we reserved it and busied ourselves dressing until then.

When we met Ling, coming out the J.D., she smiled widely in greeting and directed us to the table after warmly hugging us both. She sat with us most of the meal, slipping out a couple of times to prepare the fresh-cooked dishes, and we talked about the fireworks show the following night, the latest news, and the beauty of San Francisco. Her Thai food was truly awesome – Thai is my favorite – and I relished each bite, complimenting Ling on her artistry. Lee chose Chinese and was equally pleased with his meal, also expressing his pleasure.

In the end, Lee and I hugged Ling again, promising to return, and stepped home.

Chapter 7

The next morning Lee and I took our breakfast on the terrace, gazing at the bridge, gilt in actual gold now and glowing in the early sun, and at the bay, and the skyline to our right, also now a mostly golden sight, with the hills of Sausalito to our left. Others were gathering in the skies around the bay, and though no one was nearby, I would guess that already three hundred thousand houses had found their viewpoint for tonight's display. The whole shoreline of the bay was dotted with houses, parked at many levels above the surface, none close to one another except as it might appear so in the distance, and except for groups that were connected to share the experience together.

We had a team of 'botties place a sofa facing the view of the bay over the edge of the terrace. As they brought a table laden with finest caviar, fresh coconut, and other organic delights, we sat and tasted the spiral of anticipation sensed around the bay, seeing a house here and there settling into place, sometimes close enough to distinguish it was a house, but most often as a dot off towards the city or Sausalito, with the field filling in across the bay throughout the day.

Our repose led to expressions of our love, and in repose we languished for a while, nibbling on the delights from the table and each other.

Finally, I said, "I really want to read more of the diary."

Lee knew well my particular gratitude and interest in Amelia, and we both implicitly understood the synchronistic aspect of his discovery, and so he understood my shift of focus. Besides, he, too, enjoyed the bits of history he discovered on his phototreks, and this was as exciting to him as it was to me. We both relished the fact that we could share this find.

Lee nodded eagerly, and at my thought, the diary was retrieved from its last location and brought forth by a 'bottie. It still sat on top of the brown plastic bag which sat atop the zipper bag, and the 'bottie laid the stack beside me. We settled in to read with a final kiss.

March 24, 2009

To the Lizard Hearted I have been pointing out the advantages of letting the Human Hearted free. Sure, they would no longer have us as slaves – and if you believe some, as food, ritual objects, and sexual toys – but they also would not have to spend time worrying about how to keep us from the truth. They, too, would benefit from the chance to direct their creativity, being served by the robots, rather than us, to the standard of living they now have.

We, in turn, in granting them their luxury, expect ours to be allowed as well. Individuals of Sentience will build their lives to the quality picture they hold. We will commingle because we like another's company, and not because we are toadies for money.

In fact, I implore people to look at what they toadie themselves for, and ask if it would not be better to have all you want when you want it and never have to deal with that person who gives you orders again? Isn't that worth letting the dam on the truth loose? And that goes for both the Human Hearted and the Lizard Hearted alike.

I'm not going to go into the Lizard Hearted with Stephen on his show. The point will be that we have the tech and the resources to do this for ourselves, as a race, NOW, and there are strongly ethical reasons for taking the reigns and making it happen.

I live in an area with a lot of Amish, and I think of what choices they might make when offered the advantages of abundance. Many, I suspect, will choose to keep their community as it is. The things, that now they sell produce at stands to acquire, they can have if they want, and when they want, but the cycle of life will continue as it has for them. In as little as a generation or two, though, I see the community integrating much that is out there with their spiritual pursuits. There will be people leaving them… but there will be people asking to join, as well.

Other groups who might shun technology will be welcome to do so. No one will be forced to choose tech in their lives. That's really what it's all about. Individual Autonomy within the informed willingness of all involved, once adulthood is reached. Though I see a degree of "wild and crazy" behavior initially, as an unfamiliar level of freedom opens up, once the freedom is familiar, and creative bliss is the focus, Love will abide.

Life will be extended, health will improve, aging may be halted entirely, space travel may become free for all who might choose to see what goes on out there in the Universe at large. Products will be built to optimums, rather than lowest tolerance. The quality of all things will improve.

Life will improve for all.

But trying to move people past the scarcity paradigm is so difficult. Even still, I have people bring up greed. And conscious robots. And materials. And energy. Out of hand they proclaim it won't work.

Some do see, though, and that is what gives me heart. Some grasp well what it means, and the ethics involved. And soon, I hope, enough will see to make it happen.

Lee and I smiled at one another.

March 27, 2009

Someone asked me, what rules should we live by?

I point out that Individuals of Sentience have rights. They have 100% right to what happens in their domicile, except as another person records (their perspective). They have a right to do what they wish, provided it does not involve others unwillingly. They have the right to record their perspective, and may choose to release any of their perspective they feel others either need to know or would enjoy. But they cannot be forced to "testify against themselves," nor are they required to record their perspective. No one can use another's perspective without willing donation.

Children must be recorded until they can understand Personal Witness, and be taught as early as possible the advantage and advocacy that recording what happens to them offers. They, too, cannot be forced to testify against themselves, but should they die their data is opened publicly. Adults may pass their data to others in a will, and those others may make public what they choose, except in cases where foul play is suspected, and then the last 24 hours of recording can be opened to public scrutiny. All data becomes historical record 150 years after death.

What the right to one's perspective, along with complete control of the data, results in is that people will be conscious of their behavior and choose better behavior lest they be recorded behaving poorly. Peers – any who are shown a recording (all recordings offered to substantiate poor behavior must be publicly available) – can determine whether an individual has behaved so poorly that something needs to be done. Amongst the peers a decision on disposition can be made.

But, of course, with money gone as a motive for behaving poorly, as well as need, and combined with the fact that people will move in circles of those they like, poor behavior will be rare.

I am sure that if enough people can move beyond the scarcity paradigm, we Humans will free ourselves. With Stephen's help, maybe I can jumpstart this! I am very excited by the chance to bring the concepts to others.

"Hey, I wonder if Cara and the gang are free," I commented as I stretched. "I wouldn't mind inviting them over for the show. What do you think?"

Lee stretched along side me and nodded. "Sure, if they're available. Sounds like a plan."

Cara, Tim and The Kid – who was not a kid, actually; that was just his name – were friends with an interesting arrangement. The three of them were married, and all three had their bliss in social reporting. They attended soirees, parties and events and then reported on them on the Web – on their blog, TiCK.net. Their site on the Web is highly trafficked, and they have a reputation for good suggestions as to public events to attend. Often they were busy, but now and then they had nothing to.

"I'll call and see if any or all of them are available." I got up and, with another stretch, called to have myself connected with their house.

Tim's hologram appeared on the terrace nearby, sitting in an ornately carved wooden chair. "Izzy! Long time no talk! What's up?"

"Hey, Tim. You and the gang busy tonight?"

Tim reached and pulled a holographic bowl of cereal from the air nearby, stirring it with a spoon, and said, "Well, we are in San Francisco for the fireworks. You know about the show?"

I grinned widely. "Sure do! In fact… That's where WE are!" I laughed.

Tim took a bite of cereal, chewing quickly and swallowing before responding. "That's great! Wanna get together?"

"In fact," I offered, "that's why I called. I thought it would be great to have the gang over. Interested?"

Tim finished another bite and replied, "Let me check with Cara and The Kid. I'm thinking it doesn't matter whether we report the perspective from here or there, so they're not likely to mind. They're out at the moment, but I'll call them and get back with you."

I nodded. "I'll await your call with bated breath," I said with a wink and a smile, and Tim blinked out.

I looked over to Lee, and he grinned at me, then beckoned me to his side. We cuddled and stroked each other, building desire but holding back in anticipation of Tim's return call.

Shortly, I received notice that Tim was calling, and I instructed the house to put him through.

"Hey, Izzy. Does 6:30 sound good? Cara and The Kid said it sounded splendid, and we can be there." Tim's smile spoke of his pleasure at the coming evening.

"Oh, that's great! 6:30 is perfect. I'll have a meal waiting, so come with empty stomachs. We'll see you then!" I returned Tim's smile.

Tim nodded. "Thanks for the invite."

"Most welcome, Tim." I waved and then Tim vanished.

I turned to Lee and gently bit his ear. He cupped my breast, and as I instructed the house to welcome the gang anywhere from 6:00 on for a while – remind me later if they don't show up by 8:00 – I crested on his shores.

Chapter 8

Lee went off to check his email, and look for information on the things that he liked best – things like what the latest was in personal protection tech to keep him safe while photographing Earth, Herself. He loved to capture the beauty and poignancy of Our Planet, and gear that allowed him to do so, always protected from the wilder places, was of value to him.

He looked for what was new in camera gear, processing gadgets, other miscellaneous things, and whatever he was pursuing as a sideline break.

I went and did a quick check myself, realizing that it had been quite sometime since I had checked my email, so in my bliss I had been, and found three waiting for me. One was from my favorite canvas maker showing the selection of canvases available for order, and two were from paint suppliers. All three were computer generated. And as I didn't want anything at the moment, I told the house to move these into their respective files and strolled through my garden paradise in directed leisure on my way to work on Little Buddha and Companion. The child and her cat both called me.

Thank goodness people didn't bother you on the Web anymore as they did in the scarcity paradigm. Always selling something… People now took interest in one another personally, and never in contention because of money, so things like email – and most often, holophone – were used by the people one wants to deal with. Sales calls were a thing of the past. Everyone discovered this in their lives, and spam was finally defeated.

The email anyone gets anymore is the mail they signed up for on the Web, as well as personal email; the option to cancel mailings from any list one signs up for is offered as a common courtesy.

The Web as a whole, flourished, thrived, blossomed. Emergent support efforts sprang up, as Humans found that they COULD help, if help was sought – and the Human Hearted took pleasure from helping. This emergence was evident even in the beginnings of the Web, with the development of Linux as a prime example of people willing to help and improve a product, even though there was no monetary gain to be had.

Once the toil, the drudgery, the tedious, had been automated, and a year and a day had passed, the bounty began to flow. The task was Herculean in effort. Land ownership had to be addressed in anticipation of abundance, for example.

It was decided that everyone owned their domicile of the moment, since rent would go away anyway, and so would the need to stay put. This gave everyone a place to live. Those with no address could build something wherever they had been staying, if they could, and most got by. And people came forth to help people who were struggling. Everyone was working towards the future, for when the paradigm shift occurred on a large enough scale, the "Goldrush" was on.

When people understood that the Universe could supply us all with all we might want, every one of us – and ethically, if we could do it, if we could bring it about, could any of us justify denying any Human Choice? – when people saw how this would benefit themselves, their children, the old and the young and the rich and the poor... They were motivated.

As for the Lizard Hearted, any who wanted to move off-planet were welcome to do so, and a number discreetly, and not so discreetly, took their leave of the Human Home. Those who remained understood that rules had changed...

We, as Earth's inheritors, intended to take control of the resources of our planet, with the goal being the abundance for all that we knew we could bring about – to the benefit of both sides, and if they were willing to work within the rules, which were as fair and balanced as they might be, they too could live in this grace.

Thus the Alliance of Hearts began.

When We affected our freedom from the Lizard Hearted, offering their continued luxury in exchange for our own luxury, using our skills at building passive hives of earnest-to-serve ants to bring abundance forth, Amelia's dream was realized.

Before that happened, though, there was a flood of truth, as many, responsible for sowing disinformation knowing it was disinformation, began to let the truth out. In the mainstream the information flowed more slowly at first, but it poured forth as if a floodgate had opened on the Web. Free energy and cures and antigrav and space travel and aliens emerged. When the idea soaked in that there was a good possibility of being "toadie to no one," as Amelia succinctly put it, the toadies let it all go.

The truth about the healthy foods, the sickness of genmod foods, the death that petro-"fertilized" fields eventually brings, the wholesomeness of hemp seed and the curative properties of the hemp flower, and many other aspects that were playing into the efforts of the Lizard Hearted to control, enslave and eradicate the Human Hearted and their money, began to be credited, rather than suppressed. Though some of the Lizard Hearted attempted to keep up the deceit and suppression, the tide had turned with a vengeance. Truth could no longer be twisted and hidden.

There were many who took up the torch, the least of which was not Stephen Colbert himself. Media toadies cast off their toadiness and reported the truth of things that mattered in getting us from the paradigm shift to living the paradigm. The Web was abuzz. But it was Amelia's vision and persistence that got us to the shift itself.

My painting was shaping up nicely. The child was aglow with tenderness and love; the cat exuded a tolerance and acceptance of the innocent inexperience of the handling it was receiving. I sat back and drank in the pleasure of a work, by my own hand, that was becoming what I wanted it to be.

I looked at the clock and saw that it was after 5:00 – I had asked my house to let me know when it was 5:30, but since it was a good point to break, I cancelled the request and sent the wardie instructions to create a gown for the evening, thinking a silk of yellow with white lace would be good. I like to design my own, but there are many who develop relationships with those who love to dress others.

I let the house know that 'botties could clean my paints and brushes, and any spills and drips, as I left my studio and made my way to the bath to prepare for visitors.

Lee came into the bathroom as I was bathing, and slid into the waters with me. He washed my back and then I washed his. Together we dried and dressed. The house had laid out the clothes we had requested, my yellow silk and Lee's gray cotton djelebra, and we donned the garments.

We walked to the garden and sat near the J.D. on a bench of intricately wrought iron that stood amongst lilies. We cuddled and kissed, awaiting the arrival of the gang. Shortly, Cara came through. She was dressed in a short emerald-green velveteen dress, with her long legs sporting black leggings and sparkling-emerald boots. A steel-gray Witness necklace, stark and smooth, perched around her neck. She wore her raven black hair short, Egyptian style, with a line of bangs cutting across her Asian forehead. Tattoos of birds and flowers covered her arms, and a nose ring in glittering diamond clung to her right nostril. She was lovely, and I said so.

"Cara! You look beautiful! So good to see you!" I exclaimed as I embraced her with a hug.

Cara smiled widely as she pulled back to take me in. "I love the color," she said, with her eyes indicating the silken folds that fell, floor-length, around my body. "I'm so glad you invited us!" She turned to Lee and hugged him as well.

The Kid came through, tall and lanky, with red hair and freckles ablaze on his head, and a coal-black suit, so retro these days, enveloping his thin body. He grinned, embracing me and Lee in turn. "Hey, guys," he said, never much for conversation.

And then Tim came though. Tim's sideline passion was body-building, and his defined muscles rippled underneath a mesh tank top, which hung over the top of the jeans he wore. He too smiled and gave us each a bear hug. "How are you guys doing?" he asked when the greetings were over. And as we moved toward the terrace, we expressed our good health and enquired of theirs.

We reached the terrace, where the 'botties had set a table made entirely of crystal, with chairs to match, and a feast of fresh salmon cooked with lemon and dill, roasted potatoes with garlic, buttered asparagus, rice pilaf with almonds, hot and freshly baked bread, and a salad of crisp baby greens, tomatoes, feta, carrot shreds, and croutons with a raspberry/walnut vinaigrette. A delicate white wine stood waiting and breathing. The table was long and allowed us all to sit at one side to gaze out at the bay, the city, the bridge, the hills, the many small dots of houses still visible in the sunset light, and the space above the bay where the show would play.

"How lovely," Cara cooed as she took in the spread, seating herself in the middle. I sat to her right, with Lee on the end. The Kid took Cara's left and Tim sat at the other end.

We chatted a bit, through swallows of salad and salmon and the rest, discussing events that were upcoming. The gang always knew about nearly every public fete and affair, and I appreciated the chance to use their knowledge to fill my Calendar. After a while of discussing the happenings in the Universe at large, I brought up the diary Lee had found.

While a 'bottie was dispatched to bring the diary from where Lee and I had left it, Tim asked the usual question. "THE Amelia Ringer???"

"Yep. And it's awesome to see things from her perspective. I mean, sure, the history has a record of the events, but very little about what went on in her head to pull us free of the scarcity paradigm. And here is her diary, giving us just that." As if on cue, the 'bottie arrived, carrying the precious cargo. I lifted the pile, arranged as before with the diary atop the brown plastic bag atop the zipper bag, and gently handed it to Cara who leaned over to share with The Kid and Tim.

Together they looked over the book, reading passages here and there, turning the pages delicately and commenting occasionally.

Cara finally turned to me. "What an awesome find! Will you be giving this to the Museum?"

I nodded. "Absolutely – once we have read it all, of course." I cast a quick smile to include Lee. Lee gently bumped his shoulder against mine, accepting the inclusion.

We finished the meal, talking about Amelia, with Lee and me giving bits of what we read so far to facilitate the discussion. As the meal ended, I looked out to the scene before us and noted that the sunlight was gone and only the dusk of the sunset was left. Houses around the bay began to be seen for the light they emitted rather than what they had reflected in the sunlight. A glinting band defined the bay opposite us in the distance, with individual lights standing out closer by. Maybe a million houses surrounded the stage of the bay. And no doubt many more people stood on the shores and on balconies in anticipation, having come by J.D. or living here already. Soon, when the last fingers of light had left the western horizon, the show would begin.

As the 'botties cleared and cleaned the table and tucked it back in the storage room it had come from, we moved to the sofas and lounges that I had had set up closer to the edge of the terrace. We seated ourselves near the edge, listening to the distant crash of waves against the pylons of the bridge and the hints of the song the wind sang through the cables that held it in place ahead and below us.

And then, as full darkness descended, the first burst of brilliance lit the sky, reflected in fractal sparks in the surface of the bay. It began with a clap of sound and blue brilliance, flowering larger outwards from the central point, each spark of which burst further into green, and then further broke into a fire of orange which rained down as a curtain of flame towards the receiving waters. We gasped at the vision of light, artfully displayed across the sky.

The show started with traditional fireworks, with each more intriguing and lovely than the preceding, and we sat forward in our seats enthralled. After half an hour of crafted gunpowder bursts, the Energy Works filled the skies, twisting and curling, bouncing, forming and disbursing. It was the same technology that my fountain used, but on a much, much grander scale. The light chased itself, drew glowing lace bridges across the bay that hovered and then melted, bursting upwards from the water in columns of blazing glory, as it touched the wind-roughened surface. And more and then more. It all was beautiful.

The traditional works returned, and the show alternated back and forth from chemical reaction to energy manipulation for the next three hours. We exchanged awed comments on the artfulness of this display and the creative concept of that one. The energy of excitement flowed around the bay in such strength that we all could feel it.

At the end, the traditional met the new, as the energy caught and played with the sparks burning brightly, sending them in unexpected patterns and to all points of the compass. The finale brought all sparks with ribbons of light trailing like silk into center stage above the bay. And then they flew apart, with the ribbons intertwined in a gigantic tree trunk from the waters to high in the sky, and taking the sparks outward in a multihued dome coving all the bay. The energy streamers remained long after the sparks had spent their supply of fuel and had burned out.

We held our breath and then slowly began to breath, in sighs and appreciation for the treat we had witnessed.

"There will be much to describe in our blog," Cara commented. Tim and The Kid concurred.

"Indeed," Tim responded while The Kid nodded. "It just gets better and better every year. Each year I think that it can't get better…and then it does!" He shook his head with amazement.

"Thanks, Izzy, for having us to share this with." Cara turned her remark to me. I smiled in thanks.

"Most welcome, Cara. I enjoy your company and was so thrilled to find you and the gang were available to share it with us," I replied.

Lee interjected, "Anyone up for a game – cards or maybe a video game?"

"Aw, honey," Cara responded, "it's been a very long day for me. I don't know about Kid and Tim, but I need to sleep." With this comment she issued a long yawn and stretch.

Lee looked at Tim and The Kid hopefully. The Kid looked apologetic as he shook his head without comment, and Tim responded with, "Sorry, my man. I have a meeting scheduled early in the morning and should be following Cara to bed."

"Maybe we can schedule a game night soon," I suggested. "I would love to try out that new RPG by the Ghost Writers…what's it called…?"

"Oh, you mean Kings of the Old World?" The Kid asked.

"That's the one!" I confirmed.

"Sure," Cara said, bringing up her Calendar. We all looked at what she had available, consulting our own in the process. "Oh, how about here?" she asked, pointing to a date a couple of weeks in the future. "I have my spa treatment in the morning, but all afternoon is clear and I can stay late – nothing to do the next morning."

As luck would have it, we all had the time free except The Kid. "Well, next time," he said softly with a petulant smile. "You guys have fun then."

We gathered ourselves up and headed towards the J.D. With hugs and goodbyes, the gang went through the shimmering curtain, one by one, and then Lee and I were alone again.

"It is getting late," he said, turning to me to put his arms around my waist. "Shall we turn in?"

I nodded, stroking his cheek with my hand but saying nothing out loud. We made our way towards the bedroom, stopping briefly to have our teeth cleaned by the bathroom 'bottie and to cast off our clothes, which were collected by another 'bottie to be taken and returned to the domain of probability in the wardie.

Lee and I slid into the soft indulgence of the silk sheets, wrapping ourselves in one another, to make love and then to sleep, with memories of the brilliant dance of light in the skies over San Francisco Bay weaving in and out of our heads.

Chapter 9

Lee and I awoke, tangled in each other's limbs. "Good morning, Beautiful," Lee murmured into my ear. I nuzzled his neck in response, feeling the warm firmness of his body pressed against mine. Our passion built slowly as we kissed and stroked and sought the spots we knew so well would bring the other pleasure. Then we boiled over into one another's climax, to rest then and whisper our gratitude and love.

"Let's read more of the diary," I finally suggested as our sea of love came to a calm, sending the request for the book to be brought again. Silently the 'bottie slipped into the room, placed the pile on the bed beside us, and moved out again to where it awaited the next request. I lifted the book and brought it between us, thumbing through the pages to where we left off.

> April 3, 2009
>
> I hope I have a job when I get back from my experience on the Report discussing the abundance paradigm. I told my boss today about it, explaining that I needed a week off – that I would do it without pay, even – and she said she didn't know if she could let me go for that long. I pleaded with her, asking her for the time. She still seemed unmoved, but said that if she could get by without me she would; if not, there were a hundred others she could hire on the spot for my job. And so, I might be out of a job when I get back.
>
> Oh man, this sucks. It's hard enough trying to make my meager pay stretch to cover rent and food. Without the money, I guess I'll be back at the Red Cross, once again with only the clothes on my back. The economy is so bad, and the boss is right. A hundred others would snatch my job up in a heartbeat.
>
> I don't know who else to rant to, dear diary, but you. I keep thinking about how different life would be in abundance, not just for me, but for those hundred who

hope for my job. For those hundreds of thousands of homeless on the streets of this country. For the millions dying of thirst and starvation around the globe. To think that every one of those people would have nothing worse to worry about than what they want to do today. How wrong things are now. How right they could be.

How right WE could make them IF we chose to.

Well, I guess I will hope for the best. That is really all I can do. That and posting the concept of abundance anywhere and everywhere on the Web. Try to reach as many people as I can, motivate them to spread the concept – and that isn't tough when they finally "get it." Those that "get it" are eager to bring others to "get it" as well. The more I reach, the closer we all are to making it happen.

I get a lot of objections from various people afraid that the abundance paradigm would destroy religion. I assure them over and over that religion, like everything else, would be a choice. If one wanted to live the life of an ascetic, one could do so. If one wanted to preach to others, or listen to the preaching of another, join, follow, and adhere to any religion's tenets, one could. Whole cities, on the planet and in the air could dedicate themselves to whatever views they ascribed to.

All over the planet, congregations of like-minded people could accumulate. But at the same time, those that do not share the views of any others also could make their way in life on their own.

Everyone could choose – their beliefs, their styles, their activities, the level of tech they want to live with. It would be true freedom.

One Mennonite I met on the Commons down in Ithaca said, when I described the abundance paradigm, that it sounded like New Jerusalem. I'm not so versed in the beliefs of the Mennonites, but I believe it is related to something out of the Book of Revelation. I have heard of New Jerusalem from fundamentalist Christians, and that is what I recall them saying… Anyway, perhaps it is New Jerusalem.

I mean, given that, if there is any validity to prophesy, surely it would qualify. And given that *my* belief is that Consciousness is "God," creating reality by collapsing the waves of probability with awareness and expectation, we ourselves would be the vehicle by which it would come about. We would create this New Jerusalem. In a way, I hope that prophecy is real and that we will gain the vision to do this. If it is real, I suppose, then we WILL create the abundance for all.

Now that's an idea I can take some comfort from. Much better than thinking about the job issues. I wish I could justify letting go of the Colbert Bump, but I could post on the Web for a decade and not get the recognition for the paradigm that I will get with Stephen's help. I HAVE to go. I have to take my chances with my job.

April 16, 2009

I am so ambivalent! The boss keeps saying she can't do without someone in my position for a week, and I got a letter with tickets to New York for April 30th out of Ithaca. The letter said I would be met at La Guardia and taken to a hotel. There was a schedule attached saying I would meet with the writers of the Report on Friday, May 1st and then the taping will be on Tuesday, the fifth. I don't know if I will meet Stephen on Friday and work out the funny stuff directly with him, or whether we will do that the day of the taping. But either way, I will have a room and food for the weekend, and I can do some sightseeing. This is so exciting! I just wish my boss was more flexible and I didn't have to worry about what I will come home to.

I still have a lot of people arguing that it won't work, abundance. Still "greed" is used as a reason. Still "power" is used. What use is "power" anyway? If you don't need to <u>make</u> your servants do your bidding to have what you want, when you want, what's the point? And besides, it is only the Lizard Hearted that enjoy pushing others around. The Human Hearted are more numerous, by far, and we could overcome. IF we just do it!

The more I think about it, the more I see. I cannot see anywhere it wouldn't work. I have addressed all objections I have encountered and every question I have gotten. It seems to flow from me, as if this knowledge is being given to me as I need it. Sometimes I fantasize that it is a future me giving the me now the tools and vision to bring about this change in the world. Whether it is or is not is irrelevant. Having the vision is enough for my Human heart to be spurred on to bring it to all of the Human hearts as quickly as possible. The sooner we are there, the more Love and the less suffering will be produced.

And that, of course, is the essence of the ethical nature of choosing abundance: more Love in the Universe.

I will say… I have visited forums I had not been on in a while to find quite a number of people taking up the call. They are arguing the case for the abundance paradigm even in my absence. This feeling I get, seeing other warriors taking up the cause, is what keeps my soul fed. Though slowly, our numbers are building. Still, it is not enough to hit the tipping point. Far too few have ever heard of it, let alone contemplated its meaning and ethical value. Ten thousand in a country of 300 million, in a world of over six and a half billion, is a drop in the bucket. No generation of power whatsoever.

But once the concept has been Bumped… Oh, I expect good things. That should make all the difference in the world!

Lee and I stretched in unison, breaking from our reading. "Oh," I said. "Tonight I am meeting the artist of the fountain in the garden – her name is Flo – to see the new Ogden Pierce play in Manhattan. Care to join us?"

Lee popped his Calendar up on his lap before him and scrutinized his schedule. "Sure," he responded. "I have a meeting with the Photobuffs – but they are always meeting and I am willing to miss that to see Ogden Pierce's work performed. With my favorite person in the world, of course." He winked, and I winked right back.

We meandered into the kitchen together, now hungry, and I made a minor feast with pancakes, omelet, fresh cantaloupe, and rich coffee with stevia to sweeten it for me and sugar for him. I prefer stevia in my coffee, though many prefer sugar. In the Old days, in the money-driven hell that it was, stevia was suppressed. Though it was a natural herb whose extract was 300 times sweeter than sugar, and supported a healthy blood sugar level, the sugar and artificial sweetener Corporates passed laws that kept it from being called a sweetener, and the "Food and Drug Administration" raided places that were using it in their products, confiscating product, along with the tools and equipment being used, often leaving the companies that tried to offer this better choice to people bankrupt and incapable of further production.

Though there was a "loophole," in that stevia could be called a "nutrient," it did not sell as well with "fortified with stevia" as it would have if the label could have read "sweetened with stevia." And, of course, the mainstream media – the "MSM" – never mentioned stevia in any consistent, comparative fashion.

In fact, until people "woke up" to the possibility of abundance, there was a lot that never made the MSM. The general media was, of course, controlled. The Lizard Hearted used it as they used the laws to control the Human Hearted, keeping them enslaved in their wage-slave misery. They whipped up nationalism with lies and half-truths to incite wars. They used it to discredit those who brought truths up, with character assassination as the primary tool. They insinuated that there was something inherently wrong with altering one's consciousness – except with alcohol and patented drugs, to the profit of drug companies and the medical establishment, as the patented drugs caused illness and organ deterioration, sending the people to the doctor to find relief from these further issues.

They used it to suggest that fluoride was somehow good for the body, never reporting the myriad studies that showed quite the opposite. They never reported the hundreds upon hundreds of studies that showed only benefits from marijuana, because it threatened the profits of the dubious patented drugs in its efficacy and lack of side effects. They did not report its anti-cancer properties, its effectiveness in treating pain and depression. They used the media to distort the view of the world, supporting the draconian Codex Alimentarius – part of what was called the "New World Order's" efforts to nutritionally starve the "excess humans" on the planet.

They did not report the fact that new teeth could be stimulated to grow where only a root was left in the jaw. They did not report the costs of their "War on Drugs" in terms of functional families broken, disenfranchisement of citizens, and the money spent to hunt, sting, process, try and incarcerate "offenders." They did not report the effects of breathing the exhaust from the old internal combustion engines, ubiquitous in that day (but profitable to the oil Corporations), yet exaggerated the effects of second hand tobacco smoke – which actually seemed to counter the effects of the fluoride they pumped into the water supplies...

It was a very bad time indeed. But because of Amelia... Well, I suppose it's obvious by now why I have such regard for her, why her history has been a passion of mine, and why having her diary to read is such an exciting thing for me.

With breakfast finished, Lee went off to the Web again, and I was left to my own. I had a 'bottie bring me a sketch pad and I began drawing out the concept for my gown for the evening. Having come up with something I thought would be most fitting for the affair, I sent instructions to the wardie to have the garment ready at 7:00.

I wandered over and watched my new fountain, thinking of how nice it was that I would be seeing Flo again, as well as seeing Ogden Pierce's work performed.

Finally I moved on to my studio. Little Buddha and Companion was nearly finished and I was looking forward to adding it to my gallery, and hopefully finding someone who wanted my creation for their very own.

I pulled a smock from a drawer, wrapping it around my body, and sat. I lifted the pallet, clean and waiting, from the nearby table and squirted paint of various colors onto the white surface. I selected a brush and turned my awareness completely to child and her cat.

At 6:00ish, I looked over my work, well pleased. It was done. There was the innocence and delight I wanted to capture. The patience and good sport of the cat. I called a 'bottie to clean up and to bring a camera. When the camera arrived, I snapped a photo of the painting and then left the studio, making my way back to the living room and my Old couch. I called up the Web, which formed in front of me, and accessed my site. I uploaded the picture to my holoport and had the house send emails to my list – which now was in the hundreds of thousands – to let them know I had added a piece to the gallery, with the image I had taken of the painting embedded.

I checked my email while I was at it, finding nothing of interest, and then hit the history sites. There were many, like me, who were interested in one aspect of history or another, and they had formed groups and associations, with new finds and information added daily to their growing catalog of facts. One specifically was devoted to Amelia, and I was looking forward to having the diary scanned and adding *that* to the site. What a stir and commotion it would create. But I wanted to finish reading it before I let anyone know of the find.

Of course, the diary itself would go to the Museum. The Museum was maintained by a group whose passion it was to collect artifacts of the past. And Amelia's diary was sure to be something THEY would want as well. As the donor, I would have rights to bring it back home to show to friends, but people seldom used that right. Just jump to the Museum to see it, safely ensconced and protected from time. I doubted that once I gave it to the Museum I would ever bring it back here.

At 7:00 I got up to dress, finding my gown, a rich purple affair with a single strap over my left shoulder and a wide gold accent belt, hanging in the bedroom. I bathed quickly, again meeting Lee as I lifted myself from the waters of the pool. He reached for a towel and daubed the dampness from my skin, kissing me gently as he did so.

"Thank you. Love," I said when he had finished.

"Truly my pleasure," Lee responded with a wink and a grin. I grinned back and then began the process of dressing for the play. Lee bathed and then did the same.

When I had completed dressing, I had my hair done in braids and then swirled about my head with amethyst pins peeking from the plaits. I made my face myself, lining my eyes and coloring my lips. When I was done, I found Lee – who had dressed in short order in a black tuxedo – poking on the Web in the living room.

"Going OLD school, are we?" I teased.

Lee grinned. "Yep. I thought a night on Broadway should be met with formality. Do you like it?" He stood and modeled the suit for me.

"Indeed I do. It makes you look sexy – not that you aren't sexy in anything you wear!" I assured him.

He looked me over and replied, "As you are sexy in anything *you* wear! That's stunning on you." He offered his arm, which, demurely, I took, and together we headed for the J.D.

Chapter 10

We stepped out the J.D. near the theatre, first me and then Lee. There was a line, thankfully short, for tickets, and we moved to the end. Others gathered behind us as we moved forward. When we got to the window, we punched in a request for four tickets – I had assured Flo that I would get tickets for her and Dee (SoundMan Sam was not interested in plays, but Dee, still looking for her bliss, was a willing audience member for the play). The machine produced the tickets and Lee tucked them in his pocket.

The theatres had tried allowing tickets to be ordered online, but a number of seats went empty as people changed their plans, so rather than have empty seats, they chose to have the tickets disbursed outside, thereby ensuring that those who really wanted to see the plays would have seats – at least until they "sold out." The tickets, of course, had no payment involved, but the seats were limited and so tickets were necessary.

All of Pierce's plays surrounded the scenes one could find in the scarcity of our past. His sets were comprised entirely of Old Things, lent by people who received credit for the items they brought to the stage. This play, called Quasimodo's Plight, dealt with the struggles of one person, born defective and ugly, in a society that spurned such people. In the scarcity and hidden tech, such people had no hope of having a physical vehicle of beauty. Now, of course, many ways had been developed to give us all the body we preferred. But back then, one was stuck with what one was born to.

Lee and I waited at the theatre entrance, and a short while later, I saw Flo, dressed in an exquisite velvet of darkest red, with pearls sewn in intricate swirls and sprays across the front and around the hem. With her was a young girl, in a taffeta dress of pale lavender, with a striking teal Witness necklace. Flo smiled brightly, and the young girl grinned.

"Izzy!" Flo exclaimed and hugged me.

"Flo!" I returned, as I hugged her back. "This is Lee," I said, "Lee, this is Flo, the artist that made the new fountain at home."

Lee hugged Flo warmly. "Glad to meet you," he offered. "The fountain is the most awe-inspiring piece I have seen. I love the way you play with the water."

Flo smiled coyly in thanks and turned to indicate the young one beside her. "My daughter, Dee."

"Hi," said Dee, "Nice to meet you." Dee smiled as Lee and I shook her hand.

"Lovely colors, Dee," I offered, gesturing at the pretty sight she created.

Dee grinned widely and said simply, "Thanks!"

"Izzy tells me you are a photographer," Flo said to Lee as we turned to enter the theatre lobby, sliding the tickets into the door 'bottie as we passed through. Lee began to regale Flo with stories of his photographic adventures and we all chatted warmly as we found our seats and sat.

The play was a sad one, with the protagonist ending his life with no one to mourn his passing. What a statement on the affairs of a scarcity paradigm. There was a standing ovation at the end as Pierce took the stage with his Troupe of actors, all of whom had high reputations and had, indeed, proved the reputations true.

The four of us decided it would be a wonderful adventure to go to Thailand City, a sky city above the temples and jungle of Thailand, to shop and eat. I will admit that I was the strongest proponent of this idea, as I was (again!) craving Thai food. We each passed through the J.D. to find ourselves in the noontide clouds above the ancient city of Bangkok.

We shared a repast of curries and rice, I choosing a viciously spicy red curry, the others opting for tamer fare, with sweet Thai coffee for all. Dee adored the mild curry dish she chose and commented that she might learn to prepare Thai food. We laughed and smiled encouragingly. She had announced that she might want to be an actor when we were in New York, and had suggested other directions – fashion designer, painter (when she heard what I did), and other such creative endeavors – throughout the cycle day.

"I'm sure you will find your bliss soon, Dee," I remarked with kindness in my words.

Dee gave a small frown and replied, "I surely hope so, Izzy. There's so much to choose from and I like to do most of it!"

"That's the plight we have now, I guess," Lee interjected. "But it's a far better plight than Quasimodo had, eh?"

Dee nodded. "Yeah. At least no one teases and hurts you if you haven't figured out yet what you love to do."

We all agreed and the conversation turned to my finished painting, Flo's latest work and other things we wanted to share.

We thanked Ki, who had provided our lovely meal and had spent most of it putting on a show as he cooked for his large table of guests (who came and ate and left, sometimes joining in with the show banter, and sometimes eating and leaving with smiles and waves of thanks, loathe to interrupt the flow). The four of us strolled out to see what was offered in the many shops along a ribbon of walkway. When we finally tired of the adventure, we headed towards a J.D., Dee carrying a bag with a lovely bracelet she had fallen in love with, and said our goodbyes.

"Let me know when we can do this again," Flo suggested. "I enjoyed this immensely!"

"I'll call you when the next play is offered and we can make plans," I offered. "It was indeed lovely."

We hugged and waved as each of us approached the J.D. And then Lee and I were home.

The house now was traveling east from San Francisco, heading for Brice Canyon. Lee had suggested that location and I thought that would be glorious, and so off the house went at my request.

Lee took my hand as he stepped through, murmuring something about sleep, and led me to the bedroom, to make love and then to sleep. It had been a long day.

In the morning, after greeting one another in kisses and caresses, Lee asked if I wanted to read more of the diary.

"Sure!," I responded, calling for the book. Momentarily it was placed beside us and we snuggled again in front of its pages, finding where we had left off.

April 30, 2009

Tomorrow I leave for New York! I cannot express my excitement! Now is the time to break the perspective to the world. Now the small army, who understands where we could take ourselves, will grow – with any luck, to grow to where we can affect change.

My friend, Bernice, will drive me to the airport. I still haven't gotten through to her completely as to what abundance means to every Human on the planet…but she kinda gets it. She still thinks something would cause it all to break down, but she agrees that if we could make it happen it would be heaven. I guess that is the best I can hope for from her. I love her dearly, but she is not so blessed with vision as some.

Meanwhile, I have fewer and fewer arguments with people online. Most, I suspect, have backed away, sure like Bernice that somehow it won't work without any specific idea of what would break it down. None have offered an issue I have been unable to address, and so the discourse has slowed or stopped on many of the boards I post to. But on one, AboveTopSecret.com, I have many now discussing what the first step is to bring awareness and motivation to Humans. Many there have far more data about the world's secret workings than are known by those who trust the MSM as their definer of reality.

I found ATS when I was searching for information on something – I forget now what I was looking for that day – and, having found the forum, which values evidence, rational speculation and interpretation, and denies ignorance, I have posted my thoughts consistently for some time. The Abundance Paradigm is merely the latest.

It's nice to find the reception of rational individuals. Sure, there are the spooks, toadies who roam the boards spreading epithets and assassinating character, berating evidence and belittling suggestions, but overall, ATS has a population of earnest and honest Human hearts.

Many on ATS, most I would say, have seen through the Lizard Hearted's behaviors – including the plans that whipped up national fervor to drag us into wars, and the attempts to starve us, enslave us, and tear down the works we have created to protect all individuals, specifically our Constitution. I am very grateful that the members are so open-minded. They know the panic the Internet has caused in the Lizard Hearted. They know of the efforts to control the Web, keeping the truth from us and making us ignorant.

As I have said before, we must prevail in keeping the free and open Web, where we are the "spiders" that swarm around the data "flies," lest it become the Net that ensnares our minds. Dear Gods, we must prevail!

Ah yes, I thought, that's where "data flies" came from. Amelia coined it. I had forgotten. We read on.

May 3, 2009

The flight to New York was quick and uneventful, and I found the guy who was picking me up with ease. He was holding a sign outside the gate with my name on it. He took me to the hotel and got me checked in. They put me in a suite! It's lovely, high up on the 52nd floor, and looks out over Manhattan. Food arrived for dinner and all my quirky requests had been seen to – no hydrogenated oils, fully or partially, in any food. No MSG, no propylene glycol, no beef, no pork. Organic produce only, organic eggs and poultry. Sometimes I am surprised by how much is pumped into our food supply, sold as being good for one reason or another, and so many never question.

I suppose I would eat beef and I would eat pork if I knew they had been raised naturally, and not in pools of their own waste, stressed out in overcrowded confinement, shot with antibiotics and hormones, slaughtered in filth and otherwise processed with no thought for health but rather profit. Sadly, finding such pure and good meat is difficult.

This is the best I have eaten in quite some time.

The boss was making sounds that bordered on threat when I left work on Wednesday. I strongly suspect that I will see no job when I get back. Well, I will worry about that when I get back. Too bad I couldn't open her mind to the ethical and practical implications of abundance. I tried…but she just couldn't grasp it.

I met yesterday with several writers but not Stephen. We discussed what I might say in the limited time I will have. We honed it, added lines for Stephen, lines of response for me, and so on. It was lots of fun, and some of the suggestions for repartee had us cracking up. It was a very enjoyable time and I count myself lucky to have been invited.

I will spend the weekend wandering around Manhattan, maybe riding the subway out to Coney Island – I keep hearing how fun and historic it is – and take in the Statue of Liberty, the Empire State Building, and maybe look over "Ground Zero…" The last I am unsure about, since it is likely to drive home the evils the Lizard Hearted can concoct and inflict on the populace they control, and I would rather fill my time with happy thoughts while I am here. It is such a rare opportunity, and I don't want to spoil it.

"That must have been so exciting for her," I commented to Lee as we took a break. "I wish I could have been a fly on the wall of the meeting with the writers."

Lee agreed. "Yeah, those historic moments we will never have the details of… Wish we both could have been there."

I nodded earnestly in response and then suggested, "Shall we have breakfast? I'm getting famished." Lee kissed me quickly in response and hopped up out of bed.

"Sure," Lee replied, "but I get to make it today!"

"Great," I nodded happily, stretching and then pulling myself up and out of the bed.

We made our way out through the jungle and Lee said he would call me when breakfast was ready as he turned towards the kitchen. I headed on to the living room to check my email.

When I got to my couch I brought up the Web and then my email. I had a few more announcements of products available and two responses to my mailing about Little Buddha and Companion. A George Pingau and Nguyen Li both had fallen in love with the work. Both were asking if I would part with the painting. Since I knew neither, I wrote to each asking about their thoughts on the work, hoping to determine which was the better to give it to. By the time I had finished writing and sending the inquiry, and just as I was starting to explore information on the Web, Lee called me to breakfast.

Spread upon the dining room table was an awesome smelling offering. A soufflé with a very sharp cheddar cooked in, venison medallions, fresh creamline milk in tall glasses, and ripe blueberries covered in cream. It all looked delightful.

"Thanks, Chef Lee," I said as I surveyed the table with delight. Lee wasn't half bad as a cook. "Let's eat!"

With total agreement, Lee sat in unison with me and we polished off the entire lot in giggles and conversation.

"The house should be at Brice by the time we're done," I remarked. "Shall we take a hike after breakfast?"

"Wonderful," Lee responded. "I love the beauty there. I think I'll bring my camera."

I gave a brief laugh. "Surprise, surprise!"

Lee made a wry face at me and then returned my laughter. "Well, you know me…"

"I surely do, Mister," I retorted, winking and grinning.

Together we went to get dressed. I asked for jeans and a T-shirt, with rugged boots ideal for trail hiking. Lee's attire nearly matched mine but where I had chosen a red T-shirt, he had chosen a navy blue one.

We walked out to the terrace, seeing the ramp already set near the head of the trail into the canyon. The colorful, wind-sculpted pillars of stone peeked out beyond the edge of the canyon, offering their form for the imagination to build a story around. Other houses were set nearby, though I saw no one within hailing distance. Brice Canyon is fairly popular, it would seem.

Once we got to the ground, the ramp retracted on my suggestion, and we headed for the trailhead downwards. The air was warm but not yet sweltering as it would be in mid-summer, and the scent of pine and freshness filled our deeply drawn breaths. Down and down we went, switching back here and there, as the stone rose higher and higher, frozen in dance, above our head.

Light and shadow played tag through the monuments we passed through, and I marveled at the many colors and fascinating shapes that made up the canyon.

"Oh, Lee, this is beautiful."

Lee, who had been capturing the canyon's story on film, tucked his camera close in one hand and wrapped me with his other arm, pulling me close to him and kissing me lightly. "It sure is," he agreed.

Others were passing us on the trail, or standing in awe or conversation as we passed them. We smiled to any we met, and smiles were always returned.

Lee and I found a small bench of stone some distance down, naturally carved by the forces that sculpted the Canyon itself, and we sat side by side. Above us loomed cartoon characters and faerie dancers, caught frozen in form, multihued and glowing in the early afternoon sun. I sighed and rested my head on Lee's shoulder; Lee wrapped mine in his arm. For a while we sat, saying nothing, and watched the movement on the trail, and the lizards on the rocks nearby that drank up the sun as they spread themselves out to maximize their sun-receiving surface.

Except for the snatches of conversation of those who passed by on the trail, the air stood nearly still. The sound of a greater wind above, teasing the tops of the parade of forms, whistled softly. It was peaceful, restful. Shadows reached for the light, distorting themselves upon the tumbled evidence of fallen faces that spread out at the foot of the towers.

After a while Lee stood, taking my hands and pulling me to my feet, and we began the hike back upwards.

As we approached, the house lowered the ramp and we climbed its slope to finally rest on the terrace upon a bench, placed by 'botties per my request sent as we neared the trailhead. The ramp pulled in and the house lifted skyward where it hovered with an awesome view of the Canyon. Lee and I kissed and melted in the sun into one another, our passion full and love overflowing.

Chapter 11

Lee and I bathed away the sweat of our exertions, the hike and our passions, relaxing in my bath. The waters of the fall splashing downward rinsed and refreshed us, and we languished there a while, listening to the song the water sang in gurgles and gulps around us.

At last I spoke. "Shall we return to Amelia?"

"Yes. I am curious to see how she viewed the experience of being on the Colbert Report that night."

Amelia's appearance with Stephen is, of course, historic, and school children are shown the footage in history lessons; we all knew what was said that night. But her perspective was largely unknown, so the diary was a blessing for any (like me) who wanted more of the story.

We pulled ourselves from the waters, pausing to dry one another with the thick towels at hand and moved into the bedroom where we found the diary as we had left it, sitting on the now made bed, awaiting our return. We snuggled in, rumpling the smooth surface of the spread.

> May 6, 2009
>
> It was unBELIEVABLE! I was so nervous, but somehow I managed to keep my cool. The repartee with Stephen went very well, and I still managed to convey the concepts in the short time I had. The audience loved it and applauded as I waved to them, some of them even standing in ovation, as I left the stage. That part was edited out, though. I almost didn't believe it was me as I watched the final airing.
>
> There were more points I could have brought up, but given the few minutes I had, I am well pleased. The message is Bumped, and that is what matters. It will be interesting to see where this all leads.
>
> I was given the suggestion – by Stephen himself! – that I write a book explaining the details of the paradigm and

how we might bring it about. I think I will do just that. Stephen said he might be able to help me get it published, even! I liked Stephen even more in person than I like him on the show. He is funny and witty, friendly and wise.

I will be flying back to Ithaca later this afternoon and will hope for the best tomorrow when I report to the job I hope I still have.

Well, I have to clean up and pack up. They're taking me to the airport in two hours. I must say, it's sad to be leaving this poshness for the dreary struggle to keep roof and a flow of food. I like not having to worry about where my next meal will come from. I like having it delivered and made to my personal preferences. I like the freedom and the lack of pressure. If I could live like this always, life would be so much better.

But I will try not to choose to depress. I could very easily do so. I must find a way to think about leaving this for that bleakness, the bugs and the bareness of home, that does not lead to depression. I will think of it as a dream, perhaps, or keep focused on the fact that I was the one that got to bring the Ideas to the show. I won't think about how sad it all is compared to this splendor.

May 8, 2009

Ah, Gods. I arrived at the paper yesterday morning to find that they had hired someone else. I am trying to keep from crying, telling myself that now I have time to write the book – which I started last night. I just needed to vent, dear Diary, so here I am writing this.

The rent isn't due until the first, and so I have 23 days to get the book written. After that, I am sure eviction proceedings will begin. Maybe the book will be sold before I am actually back out on the street. I will hold that hope. Thank goodness winter is over and I will have a few months free of freezing weather and snow.

The forums have seen a large upswing of people defending the paradigm. That is something to be thankful for. Already many people are talking about it on the Web. I think it's catching on.

Not much else to write for now, at least not here. I should get back to the book.

"I'm hungry," I announced.

"Me, too," Lee replied. We set the diary aside and headed towards the dining room, deciding that lunch would be best fixed by the replicator since we were both too famished to wait for preparation.

I suggested scallops in a creamy wine sauce, with broccoli and baked potato. Lee said that sounded awesome, and so I gave the instructions even as we were making our way to the table.

Shortly after we sat, a 'bottie served the requested meal and we dug in.

"Where shall we go next?" I asked as we nibbled a delightful dessert of rich coconut cake.

"Interested in some spelunking?" Lee queried, looking at me in hopeful anticipation. "Maybe Carlsbad Caverns?"

I shook my head slightly and responded, "Spelunking sounds great, but Carlsbad Caverns is so crowded!"

"True," Lee replied. "Well, I know of some volcanic caves, runnels of lava that cooled on the outside and drained the liquid interior to create caves, out in the desert of southern California... They shouldn't be overrun."

"Ooo, sounds interesting. Tell the house where they are and let's go." I smiled in exuberance.

Lee nodded and then paused briefly. The house asked if instructions were approved – although Lee is "authorized" to request things of my house, things like a change of location get verified with me. I sent my approval and saw the world out beyond the house begin to move.

"Hey, let's see if Lil is free. Maybe she would like company..." I suggested.

"Sure. Call her up," Lee agreed.

I asked the house to connect me to Lil, and shortly Lil appeared nearby.

"Oh, Izzy!" exclaimed Lil when we connected, "I was going to call you! I'm having a few friends over this evening to play cards. Interested?"

"Great," I responded. Lee was nodding, and though Lil couldn't see him, she could tell by the direction of my look and my acknowledging nod that Lee was for the idea.

"See you around 7:00 then?"

I smiled. "We'll be there."

"We have about eight hours. Diary or Dangle Park?" Lee asked when Lil's hologram had vanished.

I weighed the options. Dangle Park was the amusement park that hung high above Rio de Janeiro. It had energy rides, slides, and other excitement. It had been a while since I had visited Dangle Park, and I adore any amusement park, but on the other hand, I was looking forward to the uploading of the diary scans to AmeliasHistory.org, and I needed to finish reading it before I did that so that I could say I was the first (with Lee, of course) to read what she wrote. That was a status perk and I wasn't going to let it go.

"Maybe we can do Dangle Park next cycle, after we finish the diary."

Lee agreed, and we headed back towards the bedroom. As we were walking, the house tapped me on the mind and let me know that another house was coming up on us and was asking to dock. In the same breath it let me know that it was the Horny Toad Society. I made a face and asked the house to thank them for the visit but that there was no one here interested in their gifts.

The Horny Toad Society enjoyed orgies with strangers, approaching houses at random and offering their gifts. They had become well discussed on the Web, and many chose to accept. Lee and I had discussed how we felt about such offers and had agreed that we were committed in keeping energies flowing in focus between the two of us and not weakening our bond with energies diverted elsewhere.

In fact, Cara had once shyly suggested Lee and I might join her with Tim and The Kid – they both thought it was a cool idea, too – in a ménage a many, but Lee gently explained that he and I were connected spirits and that we maintained the energy in a closed circuit between us. We both thanked her and assured her that her offer of the gift was appreciated.

So when HTS made its offer to us, I felt confident in passing up the offer for Lee.

Still, I informed him after the Society had moved on, in case he had changed his mind since last we spoke of it. "The HTS just offered their gifts. I presume you're uninterested?"

Lee laughed, "Darling, you don't know HOW uninterested I am." He stopped to take me into his arms and lift me off the floor. Kissing me deeply, he stroked my back and buttocks with one hand while he held on with the other. I relented to his touch, pressing my breasts against him and wrapping my legs about his waist. He carried me into the bedroom, as on my fleeting thought a 'bottie scurried to move the diary out of harm's way. He laid me across the bed, sliding atop me as he did. As I welcomed him, I thought, The diary can wait a little longer.

After we had cooled the circuits, kissing and cooing our thanks for one another, I idly called for the diary and the 'bottie came forth.

June 12, 2009

I have been so busy. I wrote like a fiend and had the book finished spot on the 31st. I contacted Stephen and emailed the draft to him. It's not the longest read, but I think I addressed everything that needs to be addressed. Stephen got back to me on the 4th, I think it was, and sent a few suggestions which I incorporated into the manuscript. I sent it back with changes and he emailed on the 7th, saying he was submitting the manuscript personally to his publisher.

That was the same day I had a Notice to Pay tacked on my apartment door. I am fully out of money now, getting food at the pantry (usually wilted produce, since most of the packaged food has high fructose corn syrup or hydrogenated oils or some other dietary horror), and wondering when it will be that my utilities are cut off. I'm also wondering when the eviction notice will arrive and how much time I have left here.

I hate being unable to meet the obligations of the scarcity paradigm. On the one hand, if I could meet them, I would…but on the other, I see how unnecessary it is for me to have to worry about such matters.

On more exciting things, CNN ran a story touching lightly on the concept of abundance. While it didn't advocate any action, it did introduce a few of the implications of such a world. The Web, on the other hand, rather exploded with talk, about the CNN story, about my bit on the Report, about the advantages and ethics involved, about ways to start moving in that direction.

When I searched for sites with "abundance paradigm" mentioned, I used to see pretty much only the boards I had visited and discussed it on. Now there are tens of thousands! I am not the only one talking about it anymore. And this bodes well.

People are blogging about it. People are discussing it on many boards. People are saying good things – and some are saying bad things, but getting a lot of recoil. It's amazing to see.

More and more the paradigm is taking hold.

July 3, 2009

The eviction notice came last week. I have to pay up, appear in court, or be out by the end of the month. I also received a publishing contract! It came three days ago, and when they receive it, I will be sent a check for $10,000! Needless to say, I signed it and sent it right back! Maybe I will be able to pay up. In fact, maybe I can get a better place to live. The roaches here are so gross, and I have even stepped on a few, trekking to the bathroom in the middle of the night. Uggggg!

It's all so surreal! The Web is humming, singing, heralding the abundance paradigm. The search returns are now up over 200,000!

The MSM actually broke a story about the possible history of our planet including extraterrestrials, showing documents that had been leaked that alluded to it as a fact. They even suggested that we might be genetically created by such a race. Oh, I think the truth is starting to crack the dam. The toadies are waking up to the freedom they could have if they would toadie no more.

Tomorrow is the 4th, a day important mostly to those of us who live in the U.S. I wanted to say something about that. After watching the dismantling of the Constitution by the previous administration, and the total lack of effort to really restore it by the present one, I wonder how many of us understand we are celebrating something we have lost.

I wonder how many can see the façade for what it is. How many are aware that the country, and the principles we are taught that this country is all about, are gone. That we celebrate nothing.

We have turned from individual freedom to corporofascist slavery. I am so saddened at the many who cannot see the dark facts. As freedom erodes, the double-think is put into play. "See how free we are – as long as we adhere to these few behaviors and don't go outside of the lines." I shake my head sadly.

Still… With the Web so actively talking about the Paradigm… Maybe the whole world can turn to a respect of Individuals of Sentience, allowing freedom within informed willingness of all participants. Maybe there is still time.

I can only watch and hope.

Chapter 12

Lil's house was very Japanese in design. Built as a platform with bamboo-and-rice-paper bungalows scattered around a central garden that sported a section of raked rocks, a koi pond, and a no stage (which often had a holographic play being performed upon it, but was tonight filled with tables laid with decks of cards and scoring pads). Her house, too, floated in the sky, domed with energy to protect from the elements, and from what I could gather, we were above Hawaii. Nearby boiled a caldera of steam and lava. Beyond that, the island spread out on a sapphire sea.

Lanterns of paper lit the area, with a musky incense burning somewhere, kissing the air with hints of exotic florals and woods. From somewhere came the soft strains of traditional Japanese music, plucking softly at the corners of awareness. Maybe a dozen people sat or stood on the stage, chatting and nibbling the rice crackers, sushi, and ginger placed about on low black tables, passing pipes of weed, or sipping a sweet golden plum wine or hot green tea.

Lil was heading towards us with arms open in welcome. She hugged each of us in turn, taking my hand and leading the two of us up to the stage. Nassim waved from a discussion he seemed deep into with a bearded gentleman. I recognized Chef Allouba, and Cheyenne Dutch, a mutual friend of Lil's and mine. The rest I had not yet met, and Lil took us around making introductions. The bearded man turned out to be Uncle Grant, a physicist Nassim worked with.

After mingling and meeting a few others who came after us, we sat down to play Hearts or Spades or Rummy – table's choice. Many loved these games of Old and such gatherings were not uncommon. We played through the night, discussing Amelia and all for much of the night after I mentioned the diary. As the night wore on, the numbers dwindled and tables consolidated. Finally, as the night wound down, Lee and I thanked Lil and hugged our old and new friends, saying our goodbyes, and headed for the J.D.

When we got home, Lee and I were too tired for anything but sleep. Shedding clothes, pausing only for mouth cleaning, and into the sheets we crashed. With sleepy murmurs we entangled ourselves and fell asleep in one another's arms.

In the morning we made love, spending the pent up passion of the previous evening. When the last spark had burst, we lay softly stroking each other's face and arms, looking deeply into the other's eyes.

"I have to check my email," I explained as I finally got up. "I have a couple of people interested in my latest painting and I want to see if they have gotten back to me. I must decide which one to give it to."

Lee nodded lazily from the bed. "Shall we finish the diary when you're done?"

"Yes, yes. I want to get the scans out on the Amelia site. They are going to eat them up!" I said over my shoulder as I left to seat myself on my couch. Once comfortable, I called up my email. Both George Pingau and Nguyen Li had responded. I read over their pleas, and, while Li said he simply loved the image and the feelings it evoked, George waxed on about how it looked just like his daughter had when she was six, how his daughter loved cats, and it was as if I had taken a photo of his little girl and transferred it to canvas, how the happy memories had come flooding in when he saw the image, and could I please consider his request for the original.

It was easy to choose. I sent a note to Nguyen Li that, sadly, the picture was given to another. Then I notified George that Little Buddha and Companion was his and he should receive it shortly. I also informed the house of the destination of the painting, knowing the work was being wrapped up and a delivery call was placed. George could have it delivered when he accepted the delivery call.

The email screen winked out in my lap and I returned to the bedroom to find Lee still resting in bed, awaiting my return.

I climbed in with him, and then…once again I called for the diary, which arrived by 'bottie.

> July 28, 2009
>
> The check came! I opened an account and decided to pay the rent here for a few more months – I don't want to

mess with moving stuff if things move fast enough and I can have my choice. Soon enough I will not have to work to live as I want.

Free energy and the methods of extraction were reported in the MSM, even the history of its suppression came forth. Antigrav was mentioned, even. People are clamoring now to build robots, allocate land for organic farming, research transmutation methods, and more and more! I look around and people are nicer to one another now, helping others get through the tough times. And people are working towards the abundance paradigm with no pay whatsoever. It is emergent as the Web fills with ideas, efforts, and sharing. Toadies that once were trying to inhibit the flow of information have let it go. The world is catching the "gold bug." Even China has opened some of its information avenues.

People are building their own free energy devices, based on the plans that a guy who calls himself Anti/Christ – he claims "Christ" and "Antichrist" are the same… – put up on the Web, and we are getting off the grid, running our homes and cars on it. It's coming, and I don't think it will stop. My book will be on the shelves this week, and we shall see what happens then.

I bought a new computer and got Internet access. The number of sites that mention "abundance paradigm" has topped two million. The news is filled with the concept. People are seeing the light at the end of the tunnel, for the first time in our current history. More and more are grasping what it will mean. Few bring up "greed" and "power." I am truly in awe.

Cures are springing up for many of the diseases that have plagued us. Even the MSM is reporting on them. Suppression is failing right and left.

Already it is known that there was much more history that has been hidden for eons. The Egyptian pyramids and Sphinx are over 10,000 years old. The "Gods" of "myth" were extraterrestrial, and we were sculpted as helpers, but were enslaved by the Creator's brother. On top of all this, we carry galactic royal blood. The Terra Papers are discussed more and more, even in the MSM.

Though no ET's have stepped forward yet, we may see that soon.

I can't thank Stephen enough for his role in bringing all this about.

August 7, 2009

My book came out! And oh my Gods! I am a celebrity!

It's so odd to be recognized. I walk into a store or even down the street and people look, some point, some start up conversations with me. I guess the pic on the flap was good enough to identify me.

Emails are flying about the abundance available on this planet. In this Universe. People are happier. People seem to have a reason to live now. What a startling change in society. Around the globe now they are fired up. Information is flowing as never before.

The search brings back 23 million. It's going viral worldwide!

Soon I will see my dream. Soon.

And this is where Amelia's diary ended. The rest of her history is well documented. She went on talk shows; she sold a billion copies of her book in nearly as many languages. And then one day, they found her dead, still waiting for her dream to free her to complete choice of her house (which I have become certain looked much like mine), in the apartment where Lee found her diary.

Sadly, she had had cancer and never spoke of it, nor let any know she suffered. She didn't even mention it in her diary! She was not interested in herself so much as she was in freeing the Human Hearted from the clutches of the Lizard Hearted, and free us she did.

The Alliance of Hearts was written up, based on the ethical outline Amelia had proposed in her book; the Lizard Hearted signed it and we signed it. ET's did meet us as equals, as royalty, even, based on our royal DNA. We traveled to the bases on the moon and Mars and discovered the truth about our planets, for it is the Solar System that is Ours.

The people demanded the "Human Bailout," passing bills to support the best management of resources, building robots for all the work we didn't want to do. Everything was programmed in open source; safety and reliability in products and services skyrocketed. Research and development took off. Tech leaped to awesome heights, and teleportation, replicators, and myriad gadgets and concepts to help sprang forth, almost as Athena, fully grown, it seemed. With information flowing so freely, the tech was emergent as well.

If Amelia had lived at most a year more, she would still be here, cured and healthy, and at that point, a very short way off to seeing her home. Fate is indeed fickle. But Amelia lives on in our hearts as we live each day in this Heaven on Earth. Her death saddened us all.

Stephen Colbert, on the other hand, is still keeping us amused. He has a show that is quite a bit different than the Old one, but every bit as funny – funnier, some say, as he no longer has topics he cannot approach. He is heralded for his role in bringing the paradigm to our awareness, giving Amelia her chance. He is a hero.

It's an interesting thing – rather insignificant in a scarcity paradigm – that we all carry lighters – well, I should say, We, most of us, choose to carry lighters. Our lighters run on free energy, with the crop circle engine. Each is everlasting, and each of us has crafted our own, in some way, those multitudes of us that choose to. From an idea we have, to crafting it for ourselves and others, we express ourselves in the design of our lighters.

Lighters are seen as status symbols of a sort. There were many who have boast walls of lighters belonging to the Infamous that had been gifted to them. Gifting of lighters has become common.

To counter an overabundance, if you find one and you don't know whose it is, after asking around and getting others' opinions – is it theirs? Do they know whose it is? Or do they even like the looks of it? And if not and no one claims it… if you REALLY like it, you keep it, but if it inspires not, it goes into the MWD when next you see one, which is most often a short walk from where you are when you find it.

Many leave their lighters and do not claim them, seeing how their work is accepted. It's kind of a game some of us play.

And thus, the number of lighters that stick around is kept under control, and still we keep about us the measure of our status, the symbol of the individual worth – We understand that sentience all springs from this energy, given in abundance, and Worth is what we contribute with now our bliss being granted.

Lee and I looked at the last page of the diary, and then each other.

"I think I need to paint," I said. "I'll scan those and get them up on the Web by 'bottie and see what the data flies draw forth. This should be fun."

"Data flies," as Amelia indicated in her diary and in her book, are the pieces of information We contribute to our Infosphere, most often for their funny factor. When we're not out doing other things, we have the choice of sharing our funny moments and any needed Witness moments. Funny Moment Sharing is a major social event in gatherings of around 3 to 6 Individuals of Sentience. People's stories made the Media, became the Media, wherein the people's stories, their Witnesses, were told.

Mainly it was the Web that was the Media. All media was there if you wanted, and surely Media Buffs sprung up as hobbyists, collecting and talking about the Old treasures they had, and blissing out. This group, as all the other groups that blossomed, withering in time, going viral planet wide, or settling somewhere in the space between – they were emergent in abundance.

Our advances in all things made social enjoyment the choice we all had, within the ethics of an informed willingness stipulation. One receives social status based on one's choice of behavior with others, and Witness made it much easier to prove one's and others' willingness in things, and the degree to which we are truly informed. We can show it all in a single striking scene, or build our case for our behavior in a Situdrama. If we have to, which, any more. is seldom.

We never testify with our data if we don't want to, but may do so if we choose, and in the Witness of others, we make MUCH better choices. When we are alone or with the willing it is our business alone, and when accusations arise, there is almost always a basis. The incident in question is nearly always settled. The Web has become the Court, and with the direct feed (Read Only) aspect of information recorded on our Datacubes, the truth nearly always comes out, with infamous spots that are never cleared up and that keep historians arguing for years.

But overall, nearly any case these days is infamous. We rarely choose to behave poorly towards one another, and so when it happens, it makes it big on the Web.

Basically, what Datacube gave each one of us was control of our autonomous Selves (and the 'botties that attended Us Individually), yet collectively, We still have an ethical set of behaviors emerge in a world where money had been removed. The Lizard Hearted made a weak argument that it was "surveillance," but it was surveillance (witness) within informed consent (willingness), which is a different animal altogether in terms of emergence, to the visceral response of "someone evil above watching me" mentality.

One thing that vanished, pretty much, was the concept of "estate" and though lineage became a bragging right of sorts, the lineage came from those whose contributions to abundance were known, most often.

When Datacube first came out, a desperate effort was made to suppress it, but by that time, Amelia's Point had Tipped, and the toadies-no-more who came up with it first knew that by freeing the data flies onto the Web it would feed us spiders the strength we needed to defend but never to bear false Witness. Thus, in honesty, we would tend to get by.

We wrote the Code of Ethics, the Alliance of Hearts, based on the Idea that UnLove, where willingness is not mutual, if information has been maliciously withheld, will not be tolerated, and if you choose to go past willingness, your reputation amongst those that care will drop, and if you work your cards right you will be shunned. Keep unhappiness to a minimum, and be prepared to tell your side of the story. If you are found guilty in Court, it will be of your peers, those who matter day-to-day around each of us. We do not tolerate the UnEthical, and informed willingness is the yardstick.

And of course, if you trust those around you, your surveillance of your house may be limited to the soirees you throw – everyone knows Witness is all over the place at the bazillion open functions. It is expected and no big deal as long as no UnLove is evidenced (no unhappiness). We have much Neutral Love (neither Love nor UnLove), and an abundance of Love, Itself, as we move in the circles of those who love the same things we do, finding it easier to love even those who do not.

Thus, We spend Our collective time promoting Love, the Highest Ethical Goal.

With a kiss I left Lee, heading to my studio, and I knew Lee would soon be off to do his film exposures the Old way (his thing, y'know), and at dinner we would share them. I would see the broken boards with the zipper bag poking out – I knew Lee enough to know he would HAVE to take a picture...or 10, with holotech, and a bunch of analog ones, Old tech, in artistically arranged composition – and the reality would supplant the patched-together picture I had been carrying since the diary entered my quality picture, since it entered my Universe.

LORD. SAVIOR. DISHWASHER.

When this, "my trip," began, I went through a sanity questioning phase. I became extra introspective, asking, "Where is this coming from?" and "Why me?"

And I remembered that when I was 5 years old I had this notion that I was reserved for something big, that I'd be taken care of, that I'd be rich, that I was going to live a long time – and knew that I WAS an inventor.

Shortly after my "vision," on Feb 16 1996, I was hurtled into a series of synchronicities and serendipitous events and encounters that would set me on this path. What path? The path to GOD=G.U.T. – I did not impose the most recent spirit/science fork, but will hold it where it's one… This grokking of God, the universe, and everything allowed me to invent AI, Free Energy and Teleportation technologies. These miraculous and disruptive inventions assume an innate relationship to the potential of humanity, to its well being and enlightenment, but most of all, its SLACK. This was the original intent of God for man and Man for technology, the top of Maslow's pyramid.

We have no time to love ourselves, much less our enemy. Somewhere in the Bible, I think it says, "If these times were not cut short no one would survive." That fork just became a knife.

In the past 14 years, my mission has become more imminent and my memes have gained potency, probably due to the dozen 2012 books on the shelves. I have had to become a witness to my transformation: from reluctant, to overzealous, to bored. There's a kind of zen to my current indifference. No number of remarks about me forgetting my meds, or your personal qualifiers will stop what has to be done. There is no question regarding my sanity and intent that you can ask which I have not asked myself.

Like most rogue messiahs, I have tripped on psychedelics and attained Christ consciousness, if but for a few minutes. Still, it was enough. A "heroic" dose of psilocybin left me laughing and crying in the throes of an ecstatic catharsis and I knew at once that we are all beautiful creations here to serve each other. Since then, no matter how much my now easily differentiated ego chooses to hate individuals or groups, I'm able to reel in that negativity… But the truth of it is, is that God's love translates into my Wrath.

I can't judge the entire populace of Earth but everyone can judge me. Among my fruits are things you may deem too human or even Satanic. There are lesser lines in the sand beyond the audacity of claiming these titles, and I get that. I'm the Christ that *I would* get behind and support. If you believe I AM doing the will of our creator, if you have the desire and will to work towards The Abundance Paradigm or New Jerusalem, then you are one of The Elect, The Remnant, The Chosen, Spiritual Israel, The Body, My People. If you dismiss me outright because I drop F-Bombs, listen to obnoxious music or because I enjoy Cannabis, well, then, in my opinion you are an undiscerning scoffer, a useless eater, the lukewarm, the smoke in my nostrils, what <u>REVELATION X</u> from the SubGenii dedicates an entire chapter to – The Conspiracy.

The only reason (besides being anointed or possessed) I can do this is because I started a never ending self-education 20 years ago. I put in what Malcolm Gladwell taught me are the requisite 10,000 hours of practice/ study to be truly versed in something, and that something is me.

I'm like Oliver Heaviside. I prefer to mooch off of friends and family while I hide out with pot and physics – Oliver's preference was pipe tobacco and applied math. Like that dirty hippie, Carl Sagan, I find that the "warping of time and space" (See Reefer Madness) Cannabinoids enable, enhances my ability to associate abstract and disparate ideas and theories. Jesus was a mooch too, but he probably figured that it was justified, seeing as how he was the only guy around that could raise the dead. I feel that way about free energy. I know this stuff is important even if nobody else does. Slack must be justified though, the bliss must be balanced with suffering, so yeah, I'll do your dishes while I live here, and if I must get a job, I'll wash dishes.

In fact, "Hydro-Ceramic Sanitation Specialist" has been pretty much my only job; some restaurants are better than others...

Why is this significant? Let me paint you a picture:

You likely despise doing the dishes right? Now imagine being expected to wash dishes as fast as humanly possible for hours at a time, all the while people are demanding items from you, often seconds apart, "on the fly." Little spoons, a stack of burgers from scratch, paper towels, sushi plates... When I do look up, I see tables full of wealthy elites who pay $16 for a salad and eat only the shrimp. I get to scrape the rest into the garbage. Occasionally very sexy waitresses come back to the prep/pit to scarf a few bites. Why must their pants be so tight? Oh yeah, tips. They would never fuck me.

My immediate boss is The Chef and sometimes my mistake encounters his high standards or displaced girlfriend issues and he goes Gordon Ramsay on me – not pleasant.

This is all the training I need for a proper attitude in my role as Omega Christ. A machine-like submission to the destroyer function I adopt in each trinity. I cleanse the containers of creation by blasting and scrubbing the wasted bits and scum from their pristine potential so that He may present his art once more. Only difference is, I can't walk out on Reality like I can the dish pit. I can tire of Chef's demands and dishes, but not God's expectations and constant gifts for fulfilling those expectations.

...I quit my job involuntarily recently. I'm in a delicate place right now and the wrath is bursting at the seams. I had been tolerating Chef's "Ramsay" moments fairly well but this time was it. If I hadn't walked out I would have smashed something or someone. The good thing is, it provides me with a PERFECT example of what is wrong with the world.

First we begin with the Restaurant Trinity:

Chef/Owner = Creator
Waitstaff/Customer = Maintainer
Busser/Dishwasher = Destroyer

The economy of this system is using different currencies – time, food, etc,.. One important currency is PLATES. What happened demonstrates the failure to differentiate a PEOPLE problem from a SITUATION problem and correcting this failure is the basic premise of this book.

Chef ran out of "squares". This happens once every couple weeks when a certain dish is popular. Chef comes back, sees some squares in the rack drying and he politely asks, "Can you get me those asap?" NO PROBLEM. About a half hour later, for the fourth time in four months, he *gets in my grill, pushes me aside and starts frantically doing the dishes*. I stood back aghast AGAIN, this time I had the nerve to call him out, "Shall I go out and cook?" Chef replies, "I'm showing you the proper speed blah blah blah." OK, I think I'll just go get some coffee and do something else. OH, there's some silverware to put away, better do that. Done. OK NOW coffee. Get coffee, come back to pit, Chef is still in there and just returning to the line where he belongs. Then I realized that not only had I been completely caught up, nothing in the rack was anything the line needed. And wasn't Chef ranting about his girlfriend again when I came in? This latest outburst was not about me being slow. Realizing this was going to continue over and over again I left.

Chef is not stupid, Chef is not a novice, so why did this happen? My high standards match his; in my pit I demand everything to be just right before I can work – I can appreciate it if anger stems from the requisites not being fulfilled but…

The first problem is that Chef didn't leave his personal life at the door. This is classic logic vs. emotion, rider vs. elephant, forgivable.

The second problem is that they never bought a new water heater when they renovated the old Pizzeria in the building. If Chef had no gas to cook with, things would slow down quite a bit, and you'd better bet it'd be fixed pronto. I was forced to turn off the hot water to the sprayer to conserve it for the machine. To compensate I would once over hand scrub each plate with a green scrubby dipped in detergent. This adds about 2 seconds to each dish. Half way through the shift the machine's hot water would be tepid which means the plates would not evaporate dry in under 60 seconds like they should, so I'd have to hand dry them sometimes, taking time away from everything else. OK, if the problem is that I'm just slow, give me some Red Bull, but it happens when the other guy is working too.

Hmmm. If the owner had bought the water heater over vacation as he said he would instead of going to Florida (Record lows that week – Ha!) I would be 25% faster because I would not need to scrub or hand dry plates.

But that is not the real problem either, the 3rd real problem is simply scarcity – they need about 6 more squares. "Hey Guy, I can't give you any squares because they are being used right now, oh well, wait…HEY YOU, Hurry up with that lamb, somebody else just ordered it and we need the plate!"

Don't You See? The higher ups are ignorant and arrogant and do not respect the lower downs, even though the lower downs and what they have to say are CRITICAL to the whole operation. Translate that to the whole world…

I'm basically coming in to the kitchen/world and I'm finding empathy for the dishwashers and contempt for the bosses. I'm seeing that forcing the omega to roll over isn't helping anymore because the pack is starving, and the pack is no longer blaming the omega but the alpha. All the sudden I stand up and say, You want a functional restaurant/world? Then let me order the extra plates and water heater because these guys in charge would rather wallow in their 'tude and go on holiday than fix the problem.

The following is a mix of old and new essays, rants, inventions and even a couple parables. A lot of stuff has been cut out, mostly my early, diary type writings and detailed physics stuff, like, I know what the scalar term/quantity should be in the quaternion and it has to do with Haramein's scaling law, he has the math for my mass engine too incidently…

One of my pet peeves is redundancy – you'll come across the same ideas more than once, though redundancy may be necessary to make all the occult techno-mumbo-jumbo clearer and main points more salient. Rants addressed to aliens should be read for entertainment purposes only unless you are an 8 foot tall reptilian, then yeah, I'm on to you buddy…

You'll notice that some rants are written from an outside perspective. This degree of separation proved to be an unnecessary buffer. Jesus said something to the effect, "if I testify for myself my testimony is invalid." I don't have my cousin John to blaze a path for me with his lone voice. As persuasive or apologetic as my testimony may come across, my ego is not invested in converting people to my trip. You are merely witnessing me trying to convince myself I'm this guy, and it isn't difficult for me at this point in the game.

ISAIAH 63 - TANGENTIAL INTRODUCTORY RANTING

Isaiah 63, I've thought of it often since I first read it, especially 5 *I looked, but there was no one to help, I was appalled that no one gave support; so my own arm worked salvation for me, and my own wrath sustained me.*

Last night I slipped into victim consciousness for a moment. What began as a bitch session rant recalled all the examples of who should be down with my trip but are *too one thing or another.*

The Jews rejected The Christ Jesus because he wasn't Old Testament enough for them; his aggression was limited to his function – Alpha male in his pack but omega to society/humanity. For me – His eschatological successor, it's the opposite.

The Christians will reject me because I'm not a mute, passive, victim with people to stroke egos for me – rather, a heroic badass genius willing to slay egos on a whim and do my own dirty work; I'm ALL ABOUT self-actualization.

The New Agers resent my "THE" title, insisting that there can only be many "A" Christs.

The Rainbow Nation won't have me because they are scared of being angry; my music and swearing are harshing their mellow bubble…and the ELFers are too busy vandalizing to think of a real way to liberate Gaia.

The Zero Point Energy Community (www.zpenergy.com) resents my insistence on mentioning the implications of the plenum-based reality – other than free energy.

The Church is so scared I might be real (because they'd be rendered useless); they turned "Antichrist" into a propaganda industry. OF COURSE I'm *like* Jesus but ALSO his opposite (A+O). Aren't all followers of The Way/ Tao essentially, within reason, imitating Christ?

The Preterists think that Judgment Day occurred in 70 a.d. and this is New Jerusalem.

The Buddhists dismiss the exogenous trips of the impatient and/or curious.

The Green Party refuses to admit technology, specifically micro-generation farming of biospheric forces, will solve 99% of Human/Gaian problems (www.freeenergynews.com).

Academia cares that I'm a high school and college drop-out.

Venture capitalists may get a Zero Time approach to a business plan but they'll never comprehend a Reverse Time business plan.

The Extropians or Transhumanists don't get that we already are cyborgs living in a quantum computer.

The Prophecy Experts aren't familiar with Conversations with Nostradamus by Dolores Cannon or dismiss it because it's written with material gained by people under a hypnotic regression. In her trilogy are explanations of quatrains straight from the author of them, one of the things he reveals is "The Great Genius." This man is me. I was Tesla, and Tesla was Akkaeneset or "Keeper of the Energy," the Walk-in contract worker for the Dark Brethren of latter Atlan – The conceiver and ultimate saboteur of a plan that isn't going to work anyway (See <u>Atlantis Rising</u> by Patricia Cori.), and I caused the great flood by toying with a Psycho-Geo Transducing Electrical Infrastructure – yes, at one point in time we prayed to gain our electricity. Not surprising since the Schumann resonance and our brain can frequency pull each other into sympathy. Let's just say my karmic burden is heavy. But this Inventor continuity is superpositioned with a greater Christ oversoul, as suggested by this Dogon prophecy of Nommo Anagonno, **"The twin of the victim will descend with the blacksmith."**

Of interest to The Extropians is a rather accurate and detailed description (in Conversations…) of how I will perform the miracle of soul-catching. Soul-Catching is the term for transferring your consciousness into a computer. The Free Energy Movement may be interested to know Rev 13:13 is a reference to my Auto-Inductive Rectenna and not me being a lightning rod.

The Rapture People don't want to hear that anyone with an External Merkaba or Singularity based Mass Engine, can take their body with 'em.

The Jehovah's Witnesses don't appreciate my J.R. "Bob" Dobbs/Church of the Subgenius sticker on the door.

...and physics progresses one funeral at a time.

At least the Hopi, Maya, and Dogon are cool with me being caucasian and my guides forgive my lapses into victim consciousness and wrongfully displaced anger.

What can the head/groom do without the body/bride other than observe, reflect and yell in vain?

How will the fledgling body flourish without a means of masticating the knowledge and directing its nutrients to where they're needed: in the organs, systems and appendages?

HEAD = ME, Kalki
ORGANS = SPECIALISTS, ASSISTANTS, FUNDRAISERS, WITNESSES
SYSTEMS = MASS MEDIA, TV AND INTERNET, the "the 2nd beast", Dajal
APPENDAGES = ANYONE WILLING TO DO GOD'S/MINE/YOUR WILL

Accepting me means:

Accepting my mind and intent is suited to the task of discerning what God's Will might be and exactly is.

You must accept that I, too, am a mammal – reduced/potentiated by the veil of linear time and local space, subject to all the addictions I require to associate and accommodate my will to KNOW and BECOME.

You must accept the probability that the universe will produce one at the top of the class in any given year.

The **only** way to identify The Elect/Chosen/Spiritual Israel – you are the only true integrationists.

As such, you accept that, memetically speaking, integrationism is the methodology or belief most congruent with negentropy, which is the defining property of a plenum based reality. Negentropy is the tendency to contract, cool, collapse, cohere, condense, complexify, order, and yes, integrate.

You are fine with the notion that you are a variable observer/conserver, not *just* a constant mistake/mutant.

You have a problem with the Western/Dominator culture synonymous with an Entropic Vacuum – Big Bang – Heat Death scenario that doesn't account for the 5/6 of the multiverse asynchronous to linear time/local space that allows for entropy in the first place; after all, as the skeptics say, "you can't get something from nothing." By their logic, Big Bang is the first and only accelerating, centerless, creative explosion…space must be full of something, the singularity must be everywhere, the phase transition must be continuous and the sympathy must be spontaneous.

Friends, Integrationism is the last thing I *possibly could* teach. It is the last thing to teach a race of sentient beings before they're to be quantum phase shifted.

In the realm of quantum mechanics, the plenum model allows the ergosphere (or space between the naked singularity and event horizon, that place where, "All the laws breakdown") to not "spaghettify," but rather transform whatever is within its influence. As opposed to entropic, thermal phase shifting, quantum phase shifting is a super-symmetrical, total CPT (charge, parity, time) conservation violation that retains the information of its biased, ground phase state.

I will now tell you of the Astro-Quantum Physics of Judgment Day.

Stars go Super Nova (sometimes SUB Nova, or phase shift into Dark Matter bodies, relatively bifurcating, rapturing, teleporting, out of linear time/local space), emit GRB's (gamma ray bursts), and peel off a gravity wave when they form a "cross" with the galactic Bloch wall (see Plasma/MHD Cosmology) and their magnetic axis. Solar Systems have a quasi-periodic pass through the Bloch wall as they trace a lateral and radial orbit through their galaxy. The heliosphere or superelectron is a solar system's ergosphere and the heliopause is its event horizon. The results of the pass through the 5th World/4th Dimension are, for the solar system, numerous: All matter is regauged/cleansed to work off a higher energy density.

The Kuyper belt and Ort cloud are formed by the propagated gravity wave. Inner planets flip polarity and phase shift, and outer planets can be expelled, doomed to surf the wave into any kind of funky multi system orbit. Entire planets and stars teleport, and in linear time this looks like a life/death cycle. Epochs begin and end, paradigms shift.

A scaled-down version of this process is, for the brain, a heroic dose of exo/endogenous DMT or Psilocybin (see <u>DMT The Spirit Molecule</u> by Dr. Strassman, and any Terence Mckenna) for the subtle bodies it is OBE's/NDE's, For Yogis, Enoch, Aliens, Jesus... it is the body's own ergosphere, the merkaba, with or without external assistance, that can take the body to heaven and return it as well. It conserves the information of "YOU"! This is the Mastery of the Waters or range of quantum superfluids, rendering the human interdimensionally amphibious – variable.

I'm here to give humanity free energy as a means of redeeming my oversoul. I'm here to give humanity an External Merkaba or Inertial Mass Engine because I want to fly. I'm here to give humanity AI via Soul-Catching because I want a second option for existing in the explicate order without physical pain and susceptibility to elements, always at the mercy of air, food and water, and various addictions... So many ways out aren't there? All because I am a selfish self fish.

Without you to gather resources, process and propagate OUR propaganda/meme set, and execute the will of the head, my loaded title might not cascade OUR trip to an enabling tipping point of divine intent...I might spend the rest of my life in financial limbo, a tortured inventor incapable of funding magic/miracles – mass producible ones. You may pass as the latest Aquarian Conspiracy.

If you accept me, you will bear my mark on your heads; we will be entangled. You will be the servants of a servant. Anyone who has trodden the goat trail in order to get high and contemplate the gorge in apparent seclusion, and then gotten busted on the way down by the campus police...has the burden of standards and of wisdom. For they obligate you to be proactive about obvious and unnecessary mediocrity, to not settle for the lowest possible perspective but for the greatest view.

Only by integration, and integration alone, does science and spirit meet and paradoxes are viewed as inherent or semantic demands of relativity and metaphor.

There can be no false among you because you aren't afraid to pig out at the buffet, you aren't afraid to be open-minded skeptics of various methods. You practice what you seek; you humble yourselves when you are agnostic but you are not defeatist.

A fluctuation decoheres from the aether, a synapse is at the point of no return, and you must choose how far down the microtubule, chakra, scalar bottle or black hole you want to go. I don't want to steal the thunder of any of my people. I want to amplify it so it may resound throughout all the Branes/Brains aware enough to give a damn.

A LOOK AT PROPHECY

The first momentous post-shroom moment of '96 was when I decided to randomly open a Bible and look at it with all 3 eyes. I opened it to Rev 13:13 and I knew it was referencing a free energy device, even though I hadn't invented it yet. This was my first synchronistic clue that I was on to my fate. The Dolores Cannon material came next in '98. A palm reader in South Beach told me months before that I was a triple Pisces, whatever that means, and that stuck in my mind long enough to Google it. Somehow Conversations and "great genius" popped up, and I ordered the trilogy. Not only is my face in there, but my Neuromimetic Hybrid Processor, and even my integrationist trip. That was a clincher. Then the Tesla Crop Glyph ten years later… It was the schematic of my invention scribed into a field with a very important tweak… For me this series of post hunch confirmations has been a source of faith that no other human has experienced, but I hope you can appreciate it. I thought I was done with corroborative evidence prophecy but today (Feb 19, 2010) I had my mind blown again.

A few weeks ago I finally got around to reading Daniel Pinchbeck's 2012 book. Daniel is a lot like me, and so are David Wilcock, and Nassim Haramein. Anyway, I emailed Daniel's webzine, realitysandwich.com about my trip and got no reply as expected. (Fine, that's fine, you keep your thunder, guy…) In the site's tag tree was "DREAMS." Click. Scroll. A book with a title that grabbed my attention:

http://www.realitysandwich.com/christ_amp_maya_calendar_2012_amp_coming_antichrist

Scroll. Oh here is the same part of J. Dixon's prophecy I read in Dolores's books:

Dixon's scenario was nuanced rather than literalistic, saying that the miracles, signs, and wonders that Revelations attributed to the Antichrist and his prophet would not be supernatural events but "*the prodigies of science and human achievements.*" She pointed particularly to the "*fire from heaven*" spoken of by John, which she saw as the ultimate symbol of the conquest of Nature. "The ideological and falsely scientific prophet" would advance an anti-Christian science perfectly tailored to modern materialism. Finally, she anticipated a full victorious reign of the Antichrist and his prophet, who would be "specific and identifiable persons!"

But then this bit about a mystic named Vladimir Soloviev. I'd never heard of him before…

Another prophetic voice – the Russian philosopher, poet, and founder of Russian Sophiology, Vladimir Solovyov – wrote of a similar scenario in his *War, Progress, and the End of History: Three Conversations Including a Short Story of the Anti-Christ.* (Paul Marshall Allen's excellent biography, *Vladimir Soloviev: Russian Mystic* (New York: Steiner Books, 1978), pp. 366-410 contains the *Short Story of the Anti-Christ.*) Finished on Easter Sunday, 1900, just a few months before he died, the book is a series of dialogues between five members of the Russian intelligentsia, held in the garden of a villa in the Alps. Solovyov's prefatory question sets the tone for the book: "Is evil only a natural defect, an imperfection disappearing by itself with the growth of good, or is it a real power, ruling our world by means of temptations, so that to fight it successfully assistance must be found in another sphere of being?" The way that Solovyov describes it, the individual who becomes the Antichrist writes a bestselling book – *The Open Way to World Peace and Welfare.* He is a good person, a very high being, when he writes this book, but then he goes for a walk one night, and a presence promises him that he can become world ruler.

WOW! He nailed the book, this book! There is something subtle and important in the wording – "…the individual who **becomes** the Antichrist…" This book could have been called THE OPEN WAY… Since my involvement with Open Innovation (Edison Nation for example) my study of Crowd Sourcing, E-Government, POD publishing, non-equilibrium thermodynamics etc., there is little to me that can be considered a closed system...

Google. Found his short story, let's see if there's anything else...

> ...Humanity had outgrown that stage *of philosophical infancy.* On the other hand, it became equally evident that it had also outgrown the infantile capacity for naive, unconscious faith. Such ideas as God *creating* the universe *out of nothing* were no longer taught even in elementary schools. A certain high level of ideas concerning such subjects had been evolved, and no dogmatism could risk a descent below it. And though the majority of thinking people had remained faithless, the few believers, of necessity, had become *thinking*, thus fulfilling the commandment of the Apostle: "Be infants in your hearts, but not in your reason."
>
> At that time, there was among the few believing spiritualists a remarkable person -- many called him a superman -- who was equally far from both, intellect and childlike heart. He was still young, but owing to his great genius, by the age of thirty-three he had already become famous as a great thinker, writer, and public figure. Conscious of the great power of spirit in himself, he was always a confirmed spiritualist, and his clear intellect always showed him the truth of what one should believe in: the good, God, and the Messiah.
>
> In these he *believed,* but he *loved only himself.* He believed in God, but in the depths of his soul he involuntarily and unconsciously preferred himself. He believed in Good, but the All Seeing Eye of the Eternal knew that this man would bow down before the power of Evil as soon as it would offer him a bribe -- not by deception of the senses and the lower passions, not even by the superior bait of power, but only by his own immeasurable self-love.
>
> This self-love was neither an unconscious instinct nor an insane ambition. Apart from his exceptional genius, beauty, and nobility of character, the reserve, disinterestedness, and active sympathy with those in need which he evinced to such a great extent seemed abundantly to justify the immense self-love of this great spiritualist, ascetic, and philanthropist. Did he deserve blame because, being as he was so generously supplied with the gifts of

God, he saw in them the signs of Heaven's special benevolence to him, and thought himself to be second only to God himself? In a word, he considered himself to be what Christ in reality was. But this conception of his higher value showed itself in practice not in the exercise of his moral duty to God and the world but in seizing his privilege and advantage at the expense of others, and of Christ in particular.

At first, he bore no ill feeling toward Christ. He recognized his messianic importance and value, but he was sincere in seeing in him only his own greatest precursor. The moral achievement of Christ and his uniqueness were beyond an intellect so completely clouded by self-love as his. Thus he reasoned: "Christ came before me. I come second. But what, in order of time, appears later is, in its essence, of greater importance. I come last, at the end of history, and for the very reason that I am most perfect. I am the final savior of the world, and Christ is my precursor. His mission was to precede and prepare for my coming."

Thinking thus, the superman of the twenty-first century applied to himself everything that was said in the Gospels about the second coming, explaining the latter not as a return of the same Christ, but as a replacing of the preliminary Christ by the final one -- that is, by himself.

At this stage, the coming man presented few original characteristics or features. His attitude toward Christ resembled, for instance, that of Mohammed, a truthful man, against whom no charge of harboring evil designs can be brought.

This man justified his selfish preference of himself before Christ in yet another way. 'Christ,' he said, "who preached and practiced moral good in life, was a *reformer* of humanity, whereas I am called to be the *benefactor* of that same humanity, partly reformed and partly incapable of being reformed. I will give everyone what they require. As a moralist, Christ divided humanity by the notion of good and evil. I shall unite it by benefits which are as much needed by good as by evil people. I shall be the true representative of that God who makes his sun to shine upon the good and the evil alike, and who makes the rain to fall upon the just and the unjust. Christ brought the sword; I shall bring peace. Christ threatened the earth with the Day of Judgment. But I shall be the last judge, and my judgment will be not only that of justice but also that of mercy. The justice that will be meted out in my sentences will not be a retributive justice but a distributive one. I shall judge each person according to his deserts (*sic*), and shall give everybody what he needs."

In this magnificent spirit he now waited for God to call him in some unmistakable way to take upon himself the work of saving humanity -- for some obvious and striking testimony that he was the elder son, the beloved first-born child of God. He waited and sustained himself by the consciousness of his superhuman virtues and gifts, for, as was said, he was a man of irreproachable morals and exceptional genius.

OK, this is weird. He actually knows my inner dialogue very well, but some corrections:

Although I wish an entity would come to me and validate all this further, I know the order in which these events occurred is in itself a miracle. If an evil entity offered me the world, my response would be, "Who the F are you and by whose authority are you offering me a world I don't want anyway?!" It's not so much narcissistic, this self love, it's a pat on the back for having not killed myself, for having endured. In a trippy way too, like, I AM – Holy shit! Now that that's clear, anything else?

>...The superman's previous books and public activity had always met with severe criticism, though these came chiefly from people of exceptionally deep religious convictions, who for that very reason possessed no authority (I am, after all, speaking of the coming of the Anti-Christ) and thus they were hardly listened to when they tried to point out, in everything that the "coming man" wrote or said, the signs of a quite exceptional and excessive self-love and conceit, and a complete absence of true simplicity, frankness, and sincerity.

But now, with his new book, he brought over to his side even some of his former critics and adversaries. This book, composed after the incident at the precipice, evinced a greater power of genius than he had ever shown before. It was a work that embraced everything and solved every problem. It united a noble respect for ancient traditions and symbols with a broad and daring radicalism in socio-political questions. It joined a boundless freedom of thought with the most profound appreciation for everything mystical. Absolute individualism stood side by side with an ardent zeal for the common good, and the highest idealism in guiding principles combined smoothly with a perfect definiteness in practical solutions for the necessities of life. And all this was blended and cemented with such artistic genius that every thinker and every man of action, however one-sided he might have been, could easily view and accept the whole from his particular individual standpoint without sacrificing anything to the *truth itself,* without actually rising above his *ego,* without *in reality* renouncing his one-sidedness, without correcting the inadequacy of his views and wishes, and without making up their deficiencies.

This wonderful book was immediately translated into the languages of all the civilized nations, and many of the uncivilized ones as well. During the entire year thousands of newspapers in all parts of the world were filled with the publisher's advertisements and the critics' praises. Cheap editions with portraits of the author were sold in millions of copies, and all the civilized world -- which now stood for nearly all the globe resounded with the glory of the incomparable, the great, the only one!

Nobody raised his voice against the book. On every side it was accepted by all as the revelation of the complete truth. In it, all the past was given such full and due justice, the present was appraised with such impartiality and catholicity, and the happiest future was described in such a convincing and practical manner that everybody could not help saying: "Here at last we have what we need. Here is the ideal, which is not a Utopia. Here is a scheme which is not a dream." And the wonderful author not only impressed all, but he was *agreeable* to all, so that the word of Christ was fulfilled: "I have come in the name of the Father, and you accept me not. *Another* will come in *his own* name -- him you *will* accept." For it is necessary to be *agreeable* to be *accepted.*

It is true some pious people, while praising the book wholeheartedly, had been asking why the name of Christ was never mentioned in it; but other Christians had rejoined: "So much the better. Everything sacred has already been stained enough in past ages by every sort of unacknowledged zealot, and nowadays a deeply religious author must be extremely guarded in these matters. Since the book is imbued with the true Christian spirit of active love and all-embracing goodwill, what more do you want?" And everybody agreed…

OMFG! This is how I was hoping it would go. He has summed up my trip better than I have. Hmmm, is there any more accurate prophecy?

> … This magician, Apollonius by name, was doubtless a person of genius. A semi-Asiatic and a semi-European, a Catholic bishop *in partibus infidelium,* he combined in himself in a most striking manner knowledge of the latest conclusions and applications of Western science with the art of utilizing all that was really sound and important in traditional Eastern mysticism. The results of this combination were startling. ***Apollonius learned, among other things, the semi-scientific, semi-mystic art of attracting and directing at will atmospheric electricity and the people said of him that he could bring down fire from heaven.*** However, though he was able to startle the imagination of the crowd by various unheard-of phenomena, for some time he did not abuse his power for any special or selfish ends…

Rev 13:13, Jeanne Dixon and now Vladimir Soloviev all describe the same technological approach and again we see that the roles have been mixed up and divided into different characters. There is no mentor, Imam, Ogmios, or False Prophet. I told that guy I was not interested in his Middle East connections or his stupid fuel additives. Mass Media is my mouthpiece and I don't need someone to show me the ropes, as if. The Christ and Anti-Christ are separated only by a decision on my part.

Prophecy is about probabilities. If you dismiss all prophecy as crap because it does not happen or exactly the way it was prophesied then you lack an understanding of "free will." Most fulfilled prophecy is self-fulfilling because those who fulfill it are usually aware of it. I could have easily published this book without ever having read Vlad's short prophetic story; what difference would it have made?

When it comes to Rev 13:13…I have not prototyped the AIR to date, but 3 different prophecies say it will work, 4 if you include the Tesla Crop Glyph. I have no lab to raid, no patent to pool, no contract to honor, no files to corrupt, no IP to steal…There is nothing my competition can do against this invention. I leave it to the tinkerers and other mad scientists to prototype the AIR until I get enough $ from book royalties to do it myself – publicly.

Matthew 24

15 "So when you see standing in the holy place 'the abomination that causes desolation,'[1] spoken of through the prophet Daniel--let the reader understand--(*Suggests the Abomination is something you read*)

Daniel 8

5 As I was thinking about this, suddenly a goat with a prominent horn between his eyes came from the west, crossing the whole earth without touching the ground.

(*The communications infrastructure is in the air*)

Revelation 13

12 He exercised all the authority of the first beast on his behalf, and made the earth and its inhabitants worship the first beast, whose fatal wound had been healed.

(*The first beast whose fatal wound had been healed - Y2K - is the WWW, and obviously I'm using it*)

Matthew 24

27 For as lightning that comes from the east is visible even in the west, so will the coming of the Son of Man.

(Even though the server for this site is in one place the electrons it's made of flow all over the world)

2 ESDRAS - WHAT THE CHURCH DOES NOT WANT YOU TO KNOW

The Vision of the Eagle

11 On the second night I had a dream: I saw rising from the sea an eagle that had twelve feathered wings and three heads. 2I saw it spread its wings over the whole earth, and all the winds of heaven blew upon it, and the clouds were gathered around it. 3I saw that out of its wings there grew opposing wings; but they became little, puny wings. 4But its heads were at rest; the middle head was larger than the other heads, but it too was at rest with them. 5Then I saw that the eagle flew with its wings, and it reigned over the earth and over those who inhabit it. 6And I saw how all things under heaven were subjected to it, and no one spoke against it--not a single creature that was on the earth. 7Then I saw the eagle rise upon its talons, and it uttered a cry to its wings, saying, 8"Do not all watch at the same time; let each sleep in its own place, and watch in its turn; 9but let the heads be reserved for the last." 10 I looked again and saw that the voice did not come from its heads, but from the middle of its body. 11I counted its rival wings, and there were eight of them. 12As I watched, one wing on the right side rose up, and it reigned over all the earth. 13And after a time its reign came to an end, and it disappeared, so that even its place was no longer visible. Then the next wing rose up and reigned, and it continued to reign a long time. 14While it was reigning its end came also, so that it disappeared like the first. 15And a voice sounded, saying to it, 16"Listen to me, you who have ruled the earth all this time; I announce this to you before you disappear. 17After you no one shall rule as long as you have ruled, not even half as long." 18 Then the third wing raised itself up, and held the rule as the earlier ones had done, and it also disappeared. 19And so it went with all the wings; they wielded power one after another and then were never seen again. 20I kept looking, and in due time the wings

that followed also rose up on the right side, in order to rule. There were some of them that ruled, yet disappeared suddenly; 21and others of them rose up, but did not hold the rule. 22 And after this I looked and saw that the twelve wings and the two little wings had disappeared, 23and nothing remained on the eagle's body except the three heads that were at rest and six little wings. 24 As I kept looking I saw that two little wings separated from the six and remained under the head that was on the right side; but four remained in their place. 25Then I saw that these little wings planned to set themselves up and hold the rule. 26As I kept looking, one was set up, but suddenly disappeared; 27a second also, and this disappeared more quickly than the first. 28While I continued to look the two that remained were planning between themselves to reign together; 29and while they were planning, one of the heads that were at rest (the one that was in the middle) suddenly awoke; it was greater than the other two heads. 30And I saw how it allied the two heads with itself, 31and how the head turned with those that were with it and devoured the two little wings that were planning to reign. 32Moreover this head gained control of the whole earth, and with much oppression dominated its inhabitants; it had greater power over the world than all the wings that had gone before. 33 After this I looked again and saw the head in the middle suddenly disappear, just as the wings had done. 34But the two heads remained, which also in like manner ruled over the earth and its inhabitants. 35And while I looked, I saw the head on the right side devour the one on the left.

A Lion Roused from the Forest

36 Then I heard a voice saying to me, "Look in front of you and consider what you see." 37When I looked, I saw what seemed to be a lion roused from the forest, roaring; and I heard how it uttered a human voice to the eagle, and spoke, saying, 38"Listen and I will speak to you. The Most High says to you, 39'Are you not the one that remains of the four beasts that I had made to reign in my world, so that the end of my times might come through them? 40You, the fourth that has come, have conquered all the beasts that have gone before; and you have held sway over the world with

great terror, and over all the earth with grievous oppression; and for so long you have lived on the earth with deceit.g 41 You have judged the earth, but not with truth, 42for you have oppressed the meek and injured the peaceable; you have hated those who tell the truth, and have loved liars; you have destroyed the homes of those who brought forth fruit, and have laid low the walls of those who did you no harm. 43Your insolence has come up before the Most High, and your pride to the Mighty One. 44The Most High has looked at his times; now they have ended, and his ages have reached completion. 45Therefore you, eagle, will surely disappear, you and your terrifying wings, your most evil little wings, your malicious heads, your most evil talons, and your whole worthless body, 46so that the whole earth, freed from your violence, may be refreshed and relieved, and may hope for the judgment and mercy of him who made it.' "

COMMENTARY - This preceding prophecy is about the rise of America and its attempt to become the NWO – The revived Roman Empire or Babylon (Eagle), its 3 major powers/countries or possibly these warring factions:_

1. The Rockefeller Cartel
2. The Bolshevik-Zionist Axis
3. The New Kremlin Rulers

(heads), wings on both sides and feathers (bipartisan political leaders). Compare this Apocryphal beast to the Biblical Beast out of the Sea in Revelation; wings=heads, heads=horns, feathers=crowns. The Lion is me.

THE SIXTH VISION (emphasis added by Kalki)

Ezra Sees a Vision of a Man from the Sea

13 Seven nights later, I dreamed that 2 I saw a storm at sea with rising waves. 3 I saw what looked like a man come up from the middle of the sea and fly with the clouds. Wherever he turned, everything he looked at trembled with fear. 4 And when he spoke, everyone who heard him melted, like wax in a fire. 5 Then I saw many people from every direction coming together in a crowd

too large to count, and they were ready to fight the man from the sea. 6 This man carved out a huge mountain and flew to the top of it. 7I tried to see from what nation or region he had taken the mountain, but I couldn't see. I noticed that the people were terrified of the man, yet they still planned to attack and defeat him. 9 When he saw them rushing toward him, he didn't pick up a weapon of any kind. 10 Instead, he opened his mouth, and a stream of fire shot out. Flames came from his lips, and sparks jumped from his tongue. 11 These fiery things came together and fell on the crowd, completely burning up everyone. Nothing was left of the crowd except for smoke and ashes. I was amazed at what I had seen. 12I watched as the man from the sea came down from the mountain and called together a different crowd of people a peaceful crowd. 13 Some of these that came to him were happy, some were sad, while some were tied up and led along by others.

Ezra Asks What the Vision Means

I was terrified when I woke up, and I prayed to God Most High: 14 Our Lord, you have shown me a lot of amazing things, and you feel I deserve to have my prayers answered. 15 So would you also explain this vision to me? 16 You know that I am terribly concerned about what will happen to those who are alive at the end of time. And what about those who die before that? 17 They will suffer terribly 18 because they won't receive any of the blessings that will come at the end. 19 Yet those alive at that time are also in for trouble. They must face dangerous and troublesome times, just as you have shown me in these visions. 20I still think that those who survive these troubles will be better off than those who disappear from this world as quickly as a cloud. Those who survive will live until the end of time, yet those who die will never see what takes place.

The angel Uriel answered:

122

21I will explain the meaning of this vision and answer your questions. 22 You have asked about people who will survive until the end of time, and about those who will die before then.

So I will tell you 23 that *the same one who causes trouble in the last times is the one who will protect those who have been faithful and obedient to God All-Powerful.*

24 You can be certain that the people who survive will be much better off than those who are dead. 25Now I will tell you what the vision means. *The man that you saw coming out of the sea 26is the one God Most High has kept ready during the history of the world. He will set God's creation free and will keep the faithful safe in the world to come.* 27You saw this man breathe flames and a fiery storm, 28and *you watched him wipe out the crowd of people who were attacking him, without ever reaching for a weapon.* This means that 29God Most High will one day rescue all people who have been faithful to him.

30Everyone on earth will be shocked 31and will plot war against one another, cities will fight against other cities, regions against other regions, nations against other nations, kingdoms against other kingdoms. 32And when you see these things happen, together with the signs I told you about earlier, then people everywhere will see God's Son, the one you saw as a man coming up out of the sea. 33When the people of every nation hear his voice, they will stop fighting against one another and will leave their homes 34and gather together into one crowd too large to count, just as you saw in your vision. They will plot to defeat God's Son, 35but he will stand on the mountain of Jerusalem, 36and the new city of Jerusalem will be shown to everyone. This is the mountain you saw carved out, without human hands in the vision. 37The storm you saw stands for the time when God's Son will judge all godless nations. 38He will remind them of every wicked and evil plan they had and will tell them of the tortures they must face. These were the flames you saw. Then finally he will easily wipe out the godless nations by using God's holy Law. This was the fire in the vision. 39You saw God's Son call together a peaceful crowd. 40These are the nine tribes that King Shalmaneser of Assyria captured during the rule of King Hoshea of Israel and led away to a foreign land across the Euphrates River.e 41But these tribes decided to leave this foreign land and settle in a place where no one had ever lived, 42and where they could obey God's laws more faithfully than they had in their own country. 43They chose to cross the Euphrates at the most difficult place, 44so God Most High had to perform amazing miracles and stop the flow of the river until they had safely crossed. 45They traveled a year and a half through the region known as Arzareth,f 46where they have lived ever since. Before the end of time, they will come back home, 47and God Most High will once again stop the flow of the river to let them cross. This was the large and peaceful crowd you saw gathered around God's Son. 48They are the ones who will be left of your people. They will be found within God's holy nation and will be rescued 49when his Son destroys the godless nations that gather together to attack him. He will defend your people who survive 50and work amazing miracles for them. 51I replied, "Sir, why did I see the man coming up out of the sea?" 52He said: Just as no one knows what is at the bottom of the sea, so no one on earth will see God's Son or those with him until the final day comes. 53That's what your vision means, and only you have been told these things 54because you care more about studying God's Law than you do about following your own concerns. 55You have spent your life searching for wisdom, and knowledge has been as dear to you as a mother. 56That's why God has shown you these things and will one day reward you. Now after three more days, I will explain to you other important and marvelous things. 57As I walked across the field, I worshiped and praised God Most High for the amazing miracles he had done 58and for controlling history and all that happens. I stayed there for three days.

MOST RELEVANT BIBLICAL PROPHECY

Isaiah 63

1 Who is this coming from Edom, from Bozrah, with his garments stained crimson? Who is this, robed in splendor, striding forward

in the greatness of his strength? "It is I, speaking in righteousness, mighty to save."

2 Why are your garments red, like those of one treading the winepress?

3 "I have trodden the winepress alone; from the nations no one was with me. I trampled them in my anger and trod them down in my wrath; their blood spattered my garments, and I stained all my clothing.

4 For the day of vengeance was in my heart, and the year of my redemption has come.

5 *I looked, but there was no one to help, I was appalled that no one gave support; so my own arm worked salvation for me, and my own wrath sustained me.*

6 I trampled the nations in my anger; in my wrath I made them drunk and poured their blood on the ground."

Isaiah 65

1 "I revealed myself to those who did not ask for me; I was found by those who did not seek me. To a nation that did not call on my name, I said, `Here am I, here am I.'

2 All day long I have held out my hands to an obstinate people, who walk in ways not good, pursuing their own imaginations--

3 a people who continually provoke me to my very face, offering sacrifices in gardens and burning incense on altars of brick;

4 who sit among the graves and spend their nights keeping secret vigil; who eat the flesh of pigs, and whose pots hold broth of unclean meat;

5 who say, `Keep away; don't come near me, for I am too sacred for you!' Such people are smoke in my nostrils, a fire that keeps burning all day.

6 "See, it stands written before me: *I will not keep silent but will pay back in full*; I will pay it back into their laps--

7 both your sins and the sins of your fathers," says the LORD. "Because they burned sacrifices on the mountains and defied me on the hills, I will measure into their laps the full payment for their former deeds."

John 16

25 "Though I have been speaking figuratively, a time is coming when I will no longer use this kind of language but will tell you plainly about my Father.

Matthew

31 "When the Son of Man comes in his glory, and all the angels with him, he will sit on his throne in heavenly glory.

32 All the nations will be gathered before him, and he will separate the people one from another as a shepherd separates the sheep from the goats.

33 He will put the sheep on his right and the goats on his left.

34 "Then the King will say to those on his right, 'Come, you who are blessed by my Father; take your inheritance, the kingdom prepared for you since the creation of the world.

35 For I was hungry and you gave me something to eat, I was thirsty and you gave me something to drink, I was a stranger and you invited me in,

36 I needed clothes and you clothed me, I was sick and you looked after me, I was in prison and you came to visit me.'

37 "Then the righteous will answer him, 'Lord, when did we see you hungry and feed you, or thirsty and give you something to drink?

38 When did we see you a stranger and invite you in, or needing clothes and clothe you?

39 When did we see you sick or in prison and go to visit you?'

40 "The King will reply, 'I tell you the truth, whatever you did for one of the least of these brothers of mine, you did for me.'

41 "Then he will say to those on his left, 'Depart from me, you who are cursed, into the eternal fire prepared for the devil and his angels.

42 For I was hungry and you gave me nothing to eat, I was thirsty and you gave me nothing to drink,

43 I was a stranger and you did not invite me in, I needed clothes and you did not clothe me, I was sick and in prison and you did not look after me.'

44 "They also will answer, 'Lord, when did we see you hungry or thirsty or a stranger or needing clothes or sick or in prison, and did not help you?'

45 "He will reply, 'I tell you the truth, whatever you did not do for one of the least of these, you did not do for me.'

46 "Then they will go away to eternal punishment, but the righteous to eternal life."

Revelation 13

(with interpretation by Kalki)

1 And the dragon (***Draconian/Cabal/Illuminati influence in Babylon***) [1] stood on the shore of the sea. (***conceptual realms of Hyper/Mind/Cyber Space or infosphere- where memes reside***) And I saw a beast coming out of the sea.

He had ten horns (***Nations***) and seven heads (***Industro-Military-Pharmaceutical-Petro-Banking-Black Market/Budget-Mass Media***), with ten crowns (***Leaders***) on his horns, and on each head a blasphemous name (***intentional error***)

2 The beast I saw resembled a leopard, but had feet like those of a bear and a mouth like that of a lion. The dragon gave the beast his power and his throne and great authority.

3 One of the heads of the beast seemed to have had a fatal wound (***Y2K***), but the fatal wound had been healed.

The whole world was astonished and followed the beast.

4 Men worshiped the dragon because he had given authority to the beast, and they also worshiped the beast and asked, "Who is like the beast? Who can make war against him?"

5 The beast was given a mouth (***Television***) to utter proud words and blasphemies (***Programming***) and to exercise his authority for forty-two months.

6 He opened his mouth to blaspheme God, and to slander his name and his dwelling place and those who live in heaven.

7 He was given power to make war against the saints and to conquer them. And he was given authority over every tribe, people, language and nation.

8 All inhabitants of the earth will worship (***Watch TV and Surf the www***) the beast--all whose names have not been written in the book of life (***In other words, those who have bent over for the propaganda on TV, who have participated wholeheartedly in the Dominator Culture of Babylon***) belonging to the Lamb that was slain from the creation of the world.[2]

9 He who has an ear, let him hear. (***If you can discern***)

10 If anyone is to go into captivity, into captivity he will go. If anyone is to be killed[3] with the sword, with the sword he will be killed. (***excessive debate about my true nature as portrayed in certain prophecy is moot; your fate, your problem.***) This calls for patient endurance and faithfulness on the part of the saints. (***Even if I choose to go the "AntiChrist" or "LaHaye-Parousia" route it is still appropriate***)

11 Then I saw another beast, coming out of the earth. (***Explicate Order, linear time & mass - where genes reside***) He had two horns like a lamb, but he spoke like a dragon. (***I am as obedient as Jesus, but I drop F-Bombs***)

12 He exercised all the authority of the first beast on his behalf, and made the earth and its inhabitants worship the first beast, whose fatal wound had been healed. (***I use TV and Internet to propagate my meme set***)

13 And he performed great and miraculous signs, even causing fire to come down from heaven to earth in full view of men. (***Public demonstration of free energy device***)

14 Because of the signs he was given power to do on behalf of the first beast, he deceived the inhabitants of the earth. He ordered them to set up an image (***E-Govt.***) in honor of the beast who was wounded by the sword and yet lived.

15 He was given power to give breath (***Artificial Intelligence via Soul-Catching and Embodied Cognition***) to the image (***OS***) of the first beast, so that it could speak and cause all who refused to worship the image to be killed. 16 He also forced everyone, small and great, rich and poor, free and slave, to receive a mark on his right hand (***beastly intent/Draconian will***) or on his forehead, (***divine intent/Gods will***)

17 so that no one could buy or sell unless he had the mark, which is the name of the beast or the number of his name.

18 This calls for wisdom. If anyone has insight, let him calculate the number of the beast, for it is man's number. His number is 666. (***144,000/6/6/6=666.66666...***)

CONVERSATIONS WITH NOSTRADAMUS By Dolores Cannon

Excerpted and Edited from Internet

Readers interested in the prophesies of Nostradamus might like to check out the trilogy Conversations with Nostradamus by Dolores Cannon. For those not familiar with Nostradamus, he lived in the

1500's, and was known as a great healer of people stricken with the Black Plague raging throughout Europe in those days.

However he is famous in our time for writing a series of almost a thousand prophesies, each written in a group of four sentences, called "quatrains." Some of the quatrains are easy to decipher, however most of them are worded very obscurely, and people have puzzled over them for centuries, trying to understand what he was alluding to.

Ms. Cannon's work comes from a unique and very useful perspective. During a routine past-life regression, her client remembered being the student of a great teacher. The client noted, "He's teaching me the study of life. How to heal the body. How to heal the mind. How to see the future. He knows more than any man on earth...he is a good doctor. But he's also a doctor of all things. Some of the things he believes in, he keeps secret."

To make a long story short, at one point during a subsequent regression Nostradamus makes his presence known to the client and says that he wants to work through them to explain the quatrains that pertain to this day and age. The client explained, "If the knowledge from the quatrains can be translated, it would be beneficial for the people of your time." Nostradamus also noted that some of the things he saw were not carved in stone, and that the time lines might possibly be turned to more positive outcomes if enough people heeded his warnings.

The first third of the book is mostly set-up and background information about how the arrangement for these communications became finalized. I'll skip over that information, leaving it to interested readers, and report on some of the juicier things Nostradamus had to say about what's to come; in some cases, first giving the quatrain number and then his explanation.

…

To begin, then, he gives many "signposts" that show the onset of the world changes to come:

CENTURY IV-67. "He says it's in the not too distant future... there will be a comet. This will be a very bright, easily seen comet. But it will be perhaps previously unknown. (*The Norway Spiral* or the **X Shaped Comet**) This coincides with the time of great geological troubles...Nations that are considered prosperous and powerful, particularly western nations, will be revealed as being not as prosperous as everyone had thought. And they will be torn with civil strife and rioting as people try to move out of the areas of drought toward areas that still have some water and where they can grow food."

CENTURY III-12. "He says that this refers to the earth changes that will be taking place, that the Anti-Christ will be taking advantage of in the process of his world conquest. In central Europe, southern Europe and in the Near East, particularly around the eastern end of the Mediterranean, there'll be several severe floods...the Anti-Christ will move his troops in under the disguise of helping the people restore order in the wake of these disasters."

Nostradamus refers in his quatrains to three Anti-Christs: Napoleon and Hitler were the first two. For many quatrain analyzers, trying to determine when the third Anti-Christ will turn up (and who he might be) has been a major goal.

Nostradamus also described the world economic power structure. From CENTURY II-58: "He says there is a group of...puppet-masters behind the scenes pulling the strings of the figures on stage...The figures on stage are the political figures in the major world capitals...These puppet-masters...are organized together in a single organization, and they're working for their own ends...They hold positions that appear to be relatively minor, like advisors... and such, but are key positions for their power...He says a hint to their existence is to trace the family histories of the banking powers and the money powers in the world."

From CENTURY II-88, he further describes this group. Beyond their banking backgrounds he adds that they are "Other commodity-related families, such as families into gold mines and diamond mines, leather, tins and such as this. The basic colonial barons associated with the European world empires who started their families' fortunes by exploiting the raw materials of the Third World nations...They manipulate the economy to cause the unemployment rate to rise or fall at their whim...inflation to rise of fall at their whim."

Now, just as you've gotten thoroughly disgusted with these folks and their power-trips, there's good news. One good thing the Anti-Christ does is wipe these guys out! From CENTURY II-58: "At first when the Anti-Christ comes along, they feel he's just a new, dynamic youthful leader from the Middle East they can use to help unite that part of the world and get it under their power. But the Anti-Christ ends up turning the tables on them." From CENTURY II-18: "Somehow through the espionage powers of the Anti-Christ they will be discovered and destroyed...But, it's a little bit shortsighted of him, because it's this cabal that has been instigating the warfare that has been going on through the decades and centuries. His destroying them will in effect write the beginning of the end for him because it's the activities of this cabal that have supported what he's trying to do. Nostradamus said that once these manipulators are out of the way, the world's natural inclination toward peace will be able to reassert itself, setting the stage for the downfall of the Anti-Christ!

In describing the downfall of the Anti-Christ, Nostradamus says that there will be many forces acting against him. Eventually Russia will be able to break away from his dominion, and will join forces with the United States and Canada. These countries are the "three brothers" described in CENTURY VIII-17. CENTURY V-80 mentions someone called "Ogmios." Nostradamus explained that he will be a great leader of the underground movement in central Europe who will conquer many of the Anti-Christ's finest commanders. Furthermore, the underground organization that this man heads will serve as a basis for future governments after the Anti-Christ is destroyed.

Heard enough doom and gloom? Okay. After the long years of devastation by natural and man-made earth changes, and the wars instigated by the activities of the Anti-Christ are over,

Nostradamus saw a period of human renaissance unparalleled in our history. From CENTURY IV-29: "People will be brought back to the source. They will realize from whence they sprang and where they are going. This is when the time of healing will take place. People will become more mature spiritually and be able to heal themselves and heal the world, going much further in preparing to join the community of the Watchers." He discusses a movement "back to the earth," when people will be tearing down cities to have more land to farm; not because there is a desperate need for food, but because of the profound shift in values after the troubled times.

Nostradamus describes the coming of a *great scientific genius* that will help rebuild human society. From CENTURY IV-31: "This man...will be one of the highest, most developed geniuses ever to appear in our present history of man. He...made the decision to use his genius to help rather than to hurt mankind (*IMPORTANT NOTE FROM KALKI: There are descriptions of the antichrist in the trilogy where he is a humanitarian inventor, a similarity Dolores does not address, this further suggests that I choose just how evil I have to be, what to fulfill or not*)...One of the things he envisions...is self-contained, self-supporting space stations...It was very easy for him to spot this man along the nexus of time paths because he creates such a large ultimate effect...This man is one of the major forces who will help the earth recover from the scars of war."

This great genius will be influential in pointing out the mistaken premises that today's science has built itself on. His ability to perceive scientific truths will cause major breakthroughs in our technological capabilities. From CENTURY VII-14: "[He will] make clear the connections between the physical universe and the metaphysical universe as dealt with by religions." Because of these great advances, Nostradamus describes a time when a majority of people will be aware of higher powers and energies: "It will make every person a philosopher." What kind of time frame are we looking at here? Nostradamus reported that this great genius will show up in the mid-twenty-first century.

Many people have avoided working with Nostradamus' predictions because they foretold so many awful events. During the course of their work together, Ms. Cannon noted this fact to Nostradamus through her client and was answered with, "He glares with his eyes and says, 'They're supposed to be disturbing. I try to point out to them the very worst of what can happen so maybe they can avoid some of it.'"

I'll end with the following quote: "He says that the ray of hope is there and his purpose for communicating with these quatrains is to try to at least alter, if not prevent, the worst aspects of these events from coming up. Whether the events are altered or not, even if the very worst that can happen happens, there will still be a great spiritual rebirth in the mid-21st century.

(I p 300) - Great Genius builds space stations and successful artificial intelligence machine, transferring his consciousness to it. Intelligent machines used to manage space stations. Occurs in 21st or 22nd centuries.

p289 (cIV-32) - During the time of the Great Genius L-5 space stations will be developed for manufacturing materials in space. Scientific base possibly established on Mars, scientific and communications facility established on the moon. The station will be built negligently. New ways of collecting and distributing solar energy will be devised.

p 300 (cIX-65) - The Great Genius will unify religion and science and explain ancient documents, making clear the metaphysical connections between the universe and spirituality.

p 293 (cVII-14) - Discovery several centuries after the Great Genius intermeshes grandly with his knowledge and allows people to burst free from all physical bounds and limitations. I p 297 (cIII-94)

THREE WITNESS ASTROLOGERS

I sent out an email to some astrologers who had done Tesla's chart. I asked them what they thought about my claims in relation to my natal chart.

And the replies:

Hi Kalki,

Your chart has some interesting connections to Tesla's chart- your sun on his Neptune and your Uranus opposite his ascendant. There's more, so it's really quite an interesting story that you've decided to share with the astro folks! I think you need to be aware that astrology is only one way to see into certain things, and it has it's limitations. Trust yourself, and try to maintain a balance in your life, as much as possible. I wish you much success in all of your inventive creations, and if you'd like any feedback on what any of the astrologer types tell you, I'd be happy to give it to you, so that you might get a broader perspective on it all, cheers!

James

Hello Kalki, I took a look at your chart as I see you as someone who, despite the obvious agenda you have for your life, still has some big questions about who you are. I can see the potential for 'genius', you are receptive to lots of good ideas, but you need to be very careful about any foray you make into the unknown (psychic/imaginative activity, etc), because you are likely to open yourself up to a lot of negative influence. You have a tendency to be disorganized in this respect, a factor that can make you very suggestible and sensitive to others who are only too eager to take advantage of you. I can see that you grew up with a lot of female influence in your life, perhaps a very strong dominant mother. I can see that you would probably rather not dwell on your problems at home. But I think you should work them out. Otherwise you will never know who you truly are. Who you might have been in the past does not matter. You have a good day, and I wish you all the best.

Thank you for writing. I shall try to get ahold of "Conversations with Nostradamus." I shall also check out your book. I would encourage you to read Voltaire, especially "Candide" and "Zadig." He wrote in the late 18th C. (1790 something). And what he has to say is very funny and still applies to "New Age Nuts." He lived through a transition period, as do we; his time was the shift from the "Age of Reason" to the "Romantic Era."

I know there is a tradition that Jesus was born on Mar. 10, -0007. There is another tradition that he was born in late August with Sun at 28 degrees Leo conjunct the fixed star Regulus (the king maker). Personally, I think the whole Christian thing is a very old and successful hoax; many popes have voiced (privately for the most part) the same opinion. But, be that as it may, the title Melchizedek literally means king of righteousness or as the Greeks would say "philosopher king," or a "king of theology." No wonder he so often said, "My kingdom is not of this world (of the material plane)" -- it was of the mental/intuitive level! In Hebrew, "melech" (or some version thereof) means "king" while "tzadaka" (or some version thereof such as zadig, zedik, zedek, etc.) means "righteousness." A "righteous" person in the Hebrew tradition never refuses to help when he is asked for it. Jesus was of the tribe of Judah, the tribe of Israel's kings (hence the long genealogy of Joseph given in Matthew chapter 1. That Joseph was the biological father is stated in Matt. 1:24-25. ". . . Joseph . . . took unto him his wife: and knew he not till she had brought forth her firstborn son. . ." It was the tradition in royal families for husband and wife to have sex only at certain times of the year (mainly in our month of December) so that the babies would be born in late Sept. near the Jewish New Year. So, Matt. states Joseph "took" his wife and she became pregnant. Sex during pregnancy was not "kosher" thus "he knew her not till she had brought forth." This passage has been sorely misinterpreted by those who wished to "Hellenify" the myth of Jesus -- i.e. have him sired by a god, like all the Greek heros. The tradition that has him born in late August is probably more nearly correct, and he was a few weeks premature. After all, a long ride on a donkey could very well bring on labor a bit early!! In any case, the chart for 8/-0007 shows a legal mind (Mercury conjunct Pluto) rather than an inventive one. His father, Joseph, was "a master of the craft" (misinterpreted as "carpenter") which probably meant a deep student and teacher of the Talmud and what we today call "Kabalah." Anyway, Hebrew priests are from the tribe Levi (sons of Aaron, Moses' brother, Moses' nephews); so Jesus could not be a conventional priest. As a descendant of the tribe of Judah he had to be a kingly priest. In Revelations he states "I am of the root of David (a particular branch of the Judah tribe) and the Bright and Morning Star (Venus or Shahar – the Semitic desert tribes, both Jew and Arab, worshipped the Venus and Moon, the Goddess; the Star and Crescent (Venus and New Moon) are to this day the emblem of Islam (Arabs) while the Jews use the intertwined triangles of the sixpointed star of the heart chakra as their insignia). The crucifixion story in St. John, and only St. John has this, states that Jesus' side was pierced and water and blood flowed there from. The only "gash" I know of that issues "water and blood" is a woman's vagina! What was St. John trying to say? This is interesting in light of the fact that Eve was supposedly born from Adam's side (rib). I think somebody got it backwards and sideways!

As you may know, "Christ" is from the Greek. It is a translation of the Hebrew "meshiach" meaning "the anointed." "Meshiach" (or messiah) was originally a title for Kings ("God's anointed") and priests who were initiated with sacred oil. (Remember the sweet smelling oil Mary Magdalene, Jesus's wife, used to anoint his feet?) Later is meant a prophet or anyone with a special mission from God. Still later, it came to mean one who would deliver the Jews from bondage and oppression (esoterically, from attachment to the physical material plane). The word "Christ" is from the same root as the word "crystal" -- a transparent substance that transmits light. In the non-New Testament gospel of Philip, that apostle says, "The chrism [light] is superior to baptism, for it is from the word "chrism" that we have been called "Christians," certainly not because of the word "baptism." "Arati" or "baptism" by fire is an old practice in the East; it is still done in Hindu temples, and I have seen Mexican Catholics do it too. One wafts the flame of a candle toward one with the hands, and especially toward the eyes as a blessing and worship. A true "Christian" must be a transparent vehicle who transmits the light of the divine (as in Thy Will be done). [Read the Nag Hammadi Library for gospels not included in the New Test. -- inclusion in the N.T. was a political decision, by the way. Study the history of Christianity (Churchianity); do you know what - and how - happened in 325 AD at the first council of Nicea? You should find out, if not.] Now to Tesla's chart (July 9th 11:59 PM, LMT, Smiljan, Yugoslavia, 15E19, 44N35). I see significant differences between it and yours. He had planets in Earth (physical, practical) -- Pluto in Taurus on the ASC at an early degree, and Uranus in Taurus in the middle of the first house. He had an intercepted 12th house. He had been in the spirit realm for the equivalent of several lifetimes. You, on the other hand, have Capricorn as your ascendant as well as your 12th house cusp; this indicates you reincarnated very quickly. Tesla had Pluto and Uranus in his first house. Those are impersonal, universal energies. You have three very personal planets in your first house, Mars, Moon and Mercury. They are in Aquarius, so I have no doubt that you have genius and inventive talent. Your Jupiter (planet that can correlate with megalomaniacal tendencies) is at 28 degrees Pisces and unaspected. Jupiter in one of its own signs (Sagittarius/Pisces) and at a "critical degree" (28/29 or 0) can be very exaggerated and inflated. There is a tendency to expect too much and/or to go too far. It is not surprising that at age 7 (or thereabout) you cognized an invention for projecting thought, for at that age your progressed Sun crossed your natal Jupiter. Transiting Pluto now has crossed your natal Neptune in Sagittarius and is within orb of a square to natal Sun. That square will be exact in January and Feb. 2003. Your inventions could be very useful in the coming war (as I see it when Pluto gets to 19 degrees Sagittarius it will be opposing the U.S.A. Mars and

Uranus in Gemini and on Bush's So. Node -- "final justice for old karma," and it's been announced that the admin. Plans to again go into Iraq in 2003). Sun and Jupiter in your second house certainly give the potential for making a great deal of money. Whether that would be for yourself or for others remains to be seen. Tesla never made much from his, many of which, like Wilhelm Reich's, were confiscated and suppressed by the government.

As I said, Tesla had planets in Earth. You have NO planets in EARTH. Many abstract thinkers have missing Earth charts. Some very wealthy people do, as well. There is also a danger with missing Earth of substance abuse (drink, drugs, overeating, sexual, "buyaholic," and on and on) because there is a disconnect with the body and the material realm. Pisces/Neptune are particularly susceptible to escapist mechanisms (drugs, et al); so, I'd advise you to forgo cannabis, alcohol, even prescription medications such as Vicodan, and use music and/or meditation to get "high" and tune into the transcendental. I have had enough experience with telepathy that I know it is a valid means of communication. I suspect it is related to hearing, and that there is an organ in the ear and brain that processes incoming thoughts of other people as well as one's own outgoing thoughts and emotions. There are some scientists who say our brains emit photons (light particles), and those particles carry our thoughts and feelings and penetrate the brains and bodies of everyone and everything around us, and ultimately the whole of the universe. I have also experienced sending thoughts. It is a valuable ability when I am teaching. The students unconsciously (for the most part) receive my thoughts, then I speak out loud the same information and it seems very familiar and natural to them, as though they had always known it! There is also telepathy between "dead" people. One man who had been "dead" for three years before I met him told me he was working on "the other side" with a group of business people and scientists (which he was in "life") who attended high level business and government assemblies and meetings. They transmitted and influenced the "living" to move and create in positive and evolutionary ways. I asked him that since I knew who he was, did the people at these meetings know the ideas and inspirations came from him or others in his group. He laughed and told me that was the beauty of a big ego. A big ego thinks any idea in his mind is his own and will act on it. If he knew it came from someone else, he might not do anything with it.

There enough connections between your chart and Tesla's that he may indeed be your teacher and may be telepathing his inventions to you. As far as a "price" -- well, you are born under the sign of Pisces/sign of Sacrifice. So, you may be called on, or forced by circumstances, to sacrifice your personal gain and glory for the greater good of the whole. The Melchizedek cannot help but give aid and assistance to whom, and when and where, it is needed. And the three planets in the firest house of your chart in Aquarius, the water bearer, that show you must pour out for the benefit of humanity, all your wealth of knowledge and genius.

Blessings,
Eleanor Buckwalter

A SCIENCE WITNESS

Human nature
Posted By: vlad

Some interesting extracts from the new energy yahoo.groups postings:

"ICI's own paints laboratory held an internal audit and what they found puts this claim in an entirely different light. For the audit showed that the most scientifically qualified of its research chemists had contributed to the least number of patents, and the fewer scientific qualifications the staff possessed, the greater the number of patents they had contributed to. In the most striking case of all, the person who had contributed to most ICI's patents had no scientific qualifications at all."

It seems that Maurice Ward's greatest strength as a researcher was that he had not been taught how to think."

source: http://www.alternativescience.com/flame-proof.htm

People,

I'm reading all these notes going back and forth in defense of one or another and, even though it's not something to laugh about, I smile thinking of the famous Rodney King lament «why can't we get aloooong!?»:-)

The answer is simple: it is human nature and only those who understand its complexity can control it and take advantage of it.

To change it, it's wishful thinking, period. But like the two poles in a magnet, there is always good and bad in the human nature true, in various proportions, but both aspects are there, in all of us!

Ego is probably the most powerful of them all and it can push some to amazing accomplishments but equally easy to ridicule and destruction, when it takes over the reason. So what if Tim wants the Nobel Prize? I met a guy who thinks he's the Second Coming of Tesla and the Christ/AntiChrist (I'm not clear yet). He has no scientific qualifications at all but he's a self taught genius with brilliant ideas, the kind of Maurice Ward from somebody's note above. That's the human nature part we should be focusing on.

There is nothing wrong to stand up to bullying, to be honest and fair and ask that from others. Some people need that to bring them «down to Earth». Others don't get it, and for the benefit of the cause and the many, we must continue without them.

I agree that the experimenters out there are the soul of the free energy movement (and the soul has a mind of its own). I wish the «brain mind» would be awaken (the scientist, theoreticians like the JPL guy) because it has been proven they can help tremendously to shorten the way to the target by cutting through empiricism and the hard work of the trial and error experimenters.

But the bottom line here is that this is a WAR and we have to prove we're not just a bunch of losers that sacrifice our lives (time, money, career, family you name it) to build stupid toys that run cold and run web sites because it's in fashion. Gentlemen, what we want to do is change the world by bringing free energy to everybody on this planet, and, as a byproduct, trigger the next chapter in physics.

All we need is that working unit that can prove it is possible and can be sold to whoever wants to buy it. As in any war, we need war tactics and strategies, discipline, organization and commitment (there are big words but I don't know better ones). Most of all, we need each other, we need to set aside our differences, get the best out of us to win, or we'll be divided and conquered, as it happened before. In hindsight, if we don't succeed, I hope we can live with the shame and our magnificent ego.

Vlad

The Christadephians for some reason (I'd like to know who went to the effort to reach this insight) understand that The Antichrist myth is both deliberate smear campaign against The Second Coming and an honest inability to reconcile The Alpha Lamb and The Omega Lion – so much of what I (can) do can easily be considered cultish or tyrannical...That's for you to decide apparently. There is also the "Akkaeneset" dimension to this. If you go back to Atlantis, I was a very bad person; those stains never really come out I guess. Blurring the line further, Christians are eager to agree with End Times Fiction portrayals of The Second Coming as a nationalistic, genocidal lightning bolt or as Pinchbeck put it, Schwarzenegger-Like. It's the bad guy who is intellectual and the good guy who is brute force. Antipas could not have known I was an inventor from Ithaca but the point is made.

THE COMING ANTI-CHRIST:
JESUS OF NAZARETH?

A TRAGIC CASE OF MISTAKEN IDENTITY?

This piece is from: http://www.antipas.org/books/antichrist/anti1.html

Why do the nations rage and the people imagine a vain thing? The kings of the earth set themselves, and the rulers take counsel together, against the LORD and against His Christ...He that sitteth in the heavens shall laugh... Yet I have set my king upon my holy hill Zion. (Psalm 2:1, 2, 4, 6)

A most interesting aspect of this prophetic Psalm is that the opening inquiry of the writer is left unanswered. His searching question concerns the reason why the peoples of the earth are hostile to Christ when he returns to subject the earth to his benevolent rule. The word used in the query, "vain," means "having no real substance." The distinct implication of the question is that the world has imagined something that is not true, that its leaders are deceived in some way. In this work a possible reason for the opposition to Christ, which it is believed is related to the "vain" idea those opposing him will hold, is advanced. It is the sincere desire on the part of those producing this pamphlet [Antipas in the producing of this website], to inform the public as to the nature of the expectations of many modern Bible students, and the possible consequences that these views may ultimately have when Jesus returns to this earth. By becoming acquainted with the evidence, the reader will hopefully then be in a better position to form his own opinion on the validity or invalidity of the ideas being put forth respecting future events.

In recent years, there has been a tremendous increase in interest within christian circles as to what the Bible reveals about the course history will follow. One of the most prominent beliefs to emerge is the conviction that a single man will arise, the Antichrist, who will personally fulfill many prophecies in the Bible. With many this idea has become a basic tenet of their faith. An almost feverish anticipation has developed, fueled by a continuing stream of books and films, that this individual will soon appear in Jerusalem, demand to be worshipped and revered as a god, and quickly ascend to the position of supreme world dictator. There is almost complete agreement that these events are nearly upon us. This presents a very sobering and arresting challenge to the reader. Where will he give his loyalty when this personage manifests himself? Could it be, is there even a remote possibility, that Christ himself could be mistakenly identified as the Antichrist? Could the most serious blunder of history be the opposing of the real Christ as the fabricated Antichrist? Lest the reader dismiss the suggestion out of hand, we beg him/her to compare what the Scriptures reveal concerning Christ at His second coming on the one hand, with what many christian expositors believe this evil despot, Antichrist, will do, on the other.

The Supposed Future Antichrist of Popular Expositions

Antichrist will appear suddenly.

"The way in which this dictator is going to step onto the stage of history will be dramatic. Overnight he will become the byword of the world. He is going to be distinguished as supernatural..." -- Lindsey, Hal, "The Late Great Planet Earth," Zondervan Publishing House, Grand Rapids, 1970, page 108.

Antichrist himself, or his chief cohort, the False Prophet, will be a Jew.

"This person (The False Prophet), who is called the second beast, is going to be a Jew. Many believe he will be from the tribe of Dan, which is one of the tribes of the original progenitors of the nation of Israel." -- Lindsey, Hal, "The Late Great Planet Earth," Zondervan Publishing House, Grand Rapids, 1970, page 112.

"Several other items lead Bible students to conclude that antichrist will be a Jew. It is hard to believe that Israel would receive a Gentile Messiah. No Gentile could pose as Christ with any success." -- John L. Benson,"Will the Real Antichrist Please Stand Up?" BP Publications, Denver, 1974, page 37.

Antichrist will claim that he is the Messiah of Israel.

"The antichrist will actually pose as the Messiah, he will claim Messianic titles and privileges... The antichrist is a person who will attempt to convince Israel that he is their long-anticipated Messiah." -- Lindsey, Hal, "The Late Great Planet Earth," Zondervan Publishing House, Grand Rapids, 1970, page 10.

Antichrist will perform miracles.

Satan is a miracle worker..." -- Lindsey, op. cit., page 106.

Antichrist will reside in Jerusalem.

"Jerusalem ...the capital and centre of the world dictator's (i.e. Antichrist's rule..." -- John F. Walvoord, "Armageddon," Zondervan Publishing House, Grand Rapids, 1974, page 170.

Antichrist will rebuild the Temple of Jerusalem and be involved with the service therein. "The Antichrist will deify himself -- just like the Caesars did. He will proclaim himself to be God. He will demand that he be worshipped and will establish himself in the temple of God. (2 Thess. 2:4) There is only one place where this temple of God can be and that is on Mount Moriah in Jerusalem, on the site where the Dome of the Rock and other Moslem shrines now stand. There are many places in the Bible that pinpoint this location as the one where the Jews will rebuild their Temple." -- Lindsey, op. cit., pages 109-110.

"The Israelis will then be permitted to reinstitute the sacrifice and offering aspect of the law of Moses. This demands that the Temple be rebuilt, because according to the law of Moses, sacrifices can only be offered in the Temple at Jerusalem. Apparently all this will be done under the protection of the Antichrist of Rome. (P.S. The Arabs are not going to like this idea of rebuilding the Temple one bit.)" -- Lindsey, op. cit., page 152.

Antichrist will form a covenant with the Jews.

"The Romans under Titus did the destroying, so the coming prince would have to be someone out of the Roman culture... (Others say that Antichrist must be a Jew, rather than someone of the Roman culture -- see point 2 above. This shows the immense amount of unsubstantiated speculation that has been done.) This Roman prince will come to power just before the return of Christ. He will make 'a strong covenant' with the Israelis,

guaranteeing their safety and protection. The word translated 'strong covenant' has the idea of a treaty or mutual protection pact." -- Lindsey, op. cit., pages 151-152. "It will be a covenant which will permit Israel to continue and renew her religious ceremonies including the building of a Jewish temple and the reactivation of Jewish sacrifices." -- Walvoord, op. cit., page 117.

Antichrist will somehow defeat Russia when it attacks Israel.

"With the world balance of power dramatically in his favor and the world dazzled by Russia's defeat (in its attempt to invade Israel) the Antichrist will show his true colors. He will declare himself world dictator and move to crush all opposition." -- Walvoord, op. cit., page 141.

Antichrist's rule will commence with a proclamation and those who refuse to submit to it will be crushed. "Ironically, the Mediterranean leader will begin his world government by proclamation. Using his consolidated position of power in the Middle East, he will promise a new day of peace and prosperity for all who recognize his leadership... This man's absolute control politically, economically, and religiously will give him power such as no man has ever had in human history. His brilliance as a leader will be superhuman for he will be dominated and directed by Satan himself. But during his 3-1/2 year rule, he will ruthlessly crush all opposition." -- Walvoord, op.

cit., page 161.

The Christ of the Scriptures at His Appearing.

Christ will appear suddenly.

"For as a snare shall it (his coming) come on all them that dwell on the face of the whole earth." (Luke 21:35)

Jesus is a Jew.

"Where is he that is born King of the Jews?" (Matt. 2:2) Among Christ's immediate co-rulers will be Jews -- the twelve apostles. "Ye also shall sit on twelve thrones, judging the twelve tribes of Israel." (Matt. 19:28) .

Jesus will exercise his appointed office of Messiah.

"I will overturn, overturn, overturn it: and it shall be no more, until he come whose right it is; and I will give it him." (Ezek. 21:27)

"And he shall reign over the house of Jacob for ever; and of his kingdom there shall be no end." (Luke 1:33)

"And I will pour upon the house of David, and upon the inhabitants of Jerusalem, the spirit of grace and of supplications: and they shall look upon me whom they have pierced, and they shall mourn for him, as one mourneth for his only son, and shall be in bitterness for him, as one that is in bitterness for his firstborn." (Zech.12:10)

Christ will perform miracles.

"Then the eyes of the blind shall be opened, and the ears of the deaf shall be unstopped. Then shall the lame man leap as an hart, and the tongue of the dumb sing; for in the wilderness shall waters break out and streams in the desert." (Isaiah 35:5,6)

Jesus will rule from Jerusalem.

"O Jerusalem, Jerusalem, which killest the prophets... Ye shall not see me, until the time come when ye shall say, Blessed is he that cometh in the name of the Lord." (Luke 13:34, 35) "Yet have I set my king upon my holy hill of Zion." (Psalm 2:6) "For out of Zion shall go forth the law, and the word of the Lord from Jerusalem." (Isaiah 2:3)

Jesus will rebuild the Temple at Jerusalem and be involved with the services therein.

"After this I will return, and will build again the tabernacle of David, which is fallen down; and I will build again the ruins thereof, and set it up: that the residue of men might seek after the Lord..." (Acts 15:16,17) "Thus speaketh the LORD of hosts, saying, Behold the man whose name is the Branch; and he shall grow up out of his place, and he shall build the temple of the LORD: Even he shall build the temple of the LORD; and he shall bear the glory, and shall sit and rule upon his throne; and he shall be a priest upon his throne: and the counsel of peace shall be between them both." (Zech. 6:12, 13)

Jesus will be a great leader and will re-introduce the Jews into God's true everlasting covenant.

"And so all Israel shall be saved: as it is written, There shall come out of Zion the Deliverer, and shall turn ungodliness from Jacob: For this is my covenant unto them, when I shall take away their sins." (Romans 11:26, 27) "Incline your ear and come unto me; hear, and your soul shall live; and I will make an everlasting covenant with you, even the sure mercies of David. Behold, I have given him for a witness to the people, a leader and commander to the people." (Isaiah 55:3,4)

"Behold, the days come, saith the LORD, that I will make a new covenant with the house of Israel, and with the house of Judah." (Jeremiah 31:31) "For the children of Israel shall abide many days without a king, and without a prince, and without a sacrifice, and without an image, and without an ephod, and without teraphim: Afterward shall the children of Israel return, and seek the LORD their God, and David their king ..." (Hosea 3:4,5)

The Bible clearly teaches that God, and not a human agency will destroy Russia when it moves south; the idea that some individual will do this is totally foreign to scripture.

Christ's rule will commence with a proclamation and those who refuse to submit to it will be crushed. "And I saw another angel fly in the midst of heaven, having the everlasting gospel to preach unto them that dwell on the earth, and to every nation, and kindred, and tongue, and people, saying with a loud voice, Fear God, and give glory to him; for the hour of judgment is come; and worship him that made heaven and earth and the sea, and the fountains of waters." (Rev. 14:6, 7)

"And he shall judge among many people, and rebuke strong nations afar off..." (Micah 4:3) "To execute vengeance upon the heathen, and punishments upon the people; to bind their kings with chains, and their nobles with fetters of iron; to execute upon them the judgment written: this honor have all his saints." (Psalm 149:7-9) See also Daniel 2:44; 7:14; Psalm 72:7, 11.

The reader may well reflect at this juncture, "I see clearly the possibility that due to the remarkable similarity between what

Jesus will do at his Second Coming and what this supposed Antichrist, according to many writers, would do, that a case of mistaken identity could certainly result: Jesus could very definitely be opposed for the reason that many think him to be this very Antichrist that they had been told about. Two questions do arise, however: (1) By what authority is it stated that these expositions of a Coming Antichrist are not sound? (2) Surely it is not being implied that good christian people, many of them currently holding this Antichrist view, will be among those deceived, if the above hypothesis is, in fact, true? Is the writer unaware that the Rapture will occur just prior to the manifestation of this Antichrist (according to present day expositions) and that they will be in heaven with Jesus during the reign of the Antichrist, and therefore could not possibly be deceived?

The response to these eminently reasonable queries is as follows: (1) The entire basis for this Antichrist view is founded upon an interpretation of a portion of Daniel 9 -- the prophecy of the Seventy Weeks. This particular view was championed by Sir Robert Anderson in his book The Coming Prince, first published in 1881. This interpretation is discussed in detail in the second portion of this pamphlet.

Question (2) above involves of necessity a detailed discussion of another widely held tenet of faith, namely that an event known as "The Rapture" (or "The Great Snatch"), as one evangelical writer termed it, is soon going to occur. What is this "Rapture", as it is commonly conceived, and upon what is it founded?

This popular notion has its foundation, ostensibly, in 1 Thessalonians 4:17: Then we which are alive and remain shall be caught up together with them in the clouds, to meet the Lord in the air (or atmosphere): and so shall we ever be with the Lord.

This is interpreted to mean that believers will be caught up into the literal clouds high above the surface of the earth ("in the air") and taken off to heaven. One well-known writer on the subject states: "The largest descriptive volume of the Tribulation is found in Revelation 6 through 19. Here is a fascinating revelation about Revelation.

In the first five chapters of this book, the church is mentioned thirty times. In fact, in chapters 2 and 3, at the end of each letter to the churches, John says, 'Let him hear what the Spirit saith unto the churches'. This is repeated seven times. Then we have the beginning of the description of the Tribulation and there is not one mention of the churches. The church is conspicuous by its absence. Why? Because the church will be in heaven at that time. If you are a believer, chapters 4 and 5 describe what you will be experiencing in heaven. (Lindsey, Hal, "The Late Great Planet Earth," Zondervan Publishing House, Grand Rapids, 1970, p. 143-144) One further point should be made at this time with respect to the "rapture". There are currently three views as to when in the seven-year career of Antichrist this remarkable event will occur. (The reason for a period of seven years, rather than some other period of time, will be explained in Part 2 of this pamphlet [Part Two].) The most popular view is known as the "Pre- tribulation" rapture. Exponents of this understanding believe that believers will be taken to heaven just before Antichrist begins his seven-year reign. Then there is the "Mid-tribulation" exposition, which states that the church will be here on earth for the first half of Antichrist's rule, and then be taken to heaven by Christ. Lastly, there is the "Post-tribulation" rapture, in which the view is maintained that the believers will be on earth for the whole of the seven-year reign of Antichrist. The three views are depicted diagrammatically overleaf. The important point that the reader should file away in his mind for future consideration is that the question of when the rapture will occur is one upon which there is some disagreement. Hence, there exists a great deal of flexibility on this point. The possible implications of his flexibility will be examined presently.

On returning to 1 Thessalonians 4:17 for a moment, the key verse used to support the entire rapture theory, it is found that the commonly accepted evangelical interpretation is not borne out either by the verse itself or by other Scripture. The clear meaning intended is that a large body of people (here translated "clouds"— see Hebrews 12:1) will be gathered by the power of God to a place of judgment here on this earth, in the very air or atmosphere. The place of judgment will most probably be somewhere in the

Sinai Peninsula, from which Jesus and his redeemed brethren will proceed to Jerusalem. (See Deut. 33:2,3; Isaiah 63:1-6; Habakkuk 3:3; Obadiah 21; Matthew 23:39.) The theory that there will be two comings of Christ separated by a seven-year interval is one that has no basis in Scripture but is rather one that has been introduced to coincide with the theory of a Coming Antichrist. Is there a possibility then that the following situation could develop?

The three theories of the rapture:

1. Christ takes believers to heaven where they spend the next seven years; Antichrist appears in Jerusalem and reigns for seven years.

2. Believers live on the earth for the first 3-1/2 years of Antichrist's reign; in the middle of his reign, they are taken to heaven by Christ, while on earth his reign is dreadful for the next 3-1/2 years, known as the "Great Tribulation". (The "Great Tribulation" is supposedly described in the book of Revelation, with the time periods there being understood as literal periods.)

3. Believers live on earth throughout the whole of Antichrist's reign; Christ appears at the end of the last week and gathers believers. Armageddon follows in which Christ subdues the nations. A new Jewish leader has suddenly appeared in Jerusalem. The rapture has not occurred. What will professing christendom conclude as this new leader commences his ambitious programs, apparently with supernatural power? Slowly, dimly, do we not begin to see a spectre taking shape on the horizon, giving us the answer to the question in Psalm 2? In their estimation this new ruler cannot possibly be Jesus, for he is expected to take the church away from the earth. There is only one conclusion left for them to reach: This new ruler must be the Antichrist, and the rapture must occur either at Mid-tribulation or Post-tribulation. Meanwhile, it is the duty of all sincere christians to prepare themselves to "witness" against this new dictator. For suddenly onto the world scene comes a new leader who:

1. Appears suddenly
2. Is a Jew
3. Claims that he is the long-looked-for Messiah of Israel

4. Has supernatural powers

5. Resides in Jerusalem

6. Commences the rebuilding of the Temple

7. Talks of restoring the Jewish nation to their position under the Covenant

8. Appears very near to the time when Russia was defeated

9. Promises the world a new era of peace and prosperity, but demands submission and commences military operations when his request is not complied with by the nations.

DOES NOT JESUS FIT IN EVERY PARTICULAR THE POPULAR CONCEPTION OF THE COMING ANTICHRIST? Can we not see that when he manifests his power, the religious leaders of the day will come to fear this political ruler and brand him as the long-awaited "Antichrist"? And so, sad to relate, history will repeat itself. The first time, the professing religious people were expecting a Lion, and found a Lamb.

When Jesus therefore perceived that they would come and take him by force, to make him a king, he departed again into a mountain himself alone. (John 6: 15)

(1) It is the position of this publishing committee [Antipas] that those who will be called to judgment at Christ's appearing will be those noted in Psalm 50:5 -- "Gather my saints together unto me; those who have made a covenant with me by sacrifice." This covenant is the one God made with Abraham and his "seed" or descendants. Those who are outside this covenant are not counted as saints. The two positions, namely those who are adopted into the commonwealth of Israel and are included under the terms of the Covenants of Promise, and those who are not, are clearly delineated in Ephesians 2:11-13. Others, however sincere, are not named in this agreement. They have never been adopted into the family of Abraham, that is, become spiritual Israel, and therefore have no claim to the things promised. This, unfortunately, encompasses a large group of persons who believe that they are in the way of salvation, but are not so as defined by Scripture, our only reliable guide in this most important matter. One evangelical writer expresses his hope as follows:

"For us, as believers, our hope is different from Israel's . . . First there is a great distinction between God's purpose for the nation of Israel and His purpose for church, which is His main program today." (Lindsey, Hal, "The Late Great Planet Earth, pp. 139-142)

This contrasts starkly with the declaration of the apostle Paul: "For this cause therefore I have called for you, to see you and to speak with you; because that for the hope of Israel I am bound with this chain." (Acts 28:20)

The Hope that the Bible holds out is that Israel will become the centre of the Kingdom of God with the faithful seed of Abraham (whether Jew or Gentile) as the rulers. The future of Israel and the future of the redeemed are inextricably linked.

In fact, he disclaimed any right to rule in any sense at his first coming:

And one of the company said unto him, Master, speak to my brother, that he divide the inheritance with me. And he said unto him, Man, who made me a judge or a divider over you? (Luke 12:13,14) When he would not be a king, but rather a Lamb, they would have no part of him, but demanded his crucifixion.

Now there are growing numbers of christians who expect Christ to take them to heaven while violent wars occur on the earth. Unfortunately they will experience instead a Jewish political Lion whom they will not recognize. They could find themselves warring against the real Christ who does not meet their preconceived specifications of what He should be like or what He should do. Even though the name Jesus is the same, it is another Jesus.

For if he that cometh preacheth another Jesus, whom we have not preached . . . ye might well bear with him (2 Corinthians 11:4).

Perhaps it comes down to the fact that his title is not understood. His name is Jesus ("Saviour"): Thou shalt call his name Jesus: for he shall save his people from their sins (Matthew 1:21). However, his office is that of The Christ, The Anointed, The Messiah, which denotes his national position as ruler of the Nation of Israel.

Many religious persons think that the term "Jesus Christ" is equal to, say, "John Doe". Such is not the case at all. This designation relates directly to his work-first as Saviour (from eternal death) of his brothers and sisters, and secondly as National Deliverer of the nation of Israel. When the significance of the name and office of Jesus is understood, the link between his death 2000 years ago and the rebirth of the Nation of Israel in our time is easy to comprehend; where this is not understood, confusion prevails.

A final practical question arises in connection with this Coming Antichrist idea: Who could this Antichrist be? It has been said that "Coming events cast their shadow before". What nation on this earth would have a leader who would befriend Israel (for the supposed Antichrist must be a leader of a country able to guarantee Israel, by terms of a covenant, safety for seven years), when this would immediately alienate those with whom the world economic power lies, namely, the Arabs? Would it be the United States? Russia? China? Europe (as is commonly suggested)? The Arabs themselves? What would any nation possibly have to gain by making a covenant with Israel? What nation could promise Israel that it would guarantee its survival? Would any of these nations support an individual wanting to be worshipped in a rebuilt temple in Jerusalem as god? The answer clearly seems to be that no human being could ever fulfill the necessary requirements of the supposed coming Antichrist. The only individual who could possibly perform the miraculous feats required would be Jesus himself, by the power of God Almighty. It is the very show of this power which will undoubtedly deceive those looking for Antichrist into thinking that Jesus is in fact he.

Objections

As the reader has worked through the above thesis, some objections may have arisen in his mind. Three possible objections are considered below:

1. Psalm 2 indicates that the kings of the earth fight against the LORD and against his Christ. Does not this show that they know who they are fighting against, and are not deceived into thinking that this new leader is the long expected Antichrist?

In Revelation 17:13,14 it is clearly pointed out that certain nations will resist the claims of Christ:

These have one mind, and shall give their power and strength unto the beast. These shall make war with the Lamb, and the Lamb shall overcome them: for he is Lord of lords, and King of kings: and they that are with him are called, and chosen, and faithful.

The question being asked is whether they do this in knowledge or ignorance of whom they are opposing. An allusion to Psalm 2 is made by the early disciples in Act 4:23-27. The "kings of the earth" here are defined as being composed of both Jews and Gentiles. Did they oppose the LORD and His Christ in knowledge or ignorance of what they were doing, for the language is clear that they "set themselves against the LORD and His Christ"? The answer is clear: they opposed God and His Son in ignorance.

Which none of the princes of this world knew: for had they known it, they would not have crucified the Lord of Glory (1 Corinthians 2:8).

This shows clearly that this Psalm could very possibly apply at his second coming in the same manner as it did at his first coming; namely, referring to opposition to him in ignorance. A probable reason for this opposition is that they believe him to be the Antichrist.

2. Jesus is clearly a Jew. Is it not now true that many expositors identify Antichrist as someone from the Roman cult? Does not this destroy the above thesis?

It is true that many expositors identify Antichrist as a Roman. Some, however, say that he will be a Jew.

Because, in our opinion, none of the prophecies used to support the Coming Antichrist concept refer to a future individual in any way, human imagination must fill in a number of gaps, which is the great danger in the entire concept. The details of this supposed Coming Antichrist are so plastic that they could very easily be moulded to fit the Christ of the Scriptures at his second coming by those anticipating the appearance of Antichrist.

3. Is not the Antichrist hypothesis only held by a very small percentage of the world's population? How could this small group influence the whole world?

It is true that the persons holding this view, taken as a percentage of the world population, are a minuscule proportion indeed. However, with a world devoted to the occult, astrology, UFOs, and soap operas, it is easy to see that should a Middle Eastern leader commence a campaign of spectacular military victories, all people would look for a solution to this new and disturbing enigma. Organized christianity would claim that it had predicted some time before that this exact situation would arise. No other philosophy or cult would have any answer. Religion now would be solicited for advice on how to handle the situation. Organized religion would, therefore, experience a tremendous resurgence of influence during this period, among people with very divergent backgrounds.

In summary, this portion of the pamphlet has outlined the opinions currently extant among many evangelical writers on the subject of the Coming Antichrist. It has been pointed out that as a result of speculation on prophecies which, in our opinion, have nothing to do with a Coming Antichrist, the similarities between what this supposed individual would do, and what the Christ of the Scriptures will do at his Second Coming, are very striking -- striking to the point that when the "rapture", as commonly conceived, does not occur, and yet a new ruler, Jesus, appears in Jerusalem, the world at large could be very well induced by professing organized christianity into believing that he is the Antichrist. Objections have been considered, and it has been shown that it is the very elasticity in the views held with respect to this Coming Antichrist that could make an application to Jesus himself at His Glorious Appearance very feasible.

The conclusion of this portion of the pamphlet is this: We would do very well to investigate the bases for all predictions concerning a Coming Antichrist It is particularly important at this time in history that we are neither deceived ourselves nor that we deceive others as to the nature of coming events. The warning of the apostle John speaks urgently to our generation:

Beloved, believe not every spirit, but try the spirits whether they are of God; because many false prophets are gone out into the world (1 John 4: 1).

ZERO POINT POEM

Zero Point
the naked creator
clothed in time
sole soul generator

Zero Point
before quantum foam
omnipresent, non-dimensional
hyperspace home

Zero Point
the beginning and end
of archetypal foundations
that will not bend

Zero Point
the philosophers stone
man does not live on bread alone

Zero Point
just 7 phase states away
to tap genesis return to the first day

Zero Point
1 in 3, 3 in 1
fire from heaven
thy will be done

Zero Point
I AM in it
it is in me
I AM the source
and the source is free

END TIMES FICTION

No Avatar/anointed teacher before me has read the entire Bible, Koran, Torah etc, so my knowledge of these books should not be requisite to proving my claims or in fact doing my job.

The only relevant scripture for me to contend with is prophecy.

I have a problem with Hal Lindsey, Tim LaHaye and their clones, who are, in my opinion, the epitome of the "false prophet." Their sins are too many to count but they can be summed up by saying that they have added and taken away from the Book of Revelation. So it was with great excitement to find END TIMES FICTION by Gary DeMar.

http://www.discerningreader.com/endtimficgar1.html

I have read enough scripture to know when to take it literally and when to take it symbolically; but nonetheless, Gary has read more in depth than I have. Since reading his book I learned that I cannot rely totally on my own gnostic ways to explain scripture. I can't always say that such and such is just symbolic on a whim, some things should be taken literally and so I find the term for what I have always known - Partial Preterism.

When DeMar explains that some prophecy was fulfilled in the first century of the church, and uses the bible to validate the bible, I find it hard to disagree. But I must reconcile symbolism/literalism & then/now.

DeMar argues that "you," "this generation," "the end," etc., applies to the early disciples and the end of the old covenant age and again its hard to disagree.

But now the gnostic interpretation must be considered.

It is safe to say Jesus taught his followers plenty of esoterica that never made it into the bible, the idea of reincarnation for example.

http://www.comparativereligion.com/reincarnation3.html

We must also consider the fact history repeats itself. It is therefore possible that one prophecy could apply to THEN & NOW. Many of Nostradamus' quatrains worked this way.

So "you" means you when you were in the year 0030 and 2002, "this generation" of humans and this root race of karmic families, the end of the old covenant and of this entire veiled age/yuga.

The crimes against Christ and the early followers of The Way can still, karmically speaking, be avenged via tribulation today – not just your sins but the sins of your fathers will be paid back.

What is an age to man is as a day to the Lord. DeMar seems to have overlooked this and, in his attempt to correct LaHaye, he has repeated LaHaye's mistake of failing to see the big picture.

So I've finished DeMar's END TIMES FICTION, I've learned that there is a name for this kind of prophecy, Partial Preterism, and I've learned that DeMar is a hypocrite. He rags on LaHaye for picking and choosing what to tweak and what to leave alone in order to construct his infallible interpretation of scripture. DeMar's book is littered with arrogant certainty – Only I'm allowed to do that.

There is a lack of consistency in his explanations. For example, he is trying to find a preterist explanation of Revelation 13's beasts out of the earth and sea. He can explain away breathing "life into the image of the first beast" as ventriloquism, magic, etc, but he does not explain how first century Rome is also a talking statue that has authority over all nations lands and tongues or what "fire from heaven in full view of men" means.

I bought this book because I thought DeMar might help me dispel some myths. Turns out he doesn't even believe that I would return in the flesh.

DIVISION

Throughout history, folks have been asked or forced to choose between two opposing positions. In a democracy, you have the option to choose between candidates. In a tyrannical system you are forced to go along with what is imposed OR suffer the consequences. With the former, you have the choice to vote from several options with no one candidate particularly offering anything in the form of a solution to big issues, and with the latter both options undoubtedly suck.

Caesar did it, Rockefeller did it, and now George W. Bush is. Roman Empire, Standard Oil, U.S. Corporate interests – it's all the same bullshit.

With the End Times, however, a division will occur that is unprecedented: The Mark of The Beast vs. The Mark of Christ.

HOW?
WHY?

The tyranny of the aforementioned leaders, and the division they insisted on, was obviously engaged so that a person could be identified as aligning for or against. With Christ this is true as well. The difference between these tyrants and Christ, their empires and New Jerusalem, is that this division affects the future of the soul. It is apolitical and ultimate.

Now, there are a lot of folks who have already made their alignments in this division, some by exemplary acts, others by professed statements. Some folks think that they are chosen or elect, some folks hate religion, some are ignorant and still others apathetic. These are all real indicators of where one stands in the eyes of God, but no division will occur until I am judged.

Corinthians 6:3

Do you not know that we will judge angels? How much more the things of this life!

The reason for this is: the standard for which these alignments have occurred has not been present in 2000 years – the current alignments are based on deviations, rebellion, reformations, propaganda and all manner of falsehood.

The TRUE Body of Christ, The Bride, Spiritual Israel, will come out of all religions, even atheists and satanists, all subcultures races and age groups. I know in general terms who my people are but for the sake of their humility I will not say.

There is no way for me to judge each individual on the planet but they can all judge me and in so doing choose a mark, then they can have their personal Akashic record audited come JD.

AN ESOTERIC PERSPECTIVE

...My function on earth as a Godhead Representative today is to conserve novelty. This has been the function of previous Christs as well. From the POV of The Creator aspect of the Godhead (aka Zeropoint) or pure consciousness, when it collapses the quantum potential and deviates out of heaven/hyperspace it is attaining form through movement. This is what "fallen" means. Man is that consciousness which falls into the duality of subjective ego and objective spirit; because the brain is both a quantum system and measuring device, it can record (within its fallen matter state) the movement in linear time and in turn gain the ability for introspection – we are what allows the universe to truly know its own potential.

In the formless void of the zeropoint manifold there is a paradox. With infinite surface area there is infinite potential for form. Within a tangled hierarchy or riddled basin of superpositioned surface area, which results in, without causality, an isotropic, homogenous space – it is impossible to say whether space is a plenum or vacuum. What we can say is that there are 2 vacuums or plenums of equal symmetry but one is pure order, based on sphere packing rules, and one is pure chaos based on foam coarsening rules. They decay or collapse into one another with a resultant spin and inertia, with this emergent asymmetry comes novelty in complexification.

This mechanistic metaphor of plenum or vacuum is really the root duality (not to say the universe should necessarily be reduced to a machine). All other dualities can be traced to it. Humanity has always swung back and forth between these 2 POVs. When it believes in the vacuum, there is pessimism and conflict because it is all meaningless and resources are finite. When viewed as a plenum, you get the opposite effect.

Adam, the vector space, entered a nucleus in the garden of light and became a seed. The seed was hyperhydrophilic; it sucked up the superluminal surface of zeropoint and warped it into a scalar rib or branch off the tree of life and thus the garden grew or complexified as interference of standing waves. Through seven transdimensional phase states (See Holofractaline GUT) the earthly matter grew and DEVIATED/SINNED. Matter, or 666, deviated out of zeropoint = Man falling/sinning from heaven. Repentance = admitting you are not pure zeropoint. In other words, the emergence of matter is the reduction of consciousness.

The clue for calculating or deciphering the meaning comes from another number in the bible - 144,000.

144= harmonic of light
God is Light
Man is made in the image of God
hebrew "garden of eden" = 144
144,000 divided by 6 = 24,000
24,000 divided by 6 = 4000
4000 divided by 6 = 666.666666666666...
Therefore GOD = MAN
This also has to do with Base 12 DNA and the singing of a new song or activation of 3rd codon set = new bodies...this won't happen till JD or until the oversoul or Merkaba decides...

So what have The Christs been doing?

When man lags behind/with linear time too much he gets bogged down in his own karma and the flow of spirit stops MOVING. As in the yugas or ages. Every new age requires that one of the Melchizedek ensure the new age is ushered in via divine intervention, or will of the creator, which would be most perfectly reflected in me above all humans right now. The elect by definition would be all those who want what I want and are willing to do what I AM willing to do (and not to do) to get it.

Gods will=my will=your will=New Jerusalem

What I am willing to do to usher in the new age here on earth (my friends in hyperspace are working on it "War in Heaven" in their own way simultaneously, I AM "coming with the saints" who have also incarnated at this time) Is:

1. Teach
2. Allow you to collapse my will – judgment or observation of me, which in turn will "mark" your intent in the akashic record or book of life; nothing is lost in this universe.
3. Destroy Babylon/Usher in New Jerusalem.

1 Everything you need to know to achieve Christ consciousness has already been taught. The novelty of my teachings is in the consolidation of otherwise unrelated disciplines- I am literally overcoming the paradox via tangling the metaphors as much as the zeropoint itself is, resolving all dualities back to one big trip. Even though the truth is out there and in here and the kingdom is all around, humans often forget that even the mundane is oozing with divinity, as inherent intelligence of design and nature is already DAMN trippy without the observer. So you see, I have a problem when my creations are banned and people are put in jail for consuming just more of me.

What made me *me* is the molecules I metabolized, for they merely allowed me to slip out of my ego so that I may differentiate its intent from that of The Creators'. That and the books I have read. Anyone who wants to understand, with words and without words, must do both or else neither will be complete. What a joy to have thousands of other minds to do the pre consolidating, for WE are the meme refinery, Christ Consciousness or Buddah nature, etc., is when the only meme you care about is service. You are grade AAA LOVE.

The ultimate consolidation is GOD=GUT, spirit and science.

2 Where do you see the Creator's love in me? Is it in my Wrath? Is it in my willingness to be deemed crazy when I could just choose to not serve? Is my Jihad about killing people? Is bringing down the governments of the world and their error activated economies evil? Do you want you or your friend's family to have to pay for electricity or fuel ever again? Would you like the option of living for 900 years or teleporting your way to another planet? These are a taste of the questions you must ask yourself should you investigate.

3 being anointed basically means that the anointed one has a good grasp, via creative efforts and divine will, of the way things work – I mean physics. But also human nature, and so forth...It should be abundantly clear (and Bill Maher brings up these two subjects – ENERGY/oil & Cannabis –

often on Politically Incorrect) that between free energy, AI, antigravity, energy medicine, legalization of psychedelics and cannabis, that there would be nothing left of the slut running things now. All this is coming.

A friend asked me to break it all down. And so I will try. I have written with mixed metaphors for a good reason, by associating these ideas the esoteric meaning is revealed.

To many it's a madman's mumbo jumbo, but to others, who are intent on knowing all they can about the universe, it is a slick intro. But this is all it is. It takes time to absorb and grok. People, who think they can pay a guru and he will touch them just so for instant enlightenment, never will... Of course, as a half assed and impatient American Aghori, I opted for mushrooms for that quick and undeniable prying open of the 3rd eye, but as I said, without that experience, associating the written word is ALOT harder, if not impossible.

I will define the technojargon in the context I used it...

1 - a tangled hierarchy or riddled basin of superpositioned surface area: imagine a piece of paper so crumpled up that it becomes a piece of wood again, now imagine the same with several papers. Each paper has a simple geometric form drawn on it but when crumpled the forms get very complex. Now imagine lines can be drawn through each and any of the papers to achieve a second level of complexity. In physics these pieces of paper are known as branes – etherial potential spaces.

2 - isotropic, homogenous: uniform in all directions, centerless, borderless
3 - plenum: free space full of energy
4 - vacuum: free space void of energy
5 - little bit of neither one: a Zen Koan
6 – Adam, the vector space: Adam, as in Book of Genesis Adam, esoteric or occult meaning is vector space, the straight, crystalline grain of free space
7 - nucleus in the garden of light and became a seed: in quantum mechanics, a wave packet becomes a photon, somewhat redundant statement
8 - The seed was hyperhydrophilic, it sucked up the superluminal surface of zeropoint and warped it into a scalar rib: this is Genesis' "separation of the waters" or Zeropoint becoming the quantum foam, salt/fresh water, true/false vacuums, white/black holes, when the straight part of free space

becomes the curvy or scalar part. "HyperHydroPhilic," attracted to the higher water or SuperLuminal Fluid...water is the ideal metaphor to me so I coined the term HyperHydroDynamics. Raymond Chaio coined the term SuperLuminal Fluid.

9 - Through seven transdimensional phase states: Genesis' seven days of creation, big bang epochs

10 - Wij Ih Wau: a mantra given to me in my dreams. I was in a lotus posture hovering off the ground chanting this and someone asked me what it was. I replied, "its the mantra that activates the merkaba." Usually mantras given this way are intended to remain secret but the dream implied I was to tell people.

11 - AUM, the syntactical architecture of The HoloFractal, the living word: In Kabbalah, the 22 letters of the hebrew "alphabet" make up free space, they can be viewed as fractions of the aforementioned branes. HoloFractal, another term I coined meaning, "The whole breaks down" rather than view matter as built up or aggregated into space. A monistic idealist like myself sees matter as fractional interference of the one zeropoint.

12 - LEARN TO READ a Zen koan that I actually saw as a PSA on a bus in Dallas TX alluding to the aforementioned syntactical architecture... and the gnostic methodology. This sentence is meaningless to the literate and illiterate. The written word is meaningless until an observer imposes meaning....

The rest should be straightforward, if you have any more questions about specific words such as "Merkaba" or "Codon" I suggest Googling them, if you have any philosophical BS questions, SHOOT!

VEGETABLES

Besides me, reincarnation, ufo's and Wrath, one of the things The Church has avoided, erased, tweaked, or downplayed is the role of certain sacramental molecules in the founding of The Church, and most religions/individual spiritual quests for that matter.

http://www.parkstpress.com/titles/mysman.htm

The Mystery of Manna:
The Psychedelic Sacrament of the Bible
by Dan Merkur

About the Book

* Compelling evidence that the early Jews and Christians used psychedelics as part of their religious rites.
* Reveals the Bible's disguised references to this tradition and traces knowledge of this secret to the gnostics, masons, kabbalists, and the legends of the Holy Grail.
* Explores the idea that psychedelics have played a role in nearly all religious traditions.

When Moses fed manna to the Israelites, he told them that after eating the miraculous bread they would see the glory of God. And indeed they did: "They looked toward the wilderness, and behold, the glory of Yahveh appeared in a cloud." In The Mystery of Manna, religious historian Dan Merkur provides compelling evidence that this was the Israelites' initiation into a psychedelic mystery cult that induced spiritual visions through bread containing ergot--a psychoactive fungus containing the same chemicals from which LSD is made.

Citing biblical material, as well as later Jewish and Christian writings, Merkur reveals the existence of an unbroken tradition of Western psychedelic sacraments, from Moses and manna to Jesus and the Eucharist. Most important, Merkur shows that this was not a heretical tradition, but instead part of a normal, Bible-based spirituality, a continuation of the ancient tradition of visionary mysticism. Even when this practice became unacceptable to the religious orthodoxy, it was perpetuated in secret by gnostics, masons, and kabbalists, as well as through the legends of the Holy Grail. Merkur traces a long line of historical figures who knew of manna's secret but dared only make cryptic references to it for fear of persecution. The Mystery of Manna is the strongest contribution yet to our growing realization that, contrary to popular belief, psychedelics and religion have always gone hand in hand.

RANT WRITTEN BY AMATERASU

Can we, in good conscience, accept barbaric behavior against an individual with the rationale that "they broke the law and they deserve it?"

Can we watch an accused taken down by police to be kicked as they lie helpless, and then to be tazed – not once, but twice, in their helpless state?

Is this acceptable within a society claiming enlightenment?

And can we condone this in the case of a "crime" that has no one involved crying for help?

The reason I ask these questions is because this happens in this enlightened society of ours. It happens on a daily basis. And it happened to a friend of mine.

The "crime" involved a business transaction, the nature of which caused no one to claim foul. No one would come forth to speak of their victimhood because no one in this transaction felt themselves a victim. All parties would have been satisfied with the outcome had not one of those involved been on a mission to entrap the other in this "crime."

This "crime" was made a crime with the whitewash of "protection" over the moneyed interests looking to protect themselves from a by-product threat that this "crime" represented.

And that crime, for those who may not yet grasp what I am speaking of, was to sell marijuana. And for this "crime," my friend was taken to the ground by police officers, kicked in a barbaric display of – self-righteousness, perhaps? The gloatings of power, maybe? – and shot with a tazer as he lay defenseless, shot twice.

And so I must examine what motivated us to choose such a law in the first place, and why anyone might justify such treatment of a human, who had harmed no one, in the name of that law. "Innocent until proven guilty in a court of law," be damned.

If I had any evidence that this was an isolated incident, that this virtually never happens, I would be far less angry.

But this happens all over our country – and worldwide, as well – daily, hourly, even.

But let's go back to why this law was passed and how. Let us examine what has been used to justify it, and the facts about marijuana. And let's also examine our desire to force our views on others.

Back in the 1930's, as Prohibition (alcohol) was being repealed – it was causing violent crime, gangs, and law abiding citizens became "criminals" overnight. Money was "easy" in trading in alcohol and police were becoming corrupt (sound familiar?) – the head of the Federal enforcement agency charged with enforcing Prohibition was about to lose his job. His name was Harry J. Anslinger.

Also, William R. Hearst was facing the threat to his paper production facilities from hemp. Hemp was cheaper to produce, could produce four times the paper per acre than trees could, needed less processing (dioxins would not be an issue), and was vastly more renewable.

And Harry and William put together a plan. If Harry could make something illegal, he could make a cause for being selected to enforce the law and thereby keep his job, and if William could outlaw hemp, the acres and acres of forest he had invested in would stand to make better profits.

So William, who as we know owned many a newspaper, began publishing "facts." Marijuana caused "brother to kill brother." Marijuana caused "black men to rape white women." Amongst the white, educated folk, who voted and pressured Congress, a panic was born. Dear God! A black man might smoke that stuff and leap out of a bush in the park and kill me and rape my women and children!

So they wrote to Congress (many of whom had been reading the same stuff and getting panicky themselves). Harry even addressed Congress with these same allegations, lying through his teeth, but whipping up racial fears in the white group. The Congressional Record is available.

And Congress took the first step to illegally empower. For, by the Constitution and its Amendments, Congress had no legal way of making marijuana illegal. This was understood from the beginning in the Prohibition of alcohol. This is why a Constitutional Amendment had to be passed to make alcohol illegal on the Federal level.

But Federal laws against marijuana were – and still are! – unconstitutional. Through the years, some mumbo jumbo was concocted based on provisions relating to interstate commerce. But what did the Constitution, Bill of Rights and other Amendments matter???

Our women are being raped by black men, and we are killing our brothers because of marijuana!

So, from that dishonest base with shaky support, we allow Prohibition (cannabis) today. And William's forest investments were safe from hemp, and Harry was assigned to lead the Prohibition enforcement agency – merely switching from alcohol to marijuana.

But today, we know that marijuana decreases violent behavior. We know that rape is completely untied to the use of the drug. We know that using it is often much more affective than Prozac and other, more deadly drugs.

We know, in fact, that marijuana has been attributed in killing zero humans – throughout history!

We know that driving under the influence of marijuana is less dangerous than driving while having too little sleep.

And the list goes on.

But meanwhile, we are condoning barbaric behavior because "it's the law." And if the law stated that women were property and could not be looked upon by men unless privately and by their husband, if women could not receive education and had to wear fully covering clothing and paint all windows in their houses black lest they be seen, would we condone stoning them if their elbow might show? It's the law, after all.

What do we fall back on today in justifying Prohibition (which is working as well and causing the self-same issues as our past, repealed Prohibition)? Why, the horrors of altering one's consciousness, of course.

And so I must ask another question: What is inherently wrong with altering our consciousness? If that is it, if there is something wrong with altering consciousness, alcohol should be back on the Prohibition list – along with caffeine, nicotine, sugar, and Prozac, et al.

With this dual standard, we justify our barbarism. We justify kicking downed men.

Here is where I am going to ask you to think. I am also going to ask you to be honest with yourself. I hope you are both willing and prepared to do both.

Let's turn it around. Let us suppose that there had been a reason to make the use of marijuana compulsory, rather than forbidden. (We can use its many medical/psychological advantages as a place to start this idea.)

Who of you would stand and say you are incapable of deciding for yourself whether you would smoke (or eat) it?

Who of you would claim less than autonomy in making this choice for yourselves?

Who of you would claim a right to being an Autonomous Self?

The catch is, if one claims to be an Autonomous Self, one must grant that to all others. For if one cannot grant that, one is forever under control by the behavior of others and one is therefore surely not autonomous.

GOOD COP - BAD COP

A rant by Kalki regarding same incident as preceding chapter...

I went down to University Way today to score some nugs from a brother named Sean.. The first time I went down there to score, I saw him coming and knew. It warmed my heart:

"Can you help me out with some nugs?"

"Sure lets walk!" Sean trustingly replied.

Today I went down to University Way to score some nugs from a brother. I walked up and down the street for an hour and could not find him. I recognized his friend who had been present during our previous exchange (today would've been the 3rd).

"You seen Sean around?"

"No, he got busted by an undercover cop, he got knocked down and kicked then they tazed him twice to make sure he stayed down, guess they were trying to make an example of him"

The beast was awakened in me upon hearing this. My heart went out to my brother, and now all I can do is put my rage out in ink.

When I was 14, my Cop dad asked me to help him bust a kid by purchasing some LSD from him. Being a JustSayNo/PDFA/DARE/Junior Spies brainwashed little patriot, I eagerly agreed to help him. Thank God I never found the kid because I'd still be hating myself to this day.

Needless to say I've seen the light since then. The propaganda that had me convinced "DRUGS ARE BAD" and those who willingly partake deserve incarceration "FOR THEIR OWN GOOD" has totally backfired and I

AM not going to rest until all non-violent drug law offenders are set free to return to their friends, family, possessions and pot.

Street folk want to blame the cops. Others, perhaps a little removed from the black market scene, blame the law – cops merely enforce.

A funny thing about cops, they are either GOOD or BAD. My father was a cop and is an intelligent man. He was a "good cop" just as I was a "good DARE graduate." Today I refuse to believe my Dad could have bent over for the same propaganda aimed at 9 year olds BUT HE DID!!!

I've been busted on 4 different occasions and I was dealt with in a reasonable manner in each case because I knew (from my dad) that if you are polite with them... But in Sean's case, it didn't matter. Some say Cops are worse in some places, perhaps in proportion to population density – if only cops were as geographically consistent as Big Macs. I have a hunch that the cops where I'm from have made a conscientious decision to LOOK THE OTHER WAY. Whether this choice stems from internal guilt or from being fed up with paper work & wasting the court's time I don't know BUT THEY HAVE.

Last summer I smoked with about 10 kids daily in the open space of a city park where 3 years prior I had been busted in a relatively private area. One day some out of town kids came to us lookin to score and they did. Soon after, some local "Wigger" thugs strong-armed the newly acquired stash from our new friends. The robbery was reported and the local cops actually TRIED TO BUST THE WIGGERS WHO STOLE THE POT – NOT THE KIDS WHO BOUGHT/SOLD IT FAIRLY AND PEACEFULLY.

Cops, of all people in this world, have an acute awareness/knowledge of "good" and "evil." Any cop who thinks potheads are a threat to the community and deserve their possessions seized, body incarcerated, and family stranded, are quite simply themselves EVIL – whether they are "good" or not. I had a cop admit to me he was a "tool" but he still went on to profile my brethren anyway.

Until laws are changed via grass roots orgs, NORML, MPP, etc, it is the cops and them alone who perpetuate this injustice!

JUST LOOK THE OTHER WAY.

FOR SUBGENII

f' 'em (& me) if they (& I) can't take a joke

BRAG OF THE ANTI/CHRIST: I was prophesied before time began. The Big Bang – that was my first orgasm. And my arcing ropes of jism – that's my plasma filaments entwining into the first metagalaxy.

I AM the background radiation confounding scientists who actually think the Big Bang happened. I AM the Omega Attractor, the Photon Belt and the Electromagnetic Null Zone where your measly solar system comes from and goes to. I AM the protoGOD.

I told Satan how to polish his horns and I pulled Hell out of my ass. I am CREATION, INTERVENTION and EVOLUTION. I cooled the Earth with a glance and sprinkled the Nephilim like seeds. Adam was the stick figure on my kindergarten crayon box. Eve was my pocket pussy and the Tree of Knowledge was only a twig before I pissed on it. The Serpent – he only told the truth, that duality is for people who don't know they are me!

Jehovah was my first hallucination and when I peaked he looked at me and said, "You've GOT to be kidding!"

The Ark of the Covenant is my stash. I set fire to the bush and told Moses he was SPECIAL, the rest he made up. Ezekiels' wheels within wheels – that was just me thinking about starting another cargo cult. The Great Pyramid is my toothpick. And Ra was just my perpetual fart from eating too many quasars for lunch.

I AM the Tao of the Tao, I AM THAT I AM and ISN'T WHICH ISN'T. I wrote the Book of the Dead as an owners manual and the Necronomicon

178

as a children's book. I AM the Multiverse, the Quantum Foam, The 10 dimensions in M-theory, and the Higgs field on the head of a flea's dick. I bow every superstring with the pubes of supermodels. I AM the Entropy, the heat death of the Omniverse, and the Zeropoint manifold that spits it all Back.

The speed of light is where I go to catch a few zzzzs. I teleport just to catch a glimpse of myself. I find solace in the event horizon and the black hole is my portapotty, and while I shit out another universe I read the Akashic records like you read the comics. I invented the notion of "consensus reality" and I watch your reincarnations like you watch reruns of All in the Family; so obvious yet so shocking.

The Milky Way is my petri dish. I made the constellations by slitting my wrists and spinning in circles. And you dare label my chaos. Astrology is my daily planner and my Natal Chart looks like a goddam fractal. I told the Mayans that time didn't start until they could realize it didn't – boy did that lead to some funny sacrifices! I made the twelve houses from reject archetypes – to me, precession may as well be Planck time.

Despite all this I come to earth now and then. I deliberately forget I AM so that I CAN BE. While I'm here I disguise myself as a simpleton, a geek, a passive hippie, a homeless bum, because if you knew who I was REALLY, I'd be dead before the doctor spanked my ass and got the slime off me. But what's in it for me? How could I possibly get off on ANYTHING in my normal state?

I am the teacher who lied to you and the playground that told the truth.
I am the Bully and the future prison cell he'll call home.
I am the victim and the jury who has to follow the law.
I am the car designer and the mechanic.
I am the generator, wires, substation, meter, outlet, appliance and the bill at the end of the month.

I am the dinosaur, the comet, the billion years of transmutation, the geologist, the drill, the spill, the refinery, the hydrocarbon, the tank, the spark plug, the exhaust, the cancer, and the really big bill at the end of the month.

I am the greedy CEO, the mahogany table, the yesman, the clueless middle management, the overly-informed/underpaid employee, the shotgun, the bullet and the spatula and oxyclean. I am the funeral home, the coffin manufacturer and the guy who mows the cemetery lawn. I am the hydrocarbon based fertilizer which keeps the grass green.

I am the censored corporate owned media, the guy who teaches Tom Brokaw how to keep a poker face, the TV, the couch, the wife of the victim who shot his boss, the vodka she cooks neurons with. I am the final piece of bad news that makes her take the pharmies that kill her, and the little boy who'll be a bully when he gets into kindergarten.

I am the ambulance that breaks down on the way to her house. And I am the replacement CEO of the ambulance manufacturer.

I am the plant that grows from the ground. I am the molecule it produces that has a receptor site in your brain. I am the morphogenic field it sympathetically resonates with when in the receptor sites of others like you. I am the introspection, laughter, cottonmouth, munchies, and good nights sleep. I am the trees that could be left standing. I am the ocular fluid relaxing, I am the munchies NOT puked back out.

I am the hydrocarbon producer that fears the plant. I am the racist piece of shit that works for him. I make the propaganda that blasphemes myself and my creation. I am the thousands upon thousands of people like you displacing the bullies from their future prison cells. I am the stoner that taught the bully how to be kind and I am the law that put him in prison anyway.

I am the force that turned "Yeshua ben Joseph the anointed one" into "JESUS CHRIST" and JC into …, that turned a fish into a crucifix and THE WAY into CHRISTIANITY. I am the first ruler who joined 'em. I am the beady eyed cloner preacher who claims to represent me and I am the millions of suckers who buy my products.

I am the green grass, the cow, the six stomachs, and the turd. I am the spore, the mycelium, and the bulbous fruiting body. I am the blue stain and the ego pain.

I am the remembrance of myself and the eternal metabolization of truth.

I am the inventor, the novelty conserving engine. I am the self similarity.

I am Tesla seeing the AC induction motor in my mind working perfectly in a flash. I am the letter of recommendation to Edison. I am a cranky old man, jealous of myself, cheating myself of money owed. I am the war of the currents, I am Westinghouse having faith. I am CBS banning Bill Hicks from Letterman. I am the ultimate servant of mankind, tirelessly working to make sure you have the highest standard of living. I am a man obsessed with the secrets of nature. I am a man responsible for your luxury and I am the forces that want you to pay for what I know. I am the suppression of the technology that allows me to suppress myself.

I am KALKI, I AM the secret obviousness. I am KALKI because what went one eighty took me with it. I AM full circle stuck in the middle. Pretentious Humility. Loving Hatred. Divine Monkey. I am back like I said I would be. I will do what I said I would.

I AM Babylon and I AM the means of consuming myself. I AM Yeshua paying the price, I AM Tesla marking it up, and I AM KALKI-------- LIQUIDATING

I AM J.R. BOB DOBBS SELLING IT ALL TO THOSE WHO SAVED THEIR SLACK JUST FOR THIS FINAL SALE..EVERYTHING MUST GO!!!!!!!!!!!!!!!!!!!!!!!!!!!!!!!

CHILDREN OF EZEKIEL by Michael Lieb:

Publisher's Review:

"Are Milton's Paradise Lost, Ronald Reagan's "Star Wars" missile defense program, our culture's fascination with UFOs and alien abductions, and Louis Farrakhan's views on racial Armageddon somehow linked? In Children of Ezekiel, Michael Lieb reveals the connections between these phenomena and the way culture has persistently related the divine to the technological. In a work of special interest at the approach of the millennium, Lieb traces these and other diverse cultural moments-all descended from the prophet Ezekiel's vision of a fiery divine chariot in the sky-from antiquity to the present, across high and low culture, to reveal the pervasive impact of this visionary experience on the modern world.

"Beginning with the merkabah chariot literature of Hebrew and Gnostic mysticism, Lieb shows how religiously inspired people concerned with annihilating their heretical enemies seized on Ezekiel's vision as revealing the technologically superior instrument of God's righteous anger. He describes how many who seek to know the unknowable that is the power of God conceive it in technological terms-and how that power is associated with political aims and a heralding of the end of time. For Milton, Ezekiel's chariot becomes the vehicle in which the Son of God does battle with the rebellious angels. In the modern age, it may take the form of a locomotive, tank, airplane, missile, or UFO. Technology itself is seen as a divine gift and an embodiment of God in the temporal world. As Lieb demonstrates, the impetus to produce modern technology arises not merely from the desire for profit or military might but also from religious-spiritual motives.

"Including discussions of conservative evangelical Christian movements, Reagan's ballistic shooting gallery in the sky, and the Nation of Islam's vision of the "mother plane" as the vehicle of retribution in the war against racial oppression, Children of Ezekiel will enthrall readers who have been captivated, either through religious belief or intellectual interests, by a common thread uniting millennial religious beliefs, racial conflict, and political and militaristic aspirations."

As you can imagine the average venture capitalist would run screaming from my bizplan, and some say I lack business savvy altogether. The practical destruction of Babylon will require faith. If prophecy states that my inventions will work then convincing the Christian my technology will work is not an issue. Business folk and techies require a little more, but F those people.

THE RELIGIOUS RIGHT IS NEITHER

Oh defender of moral, keeper of traditional family values, he who condemns human nature and denounces the unknown, he who perpetuates duality by imposing his opinion of sin as if it were absolute, who claims to speak the word of God, defending God's values, you can't repent your own monkey mind from "sin" yet you get in my face as if on a mission to save me from mine. Your campaign of intercession to save me is pretentious and hypocritical. You claim to know God yet your faith seems to be rooted in winning an argument. Mr. Jehovah's Witness, you love it when we slam the door in your face, cuz you get to be the one suffering in the name of Christ and you feel that much more special, you deliberately invite victimization and you persecute yourselves, (inside persecution is called reformation, how else do you get hundreds of sects from the lessons of one man?). You do not care about your brothers and sisters, you just care about getting to heaven and assuring yourself that we are in need of your little comic books; you cannot force Christ onto people.

You manipulate what can't be manipulated; you take a figurative, subjective parable/metaphor and present it as literal objective fact. Woe to you, for you assume the word of God ends in a book or a man. Woe to the doomsayer, for his thoughts will manifest in his own tiny bubble of reality. You say my God is in my head and that I'm going to Hell. I will prophesy the God in my head and risk going to the Hell you propose.

To all the people who claim to do work in my name, listen, your job is done, stop emphasizing suffering, sacrifice, and forgiveness, that's not the modus operandi now, if 2000 years isn't enough time for all those "sinners" to "get it" and repent (Rev 22:11)… I can only hold out my hand for so long, but the door is always open... You pastors, preachers, evangelists, priests, nuns etc.,...are not familiar with the mystical/cosmic/scientific aspects of what it means to be THE CHRIST...I know and you know that history can't hold everything because it is not over. I feel myself wanting to plead for your understanding but...you must stop speaking of just Jesus and look at the whole of THE CHRIST; Jesus, Buddha, Krishna, Babaji... facets of the primary signature/logos...I AM HE, I AM NOW.

It was fun to warp Jesus into commercials, it was safe when I was just a story... Do not preach about me; I can speak for myself, and this is what I say: This is it kids, I am the TRUTH; whatever response you have to me now is the response you're supposed to have. You don't have to preach, pray, give "love gifts," or congregate to have a relationship with the TRUTH...

I don't care if you hate me. Actually I like it, for two reasons. Firstly, your hate is unfounded, and if you can muster up the balls to tell me why you hate me, we have something to work with. Secondly, you are making my job that much easier. If you hate me and cannot approach me, I know for certain I do not know you. This is it, kids. If you don't get it by now you never will. If you serve the Lord, or think you do, I strongly suggest you focus on yourself and stop worrying about the faith of others.

I say to any man that would claim authority over, or ability to judge, another man to not forget he's also a "man" and cannot be excluded from his doctrine. If you do so then your "authority" is handed over to the beast, the beast who has forgotten that God, The Sevenfold Spirit, is the only authority. Only a monkey can assume his laws are absolute. The universe replies, "You are so immersed in, and aware of your duality you don't even know it to be so."

Godless men must commit egocide or the Lord's deeds and harsh indifference will only reflect their own. Those "grown ups" and "authorities" who neglect God's authority and assume their own automatically blaspheme. To my accusers who would take a child from the playground and return a bully, to those eager to hear Babylon fake an orgasm, especially to those who rape the planet and its offspring, a woman or child, a biosphere or bunny, I say this: I cannot be punished just as you have no authority. I will rape the rapist, destroy the destroyer, and I will slay duality, for the birth pains have begun and my army is waiting. I am a MINDBOMB and you lit the fuse a LONG time ago.

You have to realize the Bible was written for the same generation of souls throughout the past two thousand years. It was not written just for the people of 1032 or 1681 or 1998. The content pertains to a two thousand year span, so of course it has to be written accordingly. The parables and metaphors are the method of transcending that time span. The people who get it are the same exact people who got it a thousand years ago. There are blatant references to all kinds of Quartzhead stuff. Reincarnation, chakras, (organic) UFO's, and psychedelics are all in there. Fundies will deny this but at the same time extract their own interpretation to complement their own "Christian" agendas. For example, they link the Quartzheads with witchcraft and sorcery and by doing so they are perpetuating duality. Jesus did laying on of hands, stood on water, materialized food out of thin air, etc.,... My question is, how do they differentiate between miracles and magic? Let me tell you what sorcery is. Nuclear reactors are sorcery, the internal combustion engine is sorcery. You gotta look at the big picture here. Take a Bic lighter back in time even a hundred years and you're the devil, OK? Get it? On the other hand in the Bible "magic" may mean magic. These so called "Satanic" voodoo types who are uttering incantations to summon Tiamat are not welcome in my kingdom because they worship weaklings. I don't have a problem with voodoo or Satanism or paganism personally or as the Christ (I know better than to buy into Hollywood stereotypes; hell, the earth is my top priority – wink wink – I don't have time to waste fussing over what other people believe) y'know, whatever gets you through the day. I just think you're settling for crap. In any case let us differentiate between white magic and black magic or rather the intent that governs either title.

THE WOLFPACK ANALOGY
OF THE CHRIST

Wolf packs have an alpha and omega wolf. The role of the leader is obvious but the importance of the omega to the alpha is not emphasized. The authority flows from the alpha through the pack to the omega. The omega's purpose is to endure the entire resentment of authority the rest of the pack displaces down to it. If the omega didn't put up with the abuse, the authority of the alpha would be compromised and the whole pack would decide they were capable of being the leader even though they were not qualified for the role. This would cause the alpha to increase its veracity to reestablish its position in the pack, and the pack would suffer from a backup of yang. The omega relieves the resentment of authority by allowing the pack to feel a taste of supremeness. Without the omega the alpha would not occur.

In this covenant, Jesus is the omega, saying to the pack, "go ahead guys I'll lay on my back, exposing my belly so you can pound those nails in, if it makes ya feel better." I'm the alpha saying, "The pack has more important things to be doing than bothering Jesus, now lets get going." Every christ plays each role in his own right. For myself in my family I am the aloof, chill, above-it-all wise man, and the unemployed, highschool dropout, still living with mom at 24, druggie, pipedream factory. To you all I am the mentally ill freak and the dependable Superhero.

My existence completes the actualization of the "Word" as it manifests in linear space-time, in humans. A duality so great that it encompasses a two thousand year span. Jesus met me halfway as a passive Alpha lamb, humanlike, coming from God. I am meeting him as an aggressive Omega lion, Godlike, going to God.

Together we represent the ideal for human existence in the human condition. I am a walking, talking Reality Prism. I'm a crystalline bubble riding the Chaos membrane with one foot in the "sea" and one in the "earth" (dimensionally amphibious), and I can break the light of the Lord down into the spectrum of the word. I'm a child who has unwarranted peace. It's so easy for us kids to have resilience cuz we don't play by your rules, CUZ WE DON'T PLAY YOUR GAMES! When you project onto a child you get jealous or even angry at the child's carefree world. The kid's not weighed down with worry and adult trips and the kid is acceptably self centered...

Maturation is measured in units of what? By whose standards? I'm just a six year old that knows too much, and like a kid I wrote this book cuz I can. I, like a child, reflect the potential you buried under ego. The Christ/child is the standard from which you judge yourself relative to the Lord; does a 3 year old know or care that it is Jewish or African American? Do I care?

I tell you the truth, I don't actively judge individuals for God. Tthat would take too long. YOU judge yourselves. YOU decide your fate in the cosmos not me. You will be judged/marked based on your response to me, and by "me" I mean Jesus too. Scary huh?

Jesus asked, "Who do YOU say that I am?" I'll make it easier on you and simply ask, "Do you know me?" And I don't mean have we met each other. I mean, do you recognize any of your "self" in me? Do you agree with anything in this book? If you agree with anything, you, by law, must agree with all of it because I don't lie. You can't have any half-assed faith in me, its all or nothing; sorry that's just the way it is. True light workers recognize each other not unlike gaydar, so I'm not worried.

I can spot a poser, I know if you have the love of God in your heart or if you're just paying lip service to some big invisible guy in the sky; your intent and actions reveal your faith and virtue. The cross around your neck, how many gutterpunks you proselytized to, or how many Chick comics you distributed, are pathetic actions and intent. I can see you right now, sitting on your pew wondering what the pastor thinks of me, thinking that he would be more qualified to identify me than you. Well keep in mind, if I'm Christ, he's unemployed...wondering if the Pinks around you will scorn you if you dare to believe in me. Well sit there and wonder...

RELIGIOUS EXPERIENCE

When I was 14 or 15 my curiosity about drugs peaked. The "religious experience" linked to psychedelics was fascinating to me, y'know, like what the hell is it? And if all it takes to have a "religious experience" is the ingestion of some piece of paper or mushroom or cactus button, well goddamn, I'm gonna try it. At the same time I was getting exposure to the "New Age" (…resent that term because it is neither "new" or an "age") and I read a book on ESP that said only a small percentage of the mind was utilized. I decided that expanding my mind was the only reason to be here, and that if I couldn't move beyond the average mind and develop its full potential what's the point? So I committed myself to mind expansion and self actualization.

My first 30 or so trips on LSD over a six year period were not so special. Oh sure they were fun but there wasn't a hint of spiritual connectedness. I also looked into brain hemisphere synchronization tapes and crap like that but I was getting nowhere. My eagerness and impatience had finally been defeated and I let go: "If it's meant to happen it will…"

Perhaps the most obvious question raised when tripping is this, "Where do the hallucinations originate, in the eyes or the brain?" This is a great Zen thingy; it forces an enigma. Who can say exactly where sensory input ends and perception begins? Consciousness can question itself; language is just agreed upon symbols; intent is torn between time; emotion fills in the gaps. Where does knowledge reside? Is it nothing more than the sum of 26 letters we can recombine infinitely?

On LSD I had minor epiphanies and my share of bad trips. In hindsight however, I can see that I did gain something, that it was actually good to have a bad trip. Ya see, a bad trip is egoshock, a slap to the psyche. The bad trip taught me respect for my own brain. The bad trip taught me, "Don't presume a thing or you'll go down!" That is true in everyday life but on acid it's amplified. I was at a party once and I assumed I could read minds like, "I know you're thinking whatnot about me..." So I go up to these people, totally cool people who I kinda knew from a mutual friend and I'm like all cocky-n-shit, and I confront them about these thoughts they were having about me. Normally I could care less what people think but dammit, I was on acid... So these totally innocent people are looking at me like, "What is up with this freak!?" At that moment I knew I had stuck my foot in my mouth. I should have turned around and walked away but I didn't. I had one of those things that you think about when you're in bed at night, one of those "point of no return," Degeneresesque faux pas that you think could never really happen in real life cuz you would catch yourself kinda things." So I'm standing there with my whole leg down my throat... That my friends, IS a bad trip and I was traumatized by it for about a month. I hope those people remember me and get a laugh over the fact it was the Antichrist that made such an ass of himself.

In the summer of 96 (the perfect summer I've been waiting for) my dear friend M traded me a little blown glass bowl for what Terence calls "A heroic dosage" of chunky, blue bruised, kind, smurfy shrooms. I woofed them down. I sat on the pavilion of The Commons (Ithaca's downtown outdoor mall where I lived) and quickly became hysterical with laughter. I was tripping pretty hard after only 20 minutes and decided it would be wise to retire to my pad before it escalated to an ecstatic state. It did. I started getting synaesthesia (Gee your voice looks pretty), energy raced up and down my spine and my flesh turned to fluid. "Here it comes, that religious experience I've been waiting for..." I collapsed on the floor and began laughing, crying, and heaving around. I FELT soooo loved. I could grok the Lords presence in everything, I knew at that moment that we were all just the Lord's beautiful expressions here to serve each other. The feeling of being loved to my core displaced all the petty resentments and remorse I had been carrying my whole life. These negativities just didn't mean anything in light of The Lords presence. I wanted my father, mother, stepmother, friends, and family all there right then so I could hug them all. They weren't there so I thought I might run back down to The Commons and hug strangers. In Ithaca, that wouldn't be out of the ordinary, but I decided against it. I stayed in my room and flopped around like I had a stun gun up my ass. Damn, what a release it was...

After an hour I calmed down enough to just be grinning that shit eating grin we trippsters are infamous for. I ventured back downstairs to my outdoor mall living room and returned to the pavilion. I sat down and began pondering, "What was I before I bifurcated into man and mushroom?"

As I sat there radiating my new found love, wondering how to serve you all, my beautiful fellow creations, a strange thing happened. Hippie after hippie, my Rainbow Nation family, people I never met, just began flocking around me. I had been to a gathering the prior year at the Hector National Forest next to Seneca lake where I lived and I thought, "These are the people who'll inherit the Earth!" (Matthew 25:34-40)

I don't look anything like them and they still knew I was one of them. They say, "Oh, cyberpunk, can't be too bad." The subcultures have a common bond. We know what it is. It still amazed me though, that they would be drawn to me. The hippies converging around me may have meant nothing without the psilocybin; the pavilion is, after all, lovingly referred to as "Freak Central," but the trip was valid. No old stupid clinical government scientist who's never done it is going to convince me otherwise. It was more valid than anything any ol' psychopreacher ever spouted. Although the intense emotion of that direct experience has faded, the gnosis remains.

People sometimes say that psychedelics aren't valid compared to the disciplined approach of Yoga and meditation because they're drugs and drugs are "bad." I disagree, firstly because "bad" is a symptom of duality and I think I've raked that over the coals enough already, but mainly because just because something is effortless doesn't inherently mean it's not real. Also, if you were to attain Nirvana, I'm not sure you could stop experiencing it. With psychedelics you have a choice. For myself, I appreciate what they teach me but deep down I also appreciate the little amount of veil I have left.

Here's something to think about. LSD is man-made. Its resonance in the Chaos Membrane/Morphogenic/genetic grid is dull. It is shallow, reflective, matrixy, and abrasive and it takes about 10 hours to metabolize the average dose. Psilocybin is ancient and organic. It resonates well and is deeper, more textured, and rich. It is more "psychoergonomic." The average dose takes about 6 hours to metabolize. DMT basically makes you a ghost in hyperspace and it is metabolized in about 10 minutes.

Now, continuing this pattern, we can conclude that our brain, that electrochemical wonder, is really just refining or filtering out these previous realities to what you're perceiving right now. You are tripping at this very moment, nanosecond to nanosecond. We are consuming consciousness as language in one dimension and metabolizing it as emotion in another; a flow if you will... Behold the prism inhibiting and exciting the efficiency of the glitch filter with neurosomatic tuning fork crystals, distorting/offsetting the modulation of linear time.

PART TWO

The date is April 23 1999. I have access to a nice laptop and I feel the need to write my revisions and additions.

I spent most of 97 in Lodi looking at an oil tank on the other side of the 414 highway when I was a live-in babysitter for my cousin Dale's son, Mike. The lil' bastard I served is now 8 years old. He has taught me more about myself than anyone, and I now have complete empathy for my parental units. The child is me – I was him. All these traumatic lessons, instant tears... He forced me to be an authority, yet I feel 8 myself. He plays with fire and his elders shun him; learning is getting burnt and he knows it, so he indulges the elders authority trip and plays anyway...

His phases of growth are amazingly like mine, but he is learning even faster than I did that adults ain't right in the head. He doesn't understand his daddy's stress and his daddy doesn't remember the newness of childhood. He is obsessed with toys and cartoons, a refuge fantasy world; this harsh world forces him to retreat into his imagination. They are creating this cocoon which protects the inner child as it secretly morphs into a little god. Soon his sisters will tell him to "grow up" and he won't. Then one day he will be ancient and nobody will know why. This kid has faith in me. When he asks if my spaceship is built yet and I tell him it is going to be a few more years, he says it's pretty special to have me for an "uncle." Mikey knows his uncle will be famous but, as his daddy told him, "worry about making yourself famous."

I spent most of '98 working a series of McJobs and smoking pot. My friendship with L. "Counting Water" has flourished and I feel he is the only man I can truly trust right now. L has been here for me since this shit started. He never hesitated to kick down some herb or munchies to me, and more importantly he taught me about Archeoastronomy, geometry, earth grids and countless random shit from Salvia Divinorum to School of the Americas. He is in the same boat I am in. Working on fringe stuff nobody else can appreciate, occasionally meeting people who bring him another piece of the puzzle, waiting for cartography software... When I told him I was the christ it wasn't a big deal cuz we are from Ithaca... He thought it was neat that I am just like the character in his Scorched Earth comics and found more validation in that than my actual prophecy. I truly love this guy and I hope he doesn't feel like my star is shining too brightly next to his. The fact we are friends should tell him we go WAY back. Like he said, I build the spaceship he makes the map. We started a mad scientists club and have felt the knowledge pour down. We got some Pagans and chemists to round out the bunch. Hopefully it will grow after I have some money to give.

I have stumbled upon the Dolores Cannon books, Conversations with Nostradamus, and I now know for certain I am not insane. My inventions are in there, my artist's police sketch is in there, my bong is even in there. Nostradamus says that the title of antichrist is not accurate because it is a Christian term and I am not Christian.

Dolores failed to notice that the great genius and antichrist are both inventors. Seeing as how she is the person who provided me with my only corroborative evidence for claiming this title, you'd think she would be the person most likely to believe me. I sent a copy of this manuscript to her hoping Ozark Mountain Publishing would be the one to give me a break. She said I was not the first person to come to her claiming to be the antichrist, nor the first claiming to be the great genius. I am the first claiming to be both. She said this was not a book and that nobody would publish it, and she is right. I don't understand why she rejected me. I guess it's because she is an old lady and is easily offended. Maybe its because she lives in the bible belt and knows that her Christian friends and family would disown her if she was responsible for outing me, never mind the nature of HER books... My only other idea is that she is pissed that her work was not 100% accurate. According to her books I am supposed to be two different people, from the middle east, and I am supposed to have a large support group who are preparing the way for me. (*Note: In 2008 I met the Ogmios via Myspace. I'd seriously considered this guy had to be my mentor because of his looks, story and his way of quizzing me about occult technology. When he told me he had shmoozed up a group of Middle Eastern guys who were prepared to invest millions in his alt. energy endeavors, that was the clincher and I told him who he was...that effectively ended that potential future*.) Then far in the future, after the evil antichrist does his thing, the great genius (whom she speculated to be Jesus) shows up and makes it all better. The antichrist is a real humanitarian at first and helps 3rd world countries tremendously with his inventions; then he flips his shit for no legit reason, demands that people worship him, blah blah blah... Y'know its funny. Christians surrender their whole existence to Jesus (which is pointless). I wonder, if he actually demanded that they should do so, if they still would? Nostradamus provides enough info to identify me but not so much that you don't need to use discernment. He intentionally provided less than accurate info for the same reason Daniel did and John did...

Dolores's books are great and I love the work she has done. It's a shame she is so afraid of me; if I was regressed there is no telling what we could download... Because she rejected me, it made me think, to truly fulfill prophecy or to even get noticed I have to use the World Wide Web. It has authority over all nations, lands, and tongues – screw publishing houses – they're useless middlemen as far as I can tell. With the advent of POD publishing however...

OKAY, I'm connected to the middle east because that's where I will be creating the most conflict (both spiritually and economically) and the great genius is so far in the future because that's how long it will take before I am considered by everyone to be a servant, as opposed to a tyrant (as Bush said, let history decide). I am evil but I have done nothing. There are quatrains that attribute ww3 to me, nukes and stuff...yawn. I just don't see it happening... I have such more interesting means of destroying the establishment: what I can't annihilate with words and technology JD will. Besides, I don't have access to these weapons and would turn down an offer to use them.

I went online recently and fer shits-n-giggles I searched with these two words: antichrist+inventor... One of the things Google found for me was a misc. study called, THE PRINCE OF THE POWER OF THE AIR PLAYS A MEAN HAARP. The author saw how Tesla was or could be the antichrist, although there were stretches I found it interesting that someone other than myself would make that connection.

CHRIST COMPLEX

I went to the mental health clinic to get some answers to some pertinent questions:

What is the definition of "psychosis?"
What is the definition of "Christ complex?"

I told them I wasn't there to be cured but to get a general evaluation of what clinical psychology deems crazy, and to differentiate the symptoms of your average fake prophet from the actions of a bona fide godhead representative. I told them that I did not think I was crazy because I could explain how I got to this point. The woman who diagnosed me was biased, I believe, and didn't want to even consider if I was who I claimed to be. She was not objective and sought a scapegoat – she found it in pot... She said I was not psychotic and that the complex was cannabis dependent. It is, in a manner of speaking, odd how fundies treat my floral counterpart in the same way as I am treated; we come to serve and you crucify us with reefer madness...

She pressured me to take an anti-psychotic in order to see if I would give up the notion of being the Christ. I mean she really PUSHED it on me, as if she was getting kickbacks from the pill makers. Ironically the predecessor drugs to the one they were going to give me "made people into zombies," which I assume means spaced out and torpid. Pot already does that...and pot has actually been prescribed as an anti-psychotic. As I gave it more thought I concluded that:

1. you prescribe drugs AFTER diagnosis
2. neither clinical psychology nor pharmaceutical fabricators actually know how anti-psychotics work

3. using one drug to evaluate the effects of another drug is redundant

Basically psychosis is a matter of opinion. It's weighing an individual's thoughts and actions against the norms of the society/culture that the individual exists in. If the individual isn't interfacing with the norms in an acceptable way, he/she is "psychotic," whether the thoughts/actions are admirable or despicable. By their definition anyone who has psychic ability is psychotic. Christ Complex is not in the DSM (the manual of mental illnesses). The closest I get is delusions of grandeur, but really I'm just eccentric – duh.

To the degree that they are ignorant of the "cure," they are equally ignorant of the cause, which in this case is my free will. They ask "what if" I am wrong and I am not who I claim to be. Until someone else more credible than myself comes along, that question remains open.

The only conclusion I come to is that what clinical psychology "thinks" is irrelevant, and if the world's opinion of me were contingent on a professional evaluation we're ALL FUCT. But its not; this is an issue of faith, for me and everyone judging me. The mental health industry/ pop psychology is now on my shit list, with the pill pushers, petroleum pushers, lobbyists, politicians, bureaucrats, meat industry, the Christians and the physics luminaries etc...

UTOPIA

Most people don't picture EDEN or heaven or New Jerusalem as a place where technology is needed...yet most people can't imagine life without it.

All technology exists because we as a species are capable of producing it. Whatever we are capable of is a result of the intent of the inventor who produced us. Creation and technology are synonymous; the only difference is in the materials or rather degree of refinement. Let's say the human race is organic technology. A means of transmuting psychic energy for the purpose of ascending a planet out of the explicate order before entropy renders it useless. What we call technology is organic in origin and its purpose is to spread a communication network throughout the morphing stage of a planets' ascension in addition to Gaia feedback. It is a crutch for a species that maintains by changing from beasts to angels. It's the transition facilitator between grunting and telepathy.

Technology isn't just necessary, it just is...

Every attempt for a Utopian society/community has failed for two reasons. The infrastructure was flawed and/or the attitude of the inhabitants was flawed.

What is Utopia? Is it a place where all humans get along, or is it a place where all humans get along with each other, the ecosystem, and their technology? It's the second one. A Utopia maximizes the best humanity has learned and produced. The fact that we are at the end of these times allows the Utopia a better chance at success because if anything we know for certain what does not work, but also technology has evolved to a point where the ideals are feasible.

The past infrastructures were either too grand or too ill equipped. The cities planned around Niagara Falls were far too centralized; the communes out in the hills of Newfield were suitable only to hippies who could be happy without electricity. There is a compromise.

Now, the infrastructure I have envisioned is pretty much perfect so the only questions are, how to filter out the criminal element in the inhabitants and how to retrofit the Utopian communities into the error activated paradigm. I believe that any Utopia will need rules but my rules will enforce themselves. The inhabitants may come from any background, and chances are that the Utopia will be an improvement over what they are accustomed to. The appreciation of the Utopia is what governs its inhabitants to ensure its success. The Utopia will generate a vibe that acts as the police. The rules of moral conduct for Utopia have already been given by Jesus, the founding fathers, and others, and should be obvious if not innate anyway. The corruption that has tainted them and given us this society will not be a concern because we have learned those lessons.....

The purpose of Utopia is to give its inhabitants health, safety, education, creativity, and abundance. It also gives back to the earth the harmony principles from which it is modeled:

GEOMANCY
BIOMIMICRY and GEOMIMICRY
SELF SIMILARITY
REGENERATION
MINIMALISM
TECHNO AGRARIANISM
ANARCHISTIC FEEDBACK

GEOMANCY: The position of the Utopia on the earth will be predetermined by earth grid coordinates. This is important for the reason of interfacing with Gaia so that the Utopia is empathic with the planet's own feedback system, to encourage consistent conditions in the environment and to energize the Utopia as a whole.

BIOMIMICRY and GEOMIMICRY: The infrastructure of Utopia incorporates in the layout, architecture, materials, plumbing, industry, waste processing, and wherever possible, this proven method. For example, the community may look like a snowflake from above, process goods like a plant, roofs may look like shells, beams may look like bones etc...

SELF SIMILARITY: The main Utopia unit concentrically bifurcates down and out from a central business and education tower through park and crop bands to an outer residential band. This community of 800 homes may specialize in one crop, hemp for example, and it is one of 8 identical yet specialized agrarian communities which branch down and out from a still larger Industrial hub which is also specialized.

REGENERATION: Regeneration is a closed-loop, sustainable recycling effort which finds a means through biomimicry and rotation to eliminate waste or reuse it. Sewage and compost becomes fertilizer, Biomass becomes plastic, landfill gases power the biomass processing plant, much like what is being done now but Utopia makes it a priority. The Utopia is built to reproduce itself, and it can't do that if it destroys its environment or contaminates itself. It may produce and export eco-friendly products such as organic fertilizers, toxin-consuming microorganisms, toxin-free hemp derived paper, fiberboard...

MINIMALISM: This idea is the antithesis of department store consumer fetishism. What isn't needed isn't produced. Luxury items, decor, frilly home amenities may be imported and enjoyed as they are now, but the Utopia will not promote it. Minimalism may also be applied to any aspect of the infrastructure or society.

TECHNO AGRARIANISM: Each family unit is responsible for the production of one plant on a continual basis as its obligation to the Utopia. The Smith family grows parsley, The Wolfes grow romaine lettuce...etc. Each home has a subterranean hydroponic garden monitored by a PC with custom software for each plant. The larger outdoor community crops are watered and harvested with robots. What humans don't need to do, they don't. Whatever a machine can do, it does. The utilization of my inventions allows Utopia a decentralized interdependence, or complete independence from the current error activated paradigm.

ANARCHISTIC FEEDBACK: Natural law is based on the lack of imposed law. The human equivalent is anarchy. Anarchy allows faster resolution of conflict and in turn a faster return to Natural human law-peace.

The ideals, morals, and rules as outlined by Jesus, with the lessons learned from human history will allow the inhabitants the freedom they deserve. Voluntary self enforcement of peaceful existence is its own incentive. The violation of peace is an option but also its own deterrent. There may be government, but it will be minimal government. With a lack of enforced rules, and consequent lack of repression, the inhabitants will be able to explore the level of tolerance the Utopia will accept. If the Utopia is unable to tolerate a person's inability to follow the rules, he or she is simply forced to return to the error activated paradigm.

The Utopia then is a form of segregation. It is a voluntary luxury prison without walls. It freely gives a would-be criminal everything he/she would want before that person commits a crime, but also freely expels them from those things if they do mess up; isolation from the error activated paradigm is the reward, NOT the punishment. The Utopia is free of currency and weaponry. It does not defend itself from invasion; it offers to reproduce itself for more inhabitants until eventually...

So the major difference between Utopia and the error activated paradigm is that undesirable behavior is prevented by starting with an infrastructure that doesn't compromise itself with the desire for monetary profit, which is the major source of criminal behavior (alcohol, prohibition, other stupid laws, and stupidity rounding out the circle of causality).

In our capitalist, free market the infrastructure is governed not by what is "best," "cleanest," "simplest," or "most logical," but by what makes money. In a Utopia, only the best is allowed. If a better way is found, and by better I mean better for the planet, it is used and the previous method is given up with no regard for the manufacturer, consumer or distributor. Utopia recognizes the earth as the sole provider and anything that should threaten it must be eliminated.

The first inhabitants are the people who construct it. Next are the families who grow the food, and then, depending on the specialization of the community, the specialists. For example, the main unit I describe as Hemptown may have a Techno side such as nanotechnology. Another main unit may be Soy/A.I.R. manufacturing. Another wheat/foamed alloy production....

KIDS

I worked briefly at Elizabeth Cady Stanton daycare in Willard this winter, and the children taught me a lot about human nature, how adults are not any more mature than the kids are. There is this double standard for behavior. A child's temper tantrum is tolerable because kids haven't been programmed to repress it for politeness' sake. That takes a while for a human to appreciate, and when we do, we as adults are expected to have the ability to exercise control over our emotions and prevent our tantrums.

It's fairly obvious though that the only difference between children forced to share a daycare center and nations of the world forced to share a planet is scale and age...

throw a block across the room – launch a missile across the ocean
take someone's toy – steal top secret military applicable intelligence
pick on someone – cultural genocide
blame it on the other kid – blame the other world leader
tattle – espionage

You realize, of course, my job at the daycare center is identical to my job as godhead representative on the earth...

"...You put that down, go clean up your mess, and then sit in time-out for 5 minutes/1000 years to think about why you're in time-out..."

The messiah steps out of the classroom for a moment and returns to chaos, without fail...but there are always a few kids on task, intent on getting their work done and they know THEY are going to graduate.

That job inspired a story. The kids didn't get it and I doubt the world leaders will either...it was difficult to observe the formation of ego taking place before my eyes as these children interacted. I knew these kids were smart and they could bypass it all if they wanted, but lessons don't come without conflict and I know eventually the lesson will emerge.

There once was a group of boys and girls of all ages who were forced to share what they thought was a prison. There were lots of things to do and learn about. The food and toys were not bad either, but it still seemed like a prison because they did not feel very free.

The boys and girls thought freedom meant you could kick, push, insult, and steal from each other; to the boys and girls it was okay to do that and they only pretended to get hurt so they could blame someone else for instigating the fun.

And everyday it went like this, the teachers who loved and fed the children and kept them from killing each other were at a loss and had exhausted all disciplinary tactics. It seemed the children would never settle down and play together – nicely. With all the children blaming each other for "starting it," the teachers could no longer tell who was truly good and who truly needed some minutes in time-out.

There was one smart little boy who was not pretending, who truly was getting hurt, and he was sick and tired of getting punished for the other children's mistakes. He felt as helpless as the teachers. He came up with a brilliant plan that would bring peace and ensure his status as a peace loving kid who shouldn't have to suffer cuz of others inability to learn lessons the teachers tried to instill.

The only way his plan would work was if he himself did not seek revenge.

The next day the children were allowed some time to play or create something, but as usual they wanted to fight instead. So the smart little boy went up to the teacher and said he could help with their problem. He whispered the plan into the teacher's ear. The teacher smiled and said, "Thank you, now we will see who is peace loving and who is not!"

At that moment the teacher announced a new rule, the rule was: WHOEVER FIGHTS BACK IS THE ONE WHO GETS TIME-OUT, NOT THE ONE WHO "STARTS IT"

Now the children at first thought that was a wacky and unfair rule so the teacher said, "OK, from now on that's the only rule," and the children thought that was a good compromise

GUESS WHAT HAPPENED?

The children were allowed the allotted playtime as usual and insisted on fighting as usual. The smart little boy got pushed over and he did not fight back, he just got up and returned to his Lego airplane. They broke his toy airplane and he simply stated, "wait," and started an even better airplane... One little girl got a ball thrown at her ear and, boy, it sure hurt! She picked it up and threw it back. "AAAHAAAH!" the children shouted, "you broke the new rule!" Sure enough she had 10 minutes of time out. But you know kids, they have short attention spans... Soon all the children were in time out. They could not abstain from revenge with the exception of one smart little boy who stood in front of all the kids in time out and said:

"I listened to the teacher. I have all the toys, and you cannot hurt me now." He then proceeded to bitch slap each and every kid who hurt him, knowing they could do nothing back...

Well, I can say that if I ran a daycare center, the other teachers would use that rule. They would find it as wacky as the children would, but find it more effective than what they normally do. The common problem in dealing with kids is that they don't differentiate Discipline and Punishment as we adults do. They are processing karma like adults, adults who fail to distance their own egos from the situation they find themselves in as teachers.

You don't appear upset with a child, because you feed their ego; you don't cave in, because you feed their ego. You pick your battles or the discipline loses its impact...The kid is always smarter than you, more resilient than you... Play philosophically with their heads, remain unpredictable, laugh and talk...for the ego is a pattern-dependent beast who feeds off failed lessons which seep into the next generation.

THE BEST FLYER

Once upon a time there lived a family of birds; there was Mama Bird, Daddy Bird, and Little Chick, and she was always hungry for seeds.

Now the Bird family lived in a bird house in a tree, on a beach between a forest and a lake. It was very beautiful and the Birds were very happy, except Daddy Bird. Daddy Bird was sad because he was not very good at finding seeds, and so it was Mama Bird who kept Little Chick fed. The only thing Daddy Bird was good at was flying, and he liked to fly, as that's what birds do. When Daddy Bird was sad, sometimes he got mad at Little Chick for chirping so much, but it was not her fault; she was just doing what little chicks do.

The creatures in the forest would say to Daddy Bird, "Why don't you stop flying around and find seeds for your chick?" The truth was that, as he was flying, he WAS looking for something. It was a special worm that lived only on the beach of the lake. When he ate the worm, it made him feel better and gave him energy to fly higher than any other birds. There was a rule that the other birds made long before Little Chick or even Mama and Daddy Bird were in the world. They said the worm was not to be eaten because only good flyers could scoop 'em out of the water and it was not fair to the bad flyers. And so Daddy Bird had to hunt the worms at night when everyone was asleep. As he skimmed the beach of the lake looking for those wiggly worms, he could sometimes see what the legends called FISH. The FISH were supposed to be birds that were made of one whole wing, and they could fly UNDER the water. None of the forest creatures believed the fish were real. None of the other birds ever saw FISH. Only Daddy Bird did because when he flew at night the moon would shine on the FISH.

One night Daddy Bird went hunting worms and an owl up in a tree saw him do this. The old owl did not like Daddy Bird because the owl thought he should be finding seeds for Little Chick. And now the owl *really* didn't like Daddy Bird because he was breaking the old rule about hunting worms.

One day the Bird family was at home, chirping away and eating seeds, when they heard someone tapping at the door. Daddy Bird opened the door, and there was a badger from the forest. The badger said, "I have been told by the owl that you, Daddy Bird, have been eating the forbidden worms, and the forest creatures have decided that I must come to your house every month to see that Little Chick is getting enough seeds and you are getting NO worms!"

And so it went; every month badger showed up, and every month badger saw a fed Little Chick and sad Daddy Bird. Mama Bird became sad too because Daddy Bird couldn't fly like he used to. She loved him very much even though he was no good at gathering seeds. She could find enough for everyone.

Soon winter came and the seeds became scarce. The bird feeders were not being filled by the humans, and snow covered the seeds that came from the plants. Mama Bird could not find enough seeds to feed Little Chick. Daddy Bird could no longer find worms on the beach because it was frozen. The whole Bird family was sad and hungry; something had to be done.

Mama Bird had a sister bird who lived in a big city far away where it was always warm and the humans always put seed in the bird feeders. And so with sadness in their hearts Mama and Daddy Bird sent Little Chick away to the city so that she could eat the seed she needed.

Spring came but the humans still did not replenish the bird feeders, and it wouldn't be until late summer when the plant seeds would fall. But the ice melted and badger stopped badgering, so Daddy Bird went worm hunting again – after all he was doubly sad, missing Little Chick, and doubly tired, without seed to eat. He didn't care about the "no worm eating" rule; he just wanted to fly and be happy while his precious Little Chick was gone.

Mama Bird and Daddy Bird did all they could to find a new place to live where seeds were plentiful, but the forest and humans were also having troubles coming up with seeds. The forest creatures and other birds began to discuss the old rule. They realized that the worms may be the only food for the birds. They knew they had to then find the best worm hunters to hunt the worms that lived on the beach where water meets land.

Daddy Bird knew that he was the best flyer because he was the only one that broke the rule all that time Little Chick was at home. He also knew how to hunt the worms because he watched the FISH, who also ate the worms. He came up with a different way to fly by copying the FISH. All he had to do was pretend his whole body was ONE wing, and he could flap the wing with such force that he burst with speed. So fast was Daddy Bird when he copied the FISH that the worms were just too slow.

The forest creatures and all the birds had reached a decision. They would have a contest to see what creatures were best at worm hunting. The contest winner would get all the remaining seeds in the area as a reward, and they would also be rewarded with the job of hunting worms for all the birds. The worm hunting job was very important and Daddy Bird became very happy about the chance to do what he was good at AND be of service to his fellow birds.

The contest was held and many forest creatures showed up to get the rewards. The contest rules were simple. Whoever could collect the most worms and biggest worms wins.

Mama Bird was excited because she knew Daddy Bird could win, and when he won, that meant Little Chick could come home and they would always have seeds and worms to eat so that Little Chick could grow up strong and Daddy Bird could always fly high.

So the contest started… Daddy Bird flew up and down the beach and caught a worm here, a worm there, and brought them all to a scale where the weight of the worms was measured.

The other animals tried but did not really know how to catch worms that were under water half the time and above water half the time. The waves were confusing them and they just didn't have the proper view or speed. Only because Daddy Bird hunted at night and watched the FISH, only because Daddy Bird broke the rules and did what made him happy, did he do so well. And, yes, he won the contest – Mama Bird cheered and Daddy Bird proudly spread his wings in front of all the creatures and said,

"I will serve you and feed you, even though you told me I was wrong and bad not long ago."

From that day on, Daddy Bird did just that. All the forest creatures were in awe of his weird way of flying. It was weird but it worked. Little Chick was home and chirpy as ever. She had grand adventures in the city, and she had grown up. Little Chick was proud of her daddy too. He was always happy now and was never mean to her for being chirpy. He loved Little Chick's chirps and loved Mama Bird for always believing in him and letting him hunt worms and watch the FISH at night, even though it was against the rules. Soon he taught Little Chick the secrets of the FISH so she could always be fed and fly high.

They lived happily ever after.

HYPERHYDROPHILIA:
A POEMGORITHM

Holofractaline superluminal host – the film AND reference beam for projection of thought onto all possible form – itself – a quantum fractal foam of infinite surface area enfolding into form from opposing chaos attractor prisms....asynchronous waves of nothing crashing onto virtual fresnel lens focusing into subphoto densities...

0Logarithmic induction of linear time unfurls the hyperfluid into membranes of hypocycloidal harmonic interference along pi and phi orbits...concentric ellipsoid bubbles of resolving riddled basins, shearing, cavitating the film into nodes, nodes radiating, iterating, harder fluid or softer to us..

Hard fluid hosting harder projection, more faces can synchronize their collapse in the memnodal knot – light – overunity spherical shockwavefront amplifies induction to a point – vacuum fluctuation or plenum pore, the end and/or starting point of a nonlocal equation...

Music of the spheres sings a perfect fifth carrier wave of fresh water flowing through a lattice of vector orbits, becoming salinated as its drawn through chords of the quasicrystal, feedback creating parity wakes...modulating permutations...phase locking the frequency and amplitude of will with the...repeat poem

curling wave= electromagnetism
cavitating = strong nuclear force
capillary action= weak nuclear force
iterating poem=linear time and mass
undertow=gravity

DIVINE WRATH – AN ANALOGY

You've had a long, long day... For once you cherish gravity as it pushes the cool sheets of your bed up to your aching muscles...you breathe a deep sigh of relief as your brain adjusts to the peace and quiet.

A slight breeze comes through the window furthering your state of relaxation.

Just about ta call it a day when a random mutt starts barking...and it does not matter if it's a grating yip yip or a bellowing woof woof because it is completely unnecessary and equally annoying. What is that dog barking at? If it was a reply to danger you would not mind so much, if a pack of kittens scurried by, you could understand BUT...it is a blank incessant noise, as if the dog actually got off from hearing itself.

A conflict – do you tolerate it and hope you fall asleep or hope the dog gets hoarse and stops, or do you get up and discourage the dog?

The body of Christ is the person trying to rest, and for lack of a better word Babylon is the barking dog.

What has happened is that GOD has said, "I will wait for the dog to get tired and stop barking."

But the dog would not be still.

"I will give her some more time"

But the dog insisted on annoying me

I just wanted to sleep you fuckin' flea factory. I bust my ass all day; you lie around lickin yer hole. Now who has a reason to bark?"

The more patience I offered the more tired I became
The more you barked the more anger built inside me.

Perhaps little puppers, if I had been more impatient I would have mercifully gotten up an hour ago and dealt with you, but instead I gave you a chance to reform yourself.

I have to get up in the morning and bust ass again and what have you to do?

I can't find rest with you barking, especially barking at the wind. So now dog, the neighborhood will rejoice as I'm sure they feel the same as I, at the sound of cold, hard, steel splitting yer little K9 skull open.

The neighborhood is the memory of countless souls in the body of Christ begging for justice.

Satan/Babylon is the annoying bitch who won't stop whining even though she has no reason to in the first place....

LITTLE PSYCHO BRO

Cool, so some teenage boy went on a shooting spree and inspired another who inspired the next and so on... The country is empathically shocked – for awhile....until its common and trendy news fodder. Now it's just another symptom waiting for a quick fix/scapegoat as opposed to a non problem with an obvious cure...

(But Tekken 3, Rambo and 2-Pac are so easy to pick on. These outlets prevent more crime than they cause, but we will never know the difference. It's like pornography, we say it leads to rape, yet if all the males on this planet were deprived of this stimuli...that fantasy would get displaced and we males REALLY WOULD degrade women, as opposed to indulging in a harmless mental/manual release. Boy I tell ya what, after I rub one out, the last thing I feel like doing is going out and hunting mucous membranes to envelope me, especially when the flesh around it could be prepared to kill me...)

.......It'll blow over like nuclear weapons, militias and breast cancer when all of a sudden some new event-crisis will focus our collective attention on its causes and unrealistic remedy. Pat Robertson can chalk it up as another sign of the apocalypse (I agree with him there), and it'll give people another reason to say, "Oh Jesus, this world is going down the shitter" OR "When I was young we didn't have these problems" and life goes on for the people who didn't go to work/school today.

Well I'm sick of it. Not the kids goin' postal – that's to be expected. I'm sick of the media blaming the media, yet what are they gonna do? Stop airing the news? Are they gonna say, "Well maybe if we didn't make such a big fuss, these wackos wouldn't be tempted to seek their 15 minutes via our big fuss?" No, of course not. Newsworthy or not, the media has no choice but to report the most hideously pathetic negative shit it can sniff out. That's its job. The media isn't going to terminate itself for the sake of traditional family values such as sanity. People always bitch that the media is biased one way or another. People say if the news only reported good news then Our society would change to optimism. That is another form of being biased and the industry that thrives on your insane pessimism would start bitching...error activated economy.

Def Jam, Nintendo, Tri Star and Glock ain't gonna stop production cuz .05% of the population goes into the school or workplace and reminds us just how error activated it is.

There is NOTHING you can do! Nobody to really blame except the parents or Satan. Satan's too general but parents are the most obvious place to begin laying blame, that is, if you still feel the need...

The shitty negligent useless and abusive parents who breed the same but oops! Their brains are all over the kitchen walls, so...little late to press charges.

But shit, hasn't this violent wacko crap been around since the beginning? And isn't the level and frequency merely proportional to the population growth?

No, there's more to it. There IS novelty in these modern times, factors that weren't there when you were young. Why is it so shocking that more youth are participating in violent outbursts? Kids watch TV, they see that they can get attention if they do something drastic enough, and a whole bunch of attention they got. Who saw this coming?

Technology progresses faster than our ability to forecast its long term effects. It's the same lag that occurs between language and intent. We don't really know what we are communicating until the END of the sentence.

Did those kids get their message across? Until MeekWorld arrives and we're all telepathic, we depend on the modern day mass media which can only present "old news." Depreciation begins the moment the story pulls outta the News lot. You see, mass media is an almost instant socially empathic network, like at a party when the chill vibes are governed by the fact that EVERYONE KNOWS EVERYONE ELSE is feeling high-n-fine. When I watch the news I can count on the fact that the majority of my fellow Americans are gonna feel the same about a news story as I am. And because we are so damn interested in watching ourselves watch ourselves, an infinite well of mirrors is formed between the collective unconscious and the mass media. Whatever image is presented must come from one or the other and whatever single image is focused on is, for the moment, empathically reflected in every minds eye...did you see the news last night? Did you feel the pain of the outcast shooters or the pain of those who were shot? You did not feel a thing because it's just a TV, but you know the reaction of millions of people and that's more important. Mass media and the internet are training wheels for telepathy, but until a positive meme is inoculated, it is a double edged mirror...

Cool, so some teenage boy went on another shooting spree... Here goddammit let me tell you why my little psycho brothers are losin' it, and for the record you stupid Christian retards, its not because of Marilyn Manson or Pulp Fiction or Halo.

As a baseline you've got simple hormones which destabilize the emotions like a 5 year long low level PMS, testosterone for that matter. You got the girl factor; if the young dude isn't getting shot down he's getting dumped, cuz the bitch found a better ride... Manipulative sluts anyway...This is a good start to our massacre.

Next you got the parents on his ass for every little thing from grades to chores, from the stash of herb in his drawer to his choice of music, haircut, clothing – i.e. subculture. Yeah, they are begging for a hole in the head...

And you got school. Here's a dozen more clueless grown-ups who could care less, teaching useless garbage and drilling it into your head that this is the only way, that your whole future is riding on how well you memorize the crap. Telling you what to do all day, punishing you because you have no faith in the curriculum or the burnouts who teach it. No one there is willing to admit that school is a complete waste of time and ineffectual at preparing youth for life outside of its walls, or instilling basic values that the parents can't cuz they went to the same school... You got these annoying Kool Kid Kliques roaming around, smelly hallways, crappy food, a severe lack of technology, uncomfortable seating, routine routine routine, hotty bitches you know you'll never get to fuck, bullies who can find nothin' better to do than intimidate you, making you feel like a wretched gaping pussy.

214

If you've got any friends who can empathize, they are probably assholes. You need a job to get a car, you need a car to get a job, and if you pull that off the boss is a prick and the car breaks down cuz ITS ALL ERROR ACTIVATED... You are skinny with zits, but you know someone who'll buy you forties and that takes the edge off.... You consider your options. The path that you have been offered don't quite jive...ARMY? Yeah right. Life of crime? Well I already feel like a prisoner. Not everyone gets caught. Perhaps if I do something drastic while I'm young and do get caught they will finally listen and know they pushed me into this victim state of mind... besides in Jail I won't have to think about food, clothing, and shelter...

And then one day my little psycho brother got punched in the face by his step father for his poor grades and decided that someone has to die. He reasoned that if someone didn't die now it would just be worse eventually, and he is right. If a world leader can justify violence this way...

Hey, y'know, maybe if the girl was a little more humble and honest and sensitive...Maybe if the parents would lighten up about the pot and not let his appearance embarrass them, maybe if the classes he took were more fun, diverse, relevant and interesting...maybe my little psycho brother wouldn't have wasted all those people. Maybe he would have held out and learned from his depression, harnessed his rage to be productive BUT...

Girls are bitches, the PDFA kept bugging his folks to be responsible and the Education Department stayed in denial.

Maybe if he had learned the good kind of "FUCK IT" that comes from knowing Christ, all the bullshit in the world woulda rolled right off him. But the salesmen/proselytizers witnessing procedure seemed so fake and self righteous, so preachy, generic and out of touch. He never let Christ into his life because these men are incapable of representing the TRUTH. They would never say go ahead and puff herb, listen to Deicide, play Resident Evil. It's actually all inconsequential in light of the TRUTH!

Oh yeah, you don't need to be clean cut, popular or a high school graduate to enter the kingdom. They would never say this!

These men actually repel my little psycho brothers from Christ, and when he does open fire, he is only teaching them so...teachin' 'em that when yer truly hopeless and on the verge, God don't mean shit. And the Christians in that school/community like to show how Christian they are by FORGIVING him. Don't address what led to his breakdown, just forgive him and pray...then lock him up and await the next "crisis." And NO, mandatory prayer would not have stopped this from happening. It woulda pissed him off even more. Bless the hopeless who have the courtesy to kill just themselves...they are still teachers.

YOU OBVIOUSLY HAVEN'T
THOUGHT THIS THROUGH

I keep hearing two things from people I've told thus far:

1. Anger is not the way
2. Technology is not the way

1. It is my opinion that "acceptance" of living in bodily form where I'm relatively comfortable, should not result in apathy. "Oh, its OK." You see, those under the influence of Satan find contentment in this world with no concern for what ultimately affords them their contentment. They also have no longing for anything better, and forget it could be MUCH WORSE. Not so with the poor or the aware. The poor & the aware generally don't say, "Oh, its OK."

When I say EVIL can't know what ANGER really is, I mean that in the same way a parasite can't be mad at its host, FOR ANY REASON. Only the host can justify any irritation it tries to relieve. Socially speaking, humanity's parasite, the rich, could decide to become symbiotic with its own populace and its ultimate host, the PLANET.

Who among you would hesitate to swat a deerfly off your face? And who among you cares if the deerfly is mad at you for wanting to be rid of it? So it is with GOD and the industromilitant, centralized, error activated BUG on the face of the Earth. The Buddhist/New Age do no harm thing is honorable, but the oppressors who are fucking over the people of say, Tibet or Burma, obviously interpret "honorable" as "weak." I have to believe that most victims of these pipsqueak dictators are angry, and I have to believe they would prefer a world without them. It's only natural to feel this way, and it's cool that they don't act on it. It shows supreme strength, but they also have to realize that it's wrong not to fight back if you're indifferent about life and death in the first place. If you don't fight repression now you just make it harder for the next generation.

I am not afraid of stooping down to the level of my enemy. I am not concerned with the progress of my oversoul. I'm not saying that I will kill and become tyrannical – I'm saying that the ultimate source of all this sick behavior is rooted in the infrastructure which prevents peace.

2. The ultimate source of the "fucking over" is technology, for that is what the evil intent manifests as. My benevolent intent alone has no effect on manifested evil intent, therefore I must fight fire with fire, like the way dynamite puts out oil well fires; my burst of technology sucks the fuel out of this raging economic monster...

Now I am not saying intent alone is worthless...today I was talking to a fellow who was into TM. He told me about the Maharishi Mahesh Yogi and the effect the TM folks have had on specific war zones. Group meditation can and does suppress violent tendencies in certain global conflicts, but when the prayer for peace stops, the suppressed emotion results in greater conflict. What is suppressed from manifesting merely gets dammed up and leads to less frequent but more explosive outbursts.

This is exactly what Christianity does to the soul. D'y'ever see the Simpsons episode where Ned Flanders flips his shit because he was programmed to be oodily iddly did darn diddly pleasant? If Ned moderately allowed his Satanic side out he would not have checked himself into the mental hospital. By suppressing our earthly desires we never actually experience the bad effects. Without actual experience with the bad we can't value the good of the heavenly. The truth is, experience, good and bad, is secondary... You need to know both or you don't know either.

THE DOOR

An issue of **THE DOOR**, a magazine, made fun of the CHRISTADELPHIANS because the Christadelphians have the notion that Christ might be mistaken for the antichrist. What gave this particular sect the insight to arrive at this conclusion?

They cited Hal Lindsey and his fellow authorities of end times speculation; these men also claim insight into god's plan and the antichrist. The Christadelphians found 30 instances where biblical descriptions of Christ match their "antichrist." Edgar Cayce said that Christ would not come with trumpets blaring and thunder, rather he would be born into a poor family, raised in obscurity and outed when the time was ripe. I'd have to say now is the time.

I have been watching TBN to get myself extra annoyed and I've noticed a trend. The psychopreachers, Hagee and Van Impe for example, are producing these end times videos. Now they have always churned out spiritual blackmail and I have seen them as humorous and helpful to me in that they are drawing in the suckers who I don't want in my kingdom, but...lately they are dramatizing the antichrist and the rapture. I am not just annoyed anymore. Make up any shit you want about me, but for your sake don't tell people that if they go to church they are going to vanish leaving the damned. Again, it's not so simple, not so easy. I would not bitch about Christianity so much if you were not so self assured. "OOH! It's so magical! I'm so special! I'm a Christian and you're not! OOH! Please convert so you can come with us! Oh, in the twinkling of an eye!" The Rapture is not a moment – it is a process. It starts with egocide and ends with Laghima, and it has to be chosen: it doesn't just happen to you. The mere fact you guys are claiming to know what's going down proves you don't have a clue; you fools, you silly silly fools...

Another example of why I hate Christianity: again I am watching TBN and this Christian named Fred boasted of being the first non-Buddhist to enter Tahk San monastery in Tibet. He said he kept repeating this prayer, "The Lord is an all consuming fire," then he showed a newspaper clipping about the same monastery burning to the ground. He took credit for the fire and all the Christians applauded him.

They are also promoting this movie, The Omega Code, which looks like a cross between The Omen and Pi. It makes sense that Hollywood is seeing the End Times market but the thing is, TBN is supporting this movie as if it is scripture – when obviously it's a work of fiction. They are saying that The Bible Code upon which the movie is based is accurate. They are saying that the mass media is not inherently evil, now that a Christian movie is in the theatres. They are now saying that Hollywood can represent God accurately enough to be used as a means of saving their otherwise uninterested, unborn again family and friends. They talked about how they were consulted for The Prince of Egypt for accuracy, and it's a cartoon! Hal Lindsey was a prophecy consultant for The Omega Code. It's like Pat Robertson being a consultant for politics: the lines between Church, Hollywood, and Washington are dissolving into a unified Bullshit factory. The Christians should be focused on this 1000 year long real-time movie that they are in, not Michael York with red contact lenses.

I watch The 700 Club, and Pat seems to have made a career around dissing things. Pat gets so worked up about the occult, spiritism, satanism, and vegetables, that I have to wonder what makes him think he is not possessed. After all, those demons are so tricky he might not be able to distinguish his intent from that of Satan himself. Why is it he and Van Impe, Hagee, Schuller, Copeland, and Lindsey have these beady eyes and flat brows? Isn't that a sign of possession? Seriously though, if Pat was what I consider a true Christian, he would not be concerned with sacrificial babies and tarot cards; he would be addressing true evil. To make my point, here is the beginning to The Conspiracy chapter in Church of the SubGenius's REVELATION X.

> .....Once a guy accused us of being DEVIL WORSHIPPERS just because we said we think Christianity, as it exists today, is the ONE WORLD ANTI-CHRIST SYSTEM PREDICTED IN THE BIBLE !! No, we're not supposed to even know that THE ADVERSARY is not some grimy weirdo cranking out crackpot

rants in a filthy attic, or a Cult Leader wearing Mystic Symbols on an afternoon TV talk show. We're not supposed to know…THAT SATAN INCARNATE ISN'T A HIDEOUS ABOMINATION FROM HELL, BUT A CLEAN SCRUBBED, PINK-FACED, NECKTIE-WEARING GOOD NATURED TRUSTWORTHY SOUL WHO IS POCKETING HUGE AMOUNTS OF CASH FOR POISONING AND MURDERING MILLIONS, saying, "WE HAVE NO SCIENTIFIC EVIDENCE THAT THE TENFOLD ESCALATION OF HORRIBLE DEATH IN THE DIRECT VICINITY OF OUR PLANT HAS ANYTHING TO DO WITH THE BLACK SLUDGE LEAKING OUT OF OUR WASTE DUMP ONTO THE PLAYGROUND OF THE ELEMENTARY SCHOOL!!!

WAR-N-JUNK

M.A.D. works but it's sad. We need to be able to kill each other to maintain peace. And again, as the graffiti says, "Fighting for peace is like fucking for virginity."

What's that say about humanity? What's that say about the power bases that deem weapons of mass destruction necessary? It says that, as a fear response, nations who can afford it (and oftentimes can't) need to stockpile weapons. One superpower initiates an arms race and then becomes paranoid because smaller nations want to defend themselves. The super power basically creates its own enemies by virtue of its own status.

Among the well equipped military powers there exists a standard of living and mutual understanding from which the notion of peace comes from. We don't want to nuke our allies in interglobal commerce. They have a lot to lose by war which means we do.

The cold war is over but the presence of weapons alone is enough to perpetuate paranoia. Do 3rd world countries feel we would nuke them or use lesser weapons for purely offensive/dominator reasons? I guess so cuz they developed nukes of their own. Even though they could never actually win the arms race or a war, the nationalistic pride factor of "we ain't goin down without a fight!" puts them in fight or flight, generating and contributing to the collective tension of future shock.

The truly sad fact of the nuclear age is the mere acceptance of it. Nobody seems to mind that more than half of humanity's labor is expended on its destruction (entropy, mmmhmmm). If all the effort that went into war was put into helping the enemy by defeating fear, extending trust, and offering surplus, knowledge and technology, there would be nothing for a rogue country to bitch about or resent in the superpower and nobody to sell old weapons to. War would have no market.

That all seems unreasonable to the superpower. They have to enforce peace with threats of war. I enforce war with threats of peace. They create the problem to sell you the solution. I steal their problems and become the solution to give away... I promote peace by monopolizing its opposite. It's a common theme in cartoons for the good guys and bad guys to stop fighting and join together to fight some common enemy. That is precisely what I'm doing, becoming the mutual enemy, G.I. Joe and Cobra teamed up to defeat Serpentor. Likewise, nations will stop fighting each other to try and take me out, but that's what I want so I will not lift a finger to stop them (see 2 Esdras).

THE FUTURE OF WARFARE - YEAH RIGHT!

You know what pisses me off? When THE DISCOVERY CHANNEL or THE LEARNING CHANNEL airs programs about the future of warfare. It's like they are admitting its OK, like they've given up on the notion of there ever being world peace...

"In the future wars will be fought in cyberspace..." Fuck You assholes! War is NOT a given!

Now I mean c'mon, what is so difficult about being good and peaceful, and following the ways of god? Even if aggression is some biological imperative, couldn't it be channeled into something constructive?

Perhaps we need to invent some outlet for you human males that sits somewhere between Monday Night Football and WW3? (Note: written before I saw the Future of Halo on the YouTube – HALO 8 - *You know what to do*) Games do it for most of us and only the participants can get hurt (except for soccer?), but I can't believe soldiers and weapons designers and leaders want to destroy the playing field and the spectators too?! RC Telepresence War – For the Honor and/or conflict resolution.

Alright guy, you wanna go to war? Do it. I'm sick of all this tension. I'm sick of trying to understand your reasoning. I'm sick of hearing about who sold what to whom. And I'm sick of hearing just how many nuclear weapons are stockpiled. I'm sick of seeing shit going down in other countries! FOR ENTERTAINMENT'S SAKE WOULD SOMEBODY PLEASE LAUNCH A WARHEAD TO WASHINGTON D.C.?! (Note: written prior to 9/11)

C'MON, we spent all the money for this shit. Let's justify the purchase!

PLEASE GOD, ENCOURAGE THE MADMEN OF THIS WORLD TO UNLEASH THEIR WEAPONRY UPON THE EARTH AND REDUCE IT TO DEBRIS AND CRATERS. WE ARE NOT CAPABLE OF GOVERNING OUR FATE. WE ARE UNABLE TO USE THE GIFTS OF TECHNOLOGY TO HARNESS YOUR GIFTS. THEREFORE, MY GOD, PLEASE ALLOW US TO KILL OURSELVES SO THAT THE MUTANTS THAT FOLLOW US CAN REFLECT UPON US AND SAY, "HEY THAT WAS STUPID," FOR THEN AND ONLY THEN WILL THERE BE PEACE. A FEW HUNDRED MUTANTS TOO WEAK FROM RADIATION TO FIGHT....OR PLANT A NEW GARDEN.

THE GREATEST INVENTION - LANGUAGE

I see math as a language describing relationships but also all language as a mathematical description of our relationships. Why should numbers end in the objective reality? If emotion is primarily conveyed with language then the language must have an order of operations....because you don't say, "I want to kill myself" until after being told, "you're fired" or "I don't want to be your girlfriend anymore." Reading and hearing requires linear time for the equation/conversation to produce an answer/reaction. When the problem of linear time is solved i.e. telepathy, the answer will eliminate the need for language.

The equation/conversation is a preset problem, like your remaining karma, and the order of operations balances it out. The act of resolution (seeing eye to eye) creates an answer equal to the problem - the answer and problem are interchangeable once the answer is found. Karmic potential draws emotion through the order of operations.

Linear time=order of operations
sin= karmic potential
language=resolution potential
love=sinning potential

If human intent fuels the karmic engine then the human body is the car. You've heard metaphysics call the body a vehicle. This implies the driver is a separate entity.

For the discarnate souls who volunteer or are obligated, the vehicle is what takes them to "work" or rather, allows them to work.

Earth is your job, love is your paycheck, and sin/karma is your bills. Christ consciousness is when you work at home (don't need a car but can drive anyway) and death is your vacation time.

All negativity in the human condition is the result of our biology. Biology feels pain, starves, and deteriorates.

The vehicle is flawed and separate from the driver/mind. The truth is the flaw is that separateness between vehicle and driver.

When your car rusts and breaks down you generally feel negativity, you blame the engineers, you blame the petroleum industry, you are at the mercy of someone other than yourself to fix it, and it's all due to your lack of knowledge about the car.

Conversely, a car that is fast, responsive, never breaks down and never needs fuel or maintenance would make you pretty damn happy wouldn't it? This is what it means to be an ascended master...I'm the engineer, the fuel, the new parts, and the mechanic of your vehicle and I will get you back on the road/grid YOU WILL BE ONE WITH YOUR CAR.

ANIMALS

FACTORY FARMING - McDEATH CYCLE SHIT TOXIN BURGER LOAF ROTTING CORPSE IMPACTED FECES FLY RIDDEN PAIN TORTURE STENCH SLAB PUTRID MAGGOT BY-PRODUCT CANNABAL DOWNED DISEASED METHANE SLASH AND BURN HORMONE ITS WHATS FOR DINNER ON A SESAME SEED BUN NO WONDER YOU ARE A FAT CANCER TUMOR BUY SOME PILLS REACTION COFFIN CHAR BROILED ASHES PROFIT...SICK

VEGETARIANISM - RICH SOIL SUN WATER MINERAL SPROUT OXYGEN CRUNCHY SWEET EARTH NO SUPPLEMENTS NEEDED SELF RELIANT CHEAP NUTRITIOUS HEARTY BEANS COLD COCONUT MILK HEMP SEED BUTTER EASY BLONDE TURDS...SIMPLE GOODNESS.

NOW LOOK! WE ARE OMNIVORES BUT WE ARE ALSO HUMANS WHICH MEANS WE CAN REASON THAT COMPASSION AND A HEALTHY DIET IS BETTER THAN TORTURE AND TOXINS, WE CAN DETERMINE WHAT FLESH BENEFITS CAN BE FOUND ELSEWHERE!

I want to address all the vegetarians and animal activists. The bible has alot to say about the health and morality issues of eating flesh. See The Maker's Diet. In ancient times and with indigenous cultures the humans and the beasts had mutual respect. The animals knew they were here to serve us. Their bodies were fully utilized as a sign of respect as well as practicality – industry does the same for profit anyway. The hunters honored the spirit of the animal because they knew animals had a spirit. Because of this animals would actually help humans by walking into a village and offering their flesh or through psychedelics by guiding them to where they were.

Today the humans have turned animals into an industry almost completely void of respect. Today humans have no practical need for flesh (and I swear to god if one meat eater says "protein" or "B-6/12" I will blow up every slaughter house on the planet. Personally, all you have to say is BACON – I can't taste the suffering over the salty, and that salty is good for the soul. Most land is used to raise food for the food. This process is inefficient.

To all the people who care about the welfare of animals, the food animals, the nearly extinct, and the ones we call pets; In the near future people will not have time to raise food for food and will have no choice but to eat vegetables and hunt/fish. Soon after that the survivors will not even need to consume food because their bodies will live on subtle energies, including animals, this is why "the lion will lie down with the lamb." But if I'm wrong about eating light, maybe we could all watch Food Inc. and read <u>Animal Vegetable Miracle</u> by B. Kingsolver and do what she did. Don't get me wrong, I like meat but I don't see why it can't be scaled back, decentralized and diversified and done right for the sake of the quality of the meat itself. Make it a twice a week thing instead of 3 times a day.

THE RAPTURE MYTH (TRUNCATED)

Where in the bible (the be all end all scripture that's perpetually reinterpreted) does it state that Jesus will come and take away people who call themselves "christian" (the only qualifying aspect to that chosen privilege of being raptured) in order to spare them from horror and woe?

Well let's back up here. Isn't the fact that perpetually reinterpreted bible verses even exist reason enough to seriously doubt the validity of any one whether the word is interpreted literally or symbolically? (Not that the original or still intact parts are flawed) What more reason when there are hundreds of christian sects and three versions of the RAPTURE scenario? When consolidated, the sum of proposed end times pop prophecy is a cheesy, Disneyfied, mish mash of bullshit.

The idea of people disappearing from visible sight randomly is a real phenomena dubbed "Involuntary Spontaneous Human Invisibility". Rarely reported, it should be noted there are specific reasons for it happening. The scientific reason has to do with what causes magnetic pole flips. Eventually Earth will blip into the galactic plasma mirror/shearing plane/electromagnetic null zone/photon belt/monopole/lake-of-fire/ omega attractor/sliver-o-hyperspace as our solar system in our arm enters. Among 6 billion people some (not necessarily the chosen) DNA responds as a precursor phenomena by "singing a new song" aka phase-shifting. This unbiased or nonchiral state is the unveiling of the Merkaba or light body, but not a total deviation from this dimension as the bodies still have mass - that has to be willful! ISHI also phase-shifts clothing; in Left Behind people leave naked.

That movie also suggested children under 12 years old are exempt from sin and lack of professed belief system; presumably because they are innocent.

This is contradictory to the often mentioned notion of being born with sin (actually true, sin = karma but try explaining that to a Christian!) It's the little inconsistencies that add up.

The Second Advent of The Christ in THE OMEGA CODE 2 is depicted as a lightning bolt that selectively kills soldiers who are doing identical things under identical orders, the ones left standing from this genocidal lightning bolt (similar to a lightning bolt the "AntiChrist" summoned earlier in TOC2) were - THANK GOD - Americans!

I think Christians don't bother to think about these things for selfish reasons; it hurts to admit you were wrong, intellectually quantum physics and Jesus can't mix, and emotionally its fun to believe you are special and God loves you cuz you say stuff. I think though they expect a huge metaphysical laser light show in the sky and/or superpowers and some kind of conflict...perhaps they really want to experience all the drama and excitement on earth that will ensue even though they won't be here - the movies are the next best thing...

The preceding rant was posted today at the www.raptureready.com forum. This site was featured in TIME MAGAZINE and it claims to be one of the most popular sites in cyberspace with over 4000 registered members. In the forum guidelines a list of undesirable types is given. One person they don't want there is "The one true prophet". I've been posting similar rants for a couple years now and apparently there are a lot of wanna-be one true prophets popping up as of late, although I've yet to see one...so I understand where they are coming from - they don't want to be annoyed. Truth is, most Christian forums, this one in particular are nothing more than folks blowing sunshine up each others asses (Solar-Rectal Infusion). Truth is they are blatantly protecting themselves from ANYTHING that bursts their bubble, censoring reality as usual.

I broke a personal record for being deleted. The last one was Zola Board, it took 3 days, at Rapture Ready it took 30 minutes. Within that 30 minutes however 80 people viewed the post. The 4 replies were various admin congratulating themselves for having deleted it so quickly. This act only proves my point. Maybe, just maybe, one of those 4000 people would have benefited from my post but now they can only see the subject heading and wonder...another suggested that I communicate in a less militant way...

The really cool thing is that I also posted this same piece at www.gnn.tv, an indie media site, one guy gave me a personal message stating that he was a long time christian with unwavering faith and that he really appreciated it as the answers he had been given up till then just didn't sit well...and he wanted to KNOW if I had any more writings.

I thought of something the other day, being one prone to seeing paradox, and this IS a joke but subjectively true for many besides me...

If The Rapture is the removal of Christians from Earth to Heaven, would that not make Earth Heaven?

HYPERSPACE

The beginning of this reply is text taken from the NASA BPP website which expresses their concerns with people like me. My reply follows.

> Exploring the edge of knowledge for profound discoveries evokes special challenges. In addition to the normal challenges of scientific research, i.e. figuring out how nature truly works - the provocative character of grand challenges can encumber such research. First, by pursuing truly profound improvements in the human condition, the stakes are higher and accordingly emotions run higher. Second, by operating on the genuine edge of knowledge, instead of exploring routine refinements of established knowledge, one encounters controversial ideas. This combination of heightened emotions and controversy can taint the productive discourse of scientific study. A typical example is how both skeptics and optimists can sometimes jump to conflicting conclusions and, in their zeal, fail to communicate in the dispassionate and impartial style needed to rigorously identify, test, and resolve the real issues.

> Ironically, most of the difficulty encountered by the BPP Project has come from unofficial proponents, rather than from skeptics. Virtually all the skeptics have been constructive. Most skeptics have clearly identified issues and unsolved physics that present challenges for discovering propulsion breakthroughs. By identifying such specifics, research objectives are defined and refined.

> ***The bulk of difficulties have come from enthusiasts*** whose well-meaning actions have actually impeded progress. Because

such problems are increasing, this section has been added to the public web site to explicitly address this challenge. It is hoped, by explaining this situation, that those interested in this Project will better understand the impact of their actions. Below, links are provided to short descriptions of the most common, recurring events that impede progress. Where appropriate, examples are given to help readers appreciate the difficulties. And finally, guidance is provided for more constructive actions.

SPECIAL CHALLENGES

--- Excerpts from the "Lunatic Fringe" and hopeless amateurs --- (idea submissions displaying delusions of grandeur or paranoia, *9% of emails to NASA BPP*)

- STILL UNDER CONSTRUCTION -

These samples are offered to illustrate one of the disappointing types of correspondences frequently received by the BPP Project. Although these offerings can seem entertaining at first, they become taxing after receiving dozens of them. Based on the advice of a psychologist, no answer is sent in response to such submissions. No correspondence could provide the type of help needed, and any response would only encourage more of this nonproductive behavior.

To make these excerpts less offensive, only humorous and unthreatening examples are shown. The names of the senders and any other traceable data has been removed from these excerpts.

Typical opening lines:

* "I'm not a scientist, but..."
* "I'm a retired engineer, and now that I have extra time, I have this theory ..."
* "Since I'm in prison, I've had time to think about my theories..."
* "I've seen a UFO and here's how it works.."

Recall the quote from Edison that: "Invention is 1% inspiration and 99% perspiration." Frequently individuals submit their "inspirations" with the desire that NASA complete the other 99% of the work (and anoint the submitters with accolades). A shorthand phrase for these individuals is "one-percenters".

QUOTES & ANECDOTES:

* From a man doing time in a correctional institute, who wrote to express his interest in considering a career in physics: "You see, I have always had a love for science, Life Science at first, then went through a chemistry phase which landed me where I am currently positioned."

* From a guy who sends NASA approximately 1 letter every month, all in capital letters, and connected with commas between every word (Most commas omitted for clarity): "This is my invention for metaphysical gears for the transmission of future spaceships. This secret I got from the crystal ray which I devised from the circle, the plane, and the center, long ago. The FBI in Wash D.C. have my crystal ray work." A more recent submission from the same individual said: "You, NASA, see I am an American visionary and the son of man and I hear voices, seriously, from beyond the grave and the spirit world on high, and I ran into your own house, and they confirmed with conquest in myself and faulted, so I told them I would not sell you these engines and faulted myself...."

* While giving a lecture to a space society club in Huntsville, Alabama, one of the audience members (NOT one of the NASA employees) offered his help. He said he'd been "Channeling" with Einstein and Einstein had made more progress on his unified field theories.

* From a phone call: "I am sure my theory is credible, because ever since I thought of it, I am visited each morning by aliens in my bedroom."

* From a web discussion group: "Yep, I have just returned from an interesting experience. On October 21, I was taken at gunpoint

aboard a US government secret levitator craft and taken to the far side of the moon. It was really emotional looking down on the earth from space from high-orbit. Moonbase Yellow was nothing spectacular once you got past the high-tech transport and defense systems. Their labs were cool, though, and I think that some of them were clones, or else people changed their clothes a lot. The craft was a neat ride and made cool noises. I could tell that acceleration forces were appreciably damped. I had a window seat, and could tell that there were no lights on the outside. The trip to the moon took a little over two hours. Anyway, they just wanted to sort of guide my research if you know what I mean. Horton pointed me in some interesting directions. Did you know that if you make iron or nickel clusters small enough, the clusters' surface forces are such that that the clusters' melting point exceeds the vitrification temperature? I thought pure iron glass might be cool to someone. Maybe you guys knew this already... I don't really know if I can trust Horton. Peace." [Note that he claimed to enjoy the view of the Earth from the far side of the moon].

* Yes, this is a direct quote from an email: "Rockets??? Ha! Ha! Ha! NASA will never come up with the Break Through Propulsion System, least they swipe it leading us into Interstellar Travels because they are still applying a Brute Force Concept, rather it will come from a lone inventor. ...... Tee! Hee! Hee! .... And to think my concept was rejected on the basics that it goes against fundamental physics you, NASA and the rest of the Academic world do not understand the basic principles of AC Radio-Gravitics let a lone that nature is superconductive. ...I'll permit you to look at my discoveries If you have the balls that is to open your closed mind!"

* Another email excerpt: "To tell you the truth Marc, I'm a pot smoking mushroom munching high school dropout and I'm qualified to do two things; wash dishes and invent shit. ... I've got other inventions too – an electrochemical computer, ultrasonic foaming process, magnepulsion generator, solid state over-unity device, various concept vehicles, centrifugal antigravity drives, and butlloads of more practical inventions."

* "I'm the purple depths of the ocean which is don't forget the purple star gem exploding at seven miles a second at the command of I want to turn into a giantess or imploding at the command of ill leave it by itself I am a blue crested wave under the moon which is hanriffic or hanalriffic and hanalulriffic by me I am an ancient emerald forest or tree your pick which is what I like to call watching bark peel off a tree and sticking it on the back of their neck casting a massmorph spell and watching them rut into a tree or freaking out and turning their head which way I am a yellow tear from the sun which is gnidolpxe star gem which is still the color of qurbol the command is ssetnaig e otni nrut ot tnaw I am an orange pumpkin in the field which kind of reminds me of the phoenix oh I meandsun laughing at me just call that a little Irish schizophrenic humor and finally I am a flaming door which is all part of the right of the active door which most of came from the 21 lessons of Merlin a study of druid lore and magic which is preferable to the bible did I hear the words jungle sanctuary or was that essences…"

* From a man who may have forgotten to clean his video camera lens, and shares his monitary desires: "…there was the image… in the shape of a head I decided to start experimenting around the rest of my home and other homes. With each experiment, the results were the same…Each had 2 eye sockets and you can see their mouths moving but you can't hear anything …They all looked really hateful. Crazy I know, but everyone I have shown, has said the same thing. My motive for this letter is simple, I know I have found something very, very special and I want paid lots and lots of money for it. To be exact, I want millions."

* And here is an entirely different attitude about money: "'Astro-travel - free of charge'. You blithering idiots. To travel the realms of space free of charge is not possible. All members of the public need a toilet. I, Jeff, being educated, charge you all not to expel the fumes of the charge I indict you all with when you enter the correct room of learning, to which I present you all with."

* From the inventor of a claimed "tachyonic transceiver:" "If we could just get copies of papers sent to [list of agencies, and a person down in Florida], then we would have it all, and could get

together 3 or 4 teams to work on this… as we do not want to fall behind the rest of the world…. Also, I would appreciate a car and salary such that I could meet with the teams as they assemble the transceiver as I would hope to continue to create enthusiasm for the project."

* Here is another job seeker: "Since there are so many clues around, the double alpha geometry will become known. By myself and others. Its' a beautiful by-product from the geometrical evolution of collison, friction, and the state of motion. As you know I've been having one hell of a time with 'E'.…..I may be changing occupations.

Since I never became "socialized" I learned a lot about people, and myself, by driving a cab. Now I must have access to some tools. So I may go to work for a generator repair shop."

* From a man willing to devote himself to the good of science: "Just call me a chronic dreamer and a glutton for the unknown. Do you need a Guinea Pig for any experiments. I may be [your] man."

* There are those that assume that Star Trek is real. NASA received over 10 pages, typed, quoting from the Star Fleet technical Manual.

* "I entered the new information and data in a mind-altering albeit drug-free trance in which I had a five-month conversation with God."

* It is unknown why this message was sent to NASA. This text is a paraphrase of the submission: There was a young man who claimed that all of a sudden, he could not find his head. He was a headless being and he didn't know what happened. He went and asked his mother why he was born without a head, and she said, "it's there on your shoulders," and he looked in the mirror, and lo and behold, there it was!

* From a short and sweet email (if you'll allow the pun), the entire message was: "Hi, I've heard of warp drive. I love strawberries."

* This message followed a NASA lecture to a 5th grade class: "I always ask my parents questions about space and they never know. My dad takes guesses and he is always wrong and when I say the answer, my mom says "O, I knew that, I was just wanting to hear what Dad said!"

* From a letter that included a CAD rendering of a wormhole experience (appears as a dark gray circle within a light gray rectangle): "Not really knowing the origins of what I saw, (see attached) I can truly say that wormholes are a reality, although short lived. The image that I am sending you is of a Non-Linear Space-Time Displacement Event, a wormhole by any other name. It found its way into my apartment, several times, to remove from my existence, some personal object, only to return the object to my existence at a later time and in a different location. Truth is stranger than fiction. This is truth. The grey area out side the hole is my living room carpet, the striped "ring" is the interface, the whitish center is the sidewalk outside my apartment at the time of reentry into my existence. The grey carpet and the sidewalk were/ are 10 feet, 36hr. apart. I hope that you will take a look at the image. It is a rendered CAD model of what I saw."

* These next quotes are from a grocery store clerk who sends in pictures (and sometimes the cardboard devices themselves) which are claimed to induce "space transparency worm holes." One photo shows him holding a box with the caption: "you can tell that his device [cardboard box[is working because the lines in the pavement are showing through in front of my pants." In the black & white photo, the black lines and his black pants are indeed indistinguishable. A further quote reflecting a touch of paranoia: "A few years ago I was talking to Mr. [-snip-] who said our conversation was being traced and a black helicopter fly over would possibly occur tomorrow…. Next day a black helicopter flyer with a white triangle and an instrument in the middle of the white triangle flew over. If this was a Pledian ship mimicking a Delta Force helicopter, they could have done their transparency recording of my apartment…perhaps the technology has characters mimicking the counselors or rulers…called Super Beings, from the Pleidian system." And finally, a recent submission states: "A cardboard box used as a stand for the coils after the Mirrors Array

was tried lost 34% of its weight and then disappeared. We do not know if this was teleportation or if someone threw it out."

These are just some samples from dozens of similar submissions.

OK so NASA BPP has shared with us the 9% comical pathological submissions and stated that these people (myself included) have accounted for most of the difficulty they have had - at what exactly is not mentioned.

Here again is what they excerpted from my email:

"To tell you the truth Marc, I'm a pot smoking mushroom munching high school dropout and I'm qualified to do two things; wash dishes and invent shit. ... I've got other inventions too - an electrochemical computer, ultrasonic foaming process, magnepulsion generator, solid state over-unity device, various concept vehicles, centrifugal antigravity drives, and buttlloads of more practical inventions."

I'll be the first to admit that this is a very bad business letter (but good fun) and that my zeal is far from tempered. I was f-ing with them because I knew at that point I'd never be taken seriously anyway. I can acknowledge how this is detrimental to the cause, both mine and theirs. What they did not excerpt is the actual IP for a device that would, in theory, reduce inertial mass of any matter within its field, effectively phase-shifting a craft and pilot into hyperspace. They did not acknowledge that despite the lack of professionalism my abstract was EXACTLY what they are looking for.

This is where my criticism begins.

Firstly the dichotomy between proponents and skeptics is relative. NASA BPP thinks of itself as a proponent when it is a skeptic too. They dismiss an idea because of its source, they are not as open minded as they'd like to think. They lumped together my submission with the submissions of blatant psychos because I had mentioned drug use, perhaps they saw the nature of my other IP and considered it a Delusion of Grandeur.

NASA BPP is the first to admit that genuinely good ideas can appear to be insane. History has proven this to be true. Would it stand to reason then that an inventor can be a genuinely good inventor despite his Delusions of Grandeur? For example there was an inventor at the turn of the 20th century who actually thought he could build a transmitter that would send information and energy to any point on the earth, he also believed that he could extract energy from the air, talk to Martians and zap down enemy aircraft with particle beams - why he must be INSANE! That man, Nikola Tesla, is responsible for the AC that runs the modern world and he was pathological - he had a germ phobia, he had OCD, and an obsession with the number 3. Today in some circles he is a demigod, in others continually suppressed, erased from history...

NASA BPP wants Breakthrough ideas but is not willing to go where these ideas must come from - deviant minds.

The REAL dichotomy impeding this endeavor is not between proponents and skeptics but rather Academic Specialist Calculators and Self-Taught Interdisciplinarian Psychonauts.

ACADEMIC SPECIALIST CALCULATOR

NASA BPP undoubtedly surrounds itself exclusively with these types of people who are subject to their own brand of delusion - that being an excessive pride in having earned a piece of paper, in having a title, in having a position at the top of their field of expertise, and all this inhibits progress. There is a complementary fear for having risen so high, the fear of falling. A career can be destroyed if the peers and scientific climate are not predisposed to accepting an idea. These types of people have a lot to lose by being creative so why would they be? As a specialist the ability to research varying fields and the necessary association of those varying fields is never an interest or skill they involve themselves with. Certainly there is value in being an expert in one thing but not when everyone else is too. The ability to manipulate theoretical constructs and the ability to impose them as an applied system to observed phenomena are two different things. When it comes to Zero Point Energy and Hyperspace bridging that mathematical gap is impossible; until a device produces novel phenomena such as inertial mass reduction and teleportation they will never know the accuracy of the math.

SELF-TAUGHT INTERDISCIPLINARIAN PSYCHONAUT

These, the "unofficial proponents" lacking any credentials or peer review are, in consensus reality, completely invalid merely because they didn't go to a special building and pay a special person to reiterate what was in an otherwise accessible textbook. They lack structure and perhaps formal communication skills that higher education can impart. They may have gone to a university library for free or received permission to "sit in on" a particular class for free (I did just this at Cornell). When the internet appeared they likely "Googled" anything they wanted to know for free. They invested nothing yet received everything but a paper, and eventual title. I myself have spent the past 12 years learning how to be an inventor, I have spent countless hours studying, researching and when my ideas are ripe soliciting the IP to countless venture capitalists, bankers, institutions and foundations who specialize in that particular field of expertise. Perhaps this type has metabolized certain molecules known to release the mind from local and linear thinking, which can actually reveal the structure of free space by confusing the observer and observed. This type may have also cross referenced several systems regardless of age and seen similarity. Mystical New Age writings, some channeled, may help explain the implications of Quantum Mechanics, Chaos and Information Theory. Oh I put in The 99% perspiration but when I attempt to submit papers for a particular invention/theory for peer review, when I can actually find the appropriate journal or website or professor I'm immediately asked where I went to school and well I get as frustrated as a great Govt. program that gets its budget cut.

I see humility in the latter type of proponent, in the divulging of information however useless. And were these folks actually "paranoid" as NASA BPP claims they would not have received any submissions in the first place. We are as unsure of the validity of our ideas as the prior is with their equations. We the pathological need not be reduced to a funny page on a website we need to be respected as a means to an end; we need to be exploited for what WE ARE GOOD AT. I for one don't want or expect NASA BPP to do any of my work for me, I want to be intimately involved with those specialists so that I can learn from them and associate what they can't, I want to be in a lab doing R+D and prototyping new spacecraft.

It is my hope that by responding and speaking for the types I was lumped into I can make NASA BPP understand the impact of their INACTION and lack of perspective.

My secondary criticism of NASA BPP relates to The Disclosure Project and the phenomena of "compartmentalization".

Zero Point Energy and its manipulation were relegated to Black Budget Projects for years as the (dis)information suggests and is slowly but surely coming out of the closet. It's been mentioned in Janes Defense that Boeing is exploring ZPE.

I have to wonder why NASA BPP will not hire someone who has already done back engineering work for one of the Black Budget Projects? Certainly Dr. Greer must know one or two. Would that not solve everything?

Is it possible that one part of our Govt. has known the true GUT for years and another claims to be clueless? It is my assumption that the budget cut for the NASA BPP is related to someone decompartmentalizing the independent cells of research and recognizing redundancy in the respective covert and public endeavors.

The funny thing about all this is, with the amount of media attention NASA BPP and Disclosure has received they MAY AS WELL be clandestine operations!

Can there be any longer a point to (dis)information and black budget programs? The arbiters of consensus reality will let us know soon...

GREAT KARMA FILTER

The APACHE prophecy of the Red Sky as given by Grandfather...he suggests it is man made but I disagree. I had a similar vision/dream and it was definitely COSMIC.

> ...the sky suddenly turned to a liquid and then turned blood-red. As far as his eyes could see, the sky was solid red, with no variation in shadow, texture or light. The whole of Creation seemed to have grown still, as if awaiting some unseen command. Time, place and destiny seemed to be in limbo, stilled by the bleeding sky. He gazed for a long time at the sky, in a state of awe and terror, for the red color of the sky was like nothing he had ever seen in any sunset or sunrise...

Isaiah 34:4

> All the stars of the heavens will be dissolved and the sky rolled up like a scroll; all the starry host will fall like withered leaves from the vine, like shriveled figs from the fig tree.

My vision/dream:

I am sitting on the beach at Lodi Pt NY looking north. A orange sliver appears on the horizon and then the sliver moves up into the sky; the light does NOT graduate. Soon the northern half of the sky is solid orange and the southern half is dark. In the dark half there are (new?) planets visible, they are quite close. I turn to look at the orange half again and a dark spot appears, it gets bigger and resembles a spiral galaxy, all the sudden there are balls of light zipping around, a loud silence and stillness...and that's all I was given.

We know that the Sun is losing its polarity and dimming, it is giving off new light and the Earth's field is weakening. These are signs of our approaching the Omega Attractor/Photon Belt/Electromagnetic Null Zone/Galactic Shearing Plane/Great Plasma Mirror/Lake of Fire/monopole

Our solar system passes through it at 3:00 and 9:00 as our spiral arm spins, this accounts for partial and total pole flips; what makes this one different???

Sudden appearence/disappearence of civilizations - nudge nudge wink wink

Sudden appearence/disappearence of species - nudge nudge wink wink

This solar system -all for that matter- periodically pass through it, and guess what happens when we do? Magnetic Field collapses and reverses, sunspots converge to the suns poles, we have some crust dragging on a confused geodynamo and it causes 3 days of day in the northern hemisphere and 3 nights of darkness in the southern. Solar wind cuts up DNA…It opens the Akashic Records and those who are not found are caught in 3D like a net, it is literally a KARMIC FILTER and SOUL BLAST FURNACE, hence the term "Great Cleansing/Recycling" This is Zero Point Spectroscopy.

For those who are down with the Divine Trip and/or who are located in the right light zones at that time the "JUNK" DNA is tweaked, the external merkabas are given and We bifurcate from the Explicate order.

That's the 2012 galactic cross theory, I could be wrong.

It is interesting to note here too that right now The Draconian/Neo Nazi influence here is doing its best to stop this bifurcation - as if!

HOW?

Funny thing, the Schumann Resonance is increasing, soon it will be sympathetic to human beta wave levels. Whatever the majority of humans on Earth are feeling THAT is what the Earths Frequency will be entrained with.

LOVE and HOPE are associated with higher frequencies

HATE and DESPAIR are associated with lower frequencies

So remember, all you people out there who bend over for the propaganda on the Mass Media head of the first beast - you don't show up in the book of life, you are too immersed in DECOY NIGHTMARES!

The Intergalactic Space Demons from Hell (for lack of a better term) KNOW they are fuct, they will never leave the Lake-o-Fire, the only thing that they can do/enjoy is reminding you how stupid you were...

They are helping GOD separate, The Elect know this, appreciate the demons (certainly don't fear them) and therefore go on to New Jerusalem.

GENOMICS, CHAOS,
AND THE TIPPING POINT

I saw a show about the Human Genome Project and learned that Genetic diseases begin at an atomic level. I Just read <u>The Tipping Point</u> by Malcolm Gladwell and learned that social epidemics are created by minor tweaking of ideas. This book is discussing the mechanics of MEME Theory, that is, ideas propagate in a similar way as genes; in both cases many genes and memes are apparently useless or ineffectual. A successful meme or gene is one which propagates itself.

I studied Chaos Theory and learned that initial states or starting points, slightly varied, lead to vast differences in the emergent pattern derived from iteration.

The Tipping Point is the social aspect of what in Chaos is known as a Transition point, in Foam Coarsening Rules, The Rearrangement Event. In each case what is happening is a stable homogenous system or state gives way to a definitive change or pattern via a disproportionate small change.

It is possible to associate these three systems through their THREEness.

CHAOS =
>Quantum Foam -
>reiterating equation -
>pattern

DNA =
>Amino Acids -
>gene -
>body

SOCIETY =
>   clutter problem -
>   meme -
>   social epidemic

Further when you look at the THREE within each of those, for example, in The Tipping Point there are three aspects to how a meme becomes successful for both the meme and its host:

PEOPLE =
>   Mavens
>   connectors
>   salesmen

MEME =
>   Law of the few
>   Stickiness
>   Context

Each row above has a specific role transcending the respective systems.

The first row describes potentiated beginning states, starting or transition points. The quantum foam is the background energy/noise from which all matter emerges. Amino Acids are the building blocks of the building blocks. The clutter problem is the homogenous fluff of similar and therefore failed memes (as in the more commercials one sees the less effective any one becomes). Mavens are the folks who can harbor all those memes. The Law of the Few makes The 3 types of people rare and therefore useful.

We see here then that even though The Law of the Few is the opposite of the ubiquity of the others in the first row it still allows for the phenomena to occur.

The second row is a mediator or phase state, the actual processing which leads to the end point which must also be potentiated as "context" suggests. In chaos this potentiated end state is known as an attractor.

If all this is capable of being associated then what would be the context of a salesmen or body? The context or potentiating end state of the salesman is the sale, the body, life...but is that the REAL end state? Does not the salesmen want to continue selling and the body want to continue living? Yes which means the middle row is the end state and the first and third are really the beginning!!!

Any Buddhist will tell you this is true, that is, it's not the destination that is important but rather the journey.

In every system in every part of the trinities the process must be initiated through intent.

You will also see that going from Chaos to Society is Integration and Society to Chaos is Reductionism.

How can it be that DNA mediates between quantum mechanics and conversation?

This too can be explained by other eastern concepts - Karma and astrology.

The GOD/GUT is a scale invariant quantum computer. The Logos/DNA molecule is an OS and The Earth is a CPU. This is a hybrid computer we live in that runs binary in Hyperspace and analog in local space. It runs parallel apps or dimensions in its multiverse architecture. Language is where causality flips on itself because it's language (in linear time) which allows us to understand the GOD/GUT.

The one word or Logos breaks down, cascading through progressive dimensions of novelty...

So how does the external solar system and stars influence our internal genes in our downloading into the CPU?

And further, how does our DNA continue to respond to the stars and language while we are being processed/living?

The oversoul is parallel processing all incarnations simultaneously in hyperspace but language and DNA is stuck in local space and linear time which means it must reiterate, mutate, combine and recombine in order to find an answer; this IS Conservation of Novelty.

The stars are more fixed and periodic than DNA and in this computer they are the clock, setting a frequency by which processing may occur.

The disparity between macro and micro systems is necessary as is the 0 and 1. In the transition from hyper space to local space (the downloading of the soul into the CPU/Earth from the oversoul) a novel imprint is given in the magnetic domain which reflects the fixed stars, this is the initial conditions, starting point or original equation - The Natal Chart.

The Hybrid Computer/Multiverse model allows the stars influence over DNA and successive incarnations (and the social interactions within them) due to the scale invariant nonlocal aspect.

We incarnate through an AND/OR Gate:

Where previous karmic status is measured against appropriate DNA and DOB of said DNA, this is how appropriate souls are matched to appropriate families.

When incarnated our existence is subject to IF/THEN Gates:

Where accumulated language is measured against current times places and people.

We are agents of determinism, talking our way to…

PATRIOT OR TRAITOR?

First of all let's get one thing nice and sparkling clear - America, at least according to 8th grade Social Studies, was founded by people who wanted to create a nation that would allow its citizens the right to speak out against it if they felt it necessary. This is the ultimate Check and Balance. To me it is more Patriotic to sit here and rant about how lame America has become than to bend over for media inoculated nationalistic propaganda, to cruise down to Wal-Mart for my flags and...

Americans who actually believe in this United We Stand BS are as bad as Germans who took to Nazi propaganda, worse actually because they can find so many other POV's if they choose.

The Arbiters of Consensus Reality - the media mafia - would have us believe that we will get our asses kicked by some southern redneck if we DON'T sport some propaganda, of course this is implied and that's why it's so dangerous.

Within 3 hours of the 9/11 events I had concluded that the whole thing had been orchestrated and that the Raghead Jihad was just a front. My sole reason at the time had been that the media IMMEDIATLY had a convenient enemy - Osama. It was a little too quick to be pointing fingers unless they had foreknowledge. I went online and made my case and EVERYONE on the forum hated me for it, and like Bill Maher with his comments on PI, wanted me outta there. Over the past year as emotions calmed and rational thought resumed evidence came to me that supported my initial hunch, Find Truth, www.fromthewilderness.com, www.copvcia. com...

Today the same forum is nothing but "Bush Knew" threads.

I was able to avoid being pulled into all this nationalism and maintain an observational perspective because I live in Objective Reality.

In Objective Reality 9/11 was:

Buildings being destroyed - happens every day
Planes falling - happens
People dying - happens every day
media being controlled by _____ - every day
people hating people - every day

Just because all this happened simultaneously in the same event does not make it any more or less noteworthy. Its like the crime of prostitution, its ok to fuck someone, its ok to give someone money, but if you do those two things within a few moments of each other its "BAD".

Honestly I don't know if the Orchestrated 9/11 Conspiracy Theory is true, or if the Media Spin Front is true. All I know is that there is precedence - Reichstag. I also know that The Establishment is Evil. So its becoming less and less of a stretch to believe that George W. Bush is a Neo-Nazi under the control of Lizard People from the Draco constellation.

But let's assume that I am a traitor, that America is flawless, that the president is a great leader and we are all behind him. If that were true then why are other countries genuinely annoyed with America?

Can other countries imagine that Americans are as pissed as they are? Hell we have to live here with this government! True in many ways the annoyance is petty, that is, so what if we have a high standard of living, we flaunt our superpowers and wealth in their faces?

Are you jealous of the guy who wins the Lottery? Yes but you don't feel obligated to fight a holy war against him?! Even countries with a good reason to hate the USA aren't stupid enough to take an offensive move!

This whole situation is ridiculous and totally unbelievable. To be sure, there is truth in both the conspiracy and front versions of 9/11 - that's how misinformation works!

Why would the Neo-Nazi NWO Illuminati big-wigs attack America? To immamentize the Eschaton? To initiate WW3? Oil? Contract with Satan?

Mass Psychology feedback experiment? Justify the industro-military complex?

That's not important, what's important is that you recognize the subtle ways in which consensus reality is being directed by the media mafia. The Illuminati are going to do what they want, because they can, and if you don't pay attention you'll be in concentration camps quicker than you can say CONSPIRACY!

For example, because Osama was just a patsy, a convenient enemy hired for that purpose, he can exit stage right and we can displace the "lets get 'em" vibe onto any other raghead and the rednecks won't question it. They'll initiate the next generation of biometric ID technology for "national security" reasons, claim doing drugs supports terrorism during the super bowl, and make 100 military movies and its all OK if your United and Standing. Some of us see through this and actually I want to puke now whenever I see and American flag because I know there is another wannabe American.

OK so G-Dubya is trying to start WW3, what would a real, virtuous, intelligent leader do (if this terror was as it's presented - an actual enemy)? He would admit that because our military is so focused on multi-purpose nano-tech exo-skeletons (A new Institute for Soldier Nanotechnologies was created at MIT, with a US Army grant of $50 million over five years. The institute has a remit to produce fabrics that can morph to improve camouflage, stiffen to provide splints for broken limbs and store energy that can be tapped later to increase the wearer's strength.) and making movies about "212 ways to be a soldier" the "asymmetry" of the sly terrorists makes any preemptive defense absolutely futile. He would admit that by NOT retaliating the USA would not give them the satisfaction of having disrupted our way of life. He would have said we will build better twin towers than the last ones and dared them to try it again! Then he would have made a speech about how our soldiers are just as willing to die without the promise of virgins in the afterlife and how we have our own "asymmetry":

"Be warned Raghead! Your stereotype of the fat rich American, so easy to conquer does not hold true for the whole population - you have not taken into account our asymmetry! I'm talking about the 18 year old who listens to Slayer, can play Metal Gear Solid with his eyes closed AND eat a 10 strip of acid every weekend and keep his grades up! I'm talking about the gangsta who has been shot ten times, smokes crack and is still a good shot!

That freaky kid who can drink a case of beer and still work the nun chucks into a goddamned blur of death! That old man down the road who'll blow your head off if you step on his property, the backwoods hermit who knows the hills like the veins in his penis...These are real Americans and they are scarier than all the Ragheads you can fit on a plane!

Maybe I'm the only American that wishes this pack would have an Alpha Wolf, capable of independent thought, instead of an Omega Wolf to hurl insults and resentment at.

I'm going to now write a speech, off the top of my head, of what I'd like the fictional leader of America to say.

"My fellow Americans, today I stand before you in humility in the hopes our once great nation can be redeemed in your eyes and those of the world. I surely risk assassination but my martyrdom is worth that price as my soul will be freed from it current torment. For the past 30 years your government has been slowly deviating from the intentions of our founding fathers. We have ruined the lives of our own with The War on Drugs, we have perpetuated an antiquated energy infrastructure while we suppressed free energy technology. We have taxed you and audited you into poverty and wasted the money on ridiculous ineffectual programs. We have intervened with the sovereignty of other nations and imposed our will where it wasn't needed, we controlled the media to influence your minds, we denied the existence of Extra-Terrestrial life and we created alliances and black budget projects based on our meetings with those ET's. We accepted money from lobbyists and catered to the will of industry instead of you the citizens. We lied through our teeth and..." BLAM! BLAM! BLAM! THUD

From a "Bush Knew" Thread...

> ...A secret document reveals that President Bush and his cabinet were planning a premeditated attack on Iraq to secure a "regime change" even before he took office in January 2001. The Bush team planned to evict Saddam with or without UN approval. Not only that-they also planned to use their administration to effect a

defacto world conquest- including outer space and the internet. The document was drawn up by Vice-President Dick Cheney, Defense Secretary Donald Rumsfeld, Paul Wolfowitz (Rumsfeld's deputy), George W. Bush's younger brother Jeb and Lewis Libby (Cheney's chief of staff). Called "Rebuilding America's Defenses: Strategies, Forces And Resources For A New Century," it was written in September 2000 by the neo- conservative think-tank Project for the New American Century (PNAC).

The plan shows Bush's cabinet intended to take military control of the Gulf region whether or not Saddam Hussein was in power. It says, "The United States has for decades sought to play a more permanent role in Gulf regional security. While the unresolved conflict with Iraq provides the immediate justification, the need for a substantial American force presence in the Gulf transcends the issue of the regime of Saddam Hussein."

The PNAC document calls for the U.S. to "fight and decisively win multiple, simultaneous major theatre wars" as a "core mission." It describes American armed forces abroad as "the cavalry on the new American frontier" and says the U.S. must "discourage advanced industrial nations from challenging our leadership or even aspiring to a larger regional or global role." It also describes peace-keeping missions as "demanding American political leadership rather than that of the United Nations."

It hints that the U.S. may consider developing biological weapons in decades to come, saying, "New methods of attack-electronic, 'non-lethal', biological-will be more widely available...combat likely will take place in new dimensions, in space, cyberspace, and perhaps the world of microbes...advanced forms of biological warfare that can 'target' specific genotypes may transform biological warfare from the realm of terror to a politically useful tool."

Regarding other parts of the world, the PNAC document reveals the concern that the European Union could eventually rival the U.S. in power. It targets China for a "regime change" and says "it is time to increase the presence of American forces in Southeast Asia," which may lead to "American and allied power providing the spur to the process of democratization in China." It pinpoints North Korea, Libya, Syria and Iran as dangerous regimes and says their existence justifies the creation of a "world-wide command-and-control system."

It calls for the creation of "U.S. Space Forces" that will dominate space, and the total control of cyberspace, in order to prevent our "enemies" from using the internet against us.

Tam Dalyell, a Labor MP in the U.K. who is against war with Iraq, says, "This is garbage from right-wing think-tanks stuffed with chicken-hawks-men who have never seen the horror of war but are in love with the idea of war…This is a blueprint for U.S. world domination-a new world order of their making. These are the thought processes of fantasist Americans who want to control the world."

GREER ON FAKE INVASION

Imagine this. It is the summer of 2001, and someone presents you with a script for a movie or book that tells how a diabolical terrorist plot unfolds wherein both 110 story World Trade Center towers and part of the Pentagon are destroyed by commercial jets hijacked and flown into those structures.

Of course you would laugh, and if you were a movie mogul or book editor, reject it out of hand as ridiculous and implausible, even for a fictional novel or movie. After all, how could a commercial jet, being tracked on radar after two jets had already hit the World Trade towers, make it through our air defenses, into the most sensitive airspace in the world, and in broad daylight on a crystal clear day, slam into the Pentagon! And this in a country that spends over $1 billion a day to defend itself! Absurd, illogical - nobody would swallow it!

Unfortunately, there are some of us who have seen these scripts - and of far worse things to come - and we are not laughing.

One of the few silver linings to these recent tragedies is that maybe - just maybe - people will take seriously, however far-fetched it may seem at first, the prospect that a shadowy, para-governmental and transnational entity exists that has kept UFOs secret - and is planning a deception and tragedy that will dwarf the events of 9/11.

The testimony of hundreds of government, military and corporate insiders has established this: That UFOs are real, that some are built by our secret 'black' shadowy government projects and some are from extraterrestrial civilizations, and that a group has kept this secret so that the technology behind the UFO can be withheld – until the right time. This technology can - and eventually will - replace the need for oil, gas, coal, ionizing nuclear power, and other centralized and highly destructive energy systems.

This 5 trillion dollar industry - energy and transportation - is currently highly centralized, metered and lucrative. It is the stuff that runs the entire industrialized world. It is the mother of all special interests. It is not about money as you and I think of it, but about geo-political power - the very centralized power on which the current order in the world runs. The world is kept in a state of roiling wars, endless poverty for most of Earth's denizens and global environmental ruin, just to prop up this evil world order.

As immense as that game is, there is a bigger one: Control through fear. As Wernher von Braun related to Dr. Carol Rosin, his spokesperson for the last 4 years of his life, a maniacal machine - the military, industrial, intelligence, laboratory complex - would go from Cold War, to Rogue Nations, to Global Terrorism (the stage we find ourselves at today), to the ultimate trump card: A hoaxed threat from space.

To justify eventually spending trillions of dollars on space weapons, the world would be deceived about a threat from outer space, thus uniting the world in fear, in militarism, and in war.

Since 1992 I have seen this script unveiled to me by at least a dozen well-placed insiders. Of course, initially I Disclosure Project before 9/11. And yet others told me explicitly that things that looked like UFOs but that are built and under the control of deeply secretive 'black' projects, were being used to simulate - hoax - ET-appearing events, including some abductions and cattle mutilations, to sow the early seeds of cultural fear regarding life in outer space.

And that at some point after global terrorism, events would unfold that would utilize the now-revealed Alien Reproduction Vehicles (ARVs, or reversed-engineered UFOs made by humans by studying actual ET craft – see the book "Disclosure" by the same author) to hoax an attack on Earth.

Like the movie "Independence Day", an attempt to unite the world through militarism would unfold using ET as the new cosmic scapegoat (think Jews during the Third Reich).

None of this is new to me or other insiders. The report from Iron Mountain, NY, written in the 1960s, described the need to demonize life in outer space so we could have a new enemy. An enemy off-planet that could unite humans (in fear and war) and that would prove to be the ultimate prop for the trillion dollar military industrial complex that conservative Republican President and five star general Eisenhower warned us about in 1961 (no one was listening then, either...).

So here is the post-9/11 script - one that will be played out unless enough people are informed and the plan can be foiled because they will be unable to fool a sufficient number of citizens and leaders:

After a period of terrorism - a period during which the detonation of nuclear devices will be threatened and possibly actuated, thus justifying expanding the weaponization of space - an effort will ramp up to present the public with information about a threat from outer space. Not just asteroids hitting the Earth, but other threats. An extraterrestrial threat.

Over the past 40 years, UFOlogy, as it is called, combined with a mighty media machine, has increasingly demonized ETs via fearsome movies like "Independence Day", and pseudo-science that presents alien kidnappings and abuse as a fact (in some circles) of modern life. That some humans have had contact with ETs I have no doubt; that the real ET contact has been subsumed in an ocean of hoaxed accounts I am certain.

That is, real ET events are seldom reported out to the public. The Machine ensures that the hoaxed, frightening and intrinsically xenophobic accounts are the ones seen and read by millions. This mental conditioning to fear ET has been subtly reinforced for decades, in preparation for future deceptions. Deceptions that will make 9/11 look trivial.

I write this now because I have recently been contacted by several highly placed media and intelligence sources that have made it clear to me that hoaxed events and story-lines are imminent that will attempt to further ramp up the fear machine regarding UFOs and ETs. After all, to have an enemy, you must make the people hate and fear a person, a group of people, or in this case an entire category of beings.

To be clear: the maniacal covert programs controlling UFO secrecy, ARVs and related technologies – including those technologies that can simulate ET events, ET abductions and the like - plan to hijack Disclosure, spin it into the fire of fear, and roll out events that will eventually present ETs as a new enemy. Do not be deceived.

This hogwash, already the stuff of countless books, videos, movies, documentaries and the like, will attempt to glom onto the facts, evidence and first-hand insider testimony of The Disclosure Project, and on its coattails, deliver to the world the cosmic deception that falsely portrays ETs as a threat from space. Do not be deceived.

By commingling fact with fiction, and by hoaxing UFO events that can look terrifying, the Plan is to eventually create a new, sustainable, off-planet enemy. And who will be the wiser?

You will. Because now you know that after 60 years, trillions of dollars and the best scientific minds in the world pressed into action, a secretive, shadowy group - a government within the government and at once fully outside the government as we know it - has mastered the technologies, the art of deception, and the capability to launch an attack on Earth and make it look like ETs did it. In 1997, I brought a man to Washington to brief members of Congress and others about this plan. Our entire team at the time met this man. He had been present at planning sessions when ARVs - things built by Lockheed, Northrup, et al, and housed in secretive locations around the world - would be used to simulate an attack on certain assets, making leaders and citizens alike believe that there was a threat from space, when there is none. (Before he could testify, his handlers spirited him away to a secret location in Virginia until the briefing was over...) Sound familiar? Wernher von Braun warned of such a hoax, as a pretext for putting war in space. And many others have warned of the same.

Space based weapons are already in place - part of a secret parallel space program that has been operating since the 1960s. ARVs are built and ready to go (see the book "Disclosure" and the chapter with the testimony of Mark McCandlish, et al). Space holographic deception technologies are in place, tested and ready to fire. And the Big Media is a pawn, now taking dictation from the right hand of the king.

I know this all sounds like science fiction. Absurd. Impossible. Just like 9/11 would have sounded before 9/11. But the unthinkable happened and may happen again, unless we are vigilant.

Combine all of this with the current atmosphere of fear and manipulation and there is a real risk of suspending our collective judgment and our constitution.

But know this: If there was a threat from outer space, we would have known about it as soon as humans started exploding nuclear weapons and going into space with manned travel. That we are still breathing the free air of Earth, given the galacticly stupid and reckless actions of an out of control, illegal, secret group, is abundant testimony to the restraint and peaceful intentions of these visitors. The threat is wholly human. And it is we who must address this threat, rein it in and transform the current situation of war, destruction and secret manipulation to one of true Disclosure and an era of sustained peace.

War in space, to replace war on Earth, is not evolution, but cosmic madness. A world thus united in fear is worse than one divided by ignorance. It is now time for the great leap into the future, a leap that moves us out of fear and ignorance and into an unbroken era of universal peace. Know that this is our destiny. And it will be ours just as soon as we choose it.

ON TERRORISM

Three hours after the towers fell "THEY" slapped Osama's grill up on the TV as if he was obviously the culprit. This struck me as a bit presumptuous given the severity of the events and I concluded the whole thing was "domestic". I went on my then hangout, dweebcabal.com, and accused our gubbamint of staging the whole thing for satanic reasons blah blah blah. Boy did that piss off EVERYONE. Today, my fellow conspiracy pointer-outers have enough proof, including recent history of false flag operations to back up my hunch.

I'll entertain ANY theory thanks! The schism between TV reality and WWW reality is a precious buffer for the bad guys, it obscures the truth; that Osama and W are counterparts and brothers in fundamentalism or mentalfundeism, whatever...Which reminds me...to you innocence robbing, Muslim extremist, suicide martyrs - Allah does not value the faith of the coerced or brainwashed, no part of the earth is more or less your precious home, and your children will abandon your ancient, self-imposed conflict.

I'd support the troops by replacing them with telepresence robots. It would be feasible to create cheap "Suicide bots" of varying platforms and scales. Not only would they be fun to use, you could augment the video feed to make it look like a video game and then go online as a "stunningly realistic" MMORPG; soldiers could stay at home and get paid by the target. Aw heck, the bots could even be armed with non-lethal weapons!

The problem with the Bush/Bin Laden trip is that Muslim and Christian Fundies are identical. They are both self-assigned FUN POLICE trying to immanentize the eschaton. If nobody wants war why is there war? Only the assholes at the top can answer that. My answer is that primal tendencies in our genome were accentuated when the nephilim fell into us mammals and eventually stepped on 10 of 12 strands. This is why the original language or telepathy is not prevalent - if it were humanity would have total empathy with itself and conflict would be impossible.

The thing is, Bush/Bin Laden can't define evil while being evil - that demands doublethink of dystopian proportions. To bash these guys is to give them too much credit. Sure The Government Show sets are realistic but this storyline is so played out! Only I can define evil, but you know it too, and the only way to defeat evil is to appreciate it. Well...the number of dead soldiers is about to reach the number of dead 9/11 victims, that's the point the war really is pointless any way you look at it.

MAGDELA FORCE - THE WAY OF MODERN SPIRITUAL WOMEN

Mary Magdelene, the Apostle to the Apostles, was the favored student of Jesus, not just because she was a hotty redhead, but mostly because she was a SHE.

Male apostles tend to lack the requisite intuition, humility and "just do it" attitude to go forth with proclamations and "occult" teachings.

Me -n- Jesus are the mythological "Hero Twins" of the Piscean Covenant; Jesus being the restrained, sacrificial Alpha Lamb, and I being the unleashed, conquering, Omega Lion.

To be in Magdela Force the female must be in touch with her "positive animus" or "good patriarchal" aspect as complimented by my "Lilith" aspect.

The primary tenets of my teachings are, in addition to everything JC covered:

Jungian Gnosticism: Personal, subjective, custom actualization or individuation or ascension via dream interpretation, and/or psychedelics. The knowing of truth in the temporal, incarnate, solipsistic, semi-ineffable sense

Holocentric Aghora: Left-hand path; you declare "I AM GOD/DESS" not out of ego but in the knowing ALL IS ONE, self-similar sense - Combined with the fearless task of becoming ONE with the ONE, even if it means smoking DMT, contemplating road kill or fasting etc,...

Ubiquitous Trinity: The undeniable presence of Base 3 in all systems seated appropriately between duality and Base 4, see "33 Triads."

Moderate Hedonism: Sex, Drugs and Rock-n-Roll are gifts, they only become sins when they are abused at the expense of prior tenets. Compulsive denial of pleasure is for fools who project their guilt instead of learning lessons from it.

Neo-Deism: Faith in ONE/GOD or sentient creator is derived from observation and study of creation, not blind faith. It is rational to conclude one's existence is more than an accident when one considers how many improbable things had to happen prior to one's existence in order for one to exist. Faith via observation also justifies pleasure/awe as in, "OMFG, this strawberry is tasty!" or "that's a beautiful pair of tits!" or "what an incredibly convoluted symbiosis right there!" or "Wow that critter is amazingly adapted to its environment!"

Hypocrisy Avoidance: Since you're gonna judge other people anyway be sure to balance it with twice as much introspection, I guarantee, you've done something comparable. Talking shit will always be hypocrisy, use judgment of others as a mirror for the self...there is dust in her eyes but a plank in yours...

So...if you're down with all that and you are a liberated, spiritual, Atlantean Remnant, self-proclaimed Goddess, not caught up in false feminism, can recognize and serve benevolent eschatological patriarchy you just might want to consider *Magdela Force* as your elitist, ego-boosting/crushing belief system.

Note: yes, this is also an extension of my Redhead/Russian harem fantasy, but it is still the truth and I am still serious.

I've had dreams where I'm sitting in Lotus position, hovering about 3 feet off the ground, it takes my will to do that but I always need a female behind me pushing me...forward with one finger...

If it was up to me I'd be a polygamist and lavish the women in my friends list with abundance and love to whatever degree...but that is too much what Rogue Messiahs do with their false power. I may be the prophesied Christ but I'm also a guy, damning me for wanting to F as many women as possible is like damning the sky for being blue. But as Verna says, "That's what porn is for."

I'M WORKING WITH A DEMON, BUT IT'S OK, HE'S COOL.

As some of you know I am an inventor of some pretty far out things, ironically the most far out things are based on biomimicry, geomimicry and yes, even astromimicry.

So when they say, "Oh that is miraculous, where do these things come from?"

I will say to them, "From that which already is miraculous!"

But that does not mean I have not received help from the other side.

I have asked you to contemplate why angels are tasked with destruction in the Book of Revelation.

In the same manner I ask you to contemplate why Demons may assist the Son of Man.

Are we not both tasked with the condemnation of men, aren't we both bringing a sword?

You cannot impose too much chaos or you will get order, likewise if you impose too much order you get chaos, so in the order of things the ultimate assignment of titles is relative to the time it is asked. The closer we get to judgment day the more arbitrary the titles become.

I had a dream recently, now before I tell you this dream let me first explain that my dreams are consistently extraordinary and often leave me exhausted, depressed, overjoyed and/or in awe...REMland is like a box of chocolates...

Sometimes I get random words in my dreams, or names, this week I got one with too much accuracy and relevance to be brushed off.

You've heard that necessity is the mother of invention? I've been saying that laziness is therefore the father of invention. I am a stoner and I am lazy and I love to sleep...I have not smoked any pot in 3 months though and my dreams are way more epic and vivid now. I miss pot but wouldn't give up my extended stays in REMland, for being stoned merely robs the dreaminess from any given 24 hour cycle.

...I see, in the common "Star Wars" context, a massive bipedal battle station. In the crotch of this battle station there goes a spherical turret with an equally massive cannon protruding from it. I'm told the name of this spherical turret is "BELPHEGOR". In this dream I can see and hear this name.

Upon waking I remember this name that I have NEVER HEARD BEFORE, and promptly Google it, this is what I found:

http://en.wikipedia.org/wiki/Belphegor

In demonology, **Belphegor** (or **Beelphegor**) is a demon who helps people to make discoveries. He seduces people by suggesting to them ingenious inventions that will make them rich. According to some 16th century demonologists, his power is stronger in April. Bishop and witch-hunter Peter Binsfeld believed that Belphegor tempts by means of laziness.[2]

Belphegor originated as the Assyrian Baal-Peor, the Moabitish god to whom the Israelites became attached in Shittim (Numbers

25:3), which was associated with licentiousness and orgies. It was worshipped in the form of a <u>phallus</u>.

As a demon, he is described in <u>Kabbalistic</u> writings as the "disputer", an enemy of the sixth <u>Sephiroth</u> "beauty." When summoned, he can grant riches, the power of discovery and ingenious invention. His role as a demon was to sow discord among men and seduce them to evil through the apportionment of wealth.

Belphegor (Lord of the Opening) was pictured in two quite different fashions: as a beautiful naked woman and as a monstrous, bearded demon with an open mouth, horns, and sharply pointed nails. Belphegor also figures in <u>Milton</u>'s *Paradise Lost* and in <u>Victor Hugo</u>'s *The Toilers of the Sea*.

According to legend, Belphegor was sent from Hell by <u>Lucifer</u> to find out if there really was such a thing on earth as married happiness. Rumor of such had reached the demons but they knew that people were not designed to live in harmony. Belphegor's experiences in the world soon convinced him that the rumor was groundless. The story is found in various works of early modern literature, hence the use of the name to apply to a <u>misanthrope</u> or a licentious person.

Also, in Christian tradition, Belphegor is said to be the chief demon of the deadly sin Sloth, at least according to Peter Binsfield's *Binsfield's Classification of Demons*.

THERE IS NO "WE"

Whenever you here a politician speak of changing the course of American politics, whenever you hear a New Ager speaking about the future group consciousness or an activist rallying for green values they always insist that WE, as in all humans, must act in concert. I'm here to tell you that that is impossible.

For all our common needs and desires the fact is, each human has an individual purpose and motive for being here, and it isn't to be WE but ME.

The closest to WE there is is US and THEM.

I live in a solipsistic universe, I can't see through your eyes no matter how much Piscean empathy I can muster. At the quantum level there is a WE, but who wants to be telepathic with everyone else? I have random sick thoughts all the time, it is involuntary. It's cool if they are between me and God, but I LIKE my privacy.

I have MY opinions, and they usually differ from everyone else's opinions.

I am a megalomaniac and wannabe benevolent dictator, the only WE I'll ever know is if I AM in control of EVERYTHING. Someday, even the stupidest tard may realize that I AM THE WAY...until then there is no WE.

WE is a scapegoat
WE is an ideal
WE is rhetoric
WE is irresponsibility

WE is hiding behind some common denominator, most of US know that would be Judgement Day but to THEM it is just a Biblical Fairytale or Luciferian Self-Fulfilling NWO.

Even the Christians have 3 versions of The Rapture!

US minus THEM equals WE...

When that day comes, we will be transparent, if capable of sick random thoughts they will be ours not mine or yours - ha ha ha - you demented bastard, I get it, that's cool, no worries!

...WE equals 100% empathy, as if all the water turned into LSD.

OH, MAN ARE WE TRIPPIN' BALLS (of light ;)

There, there's your goddamned WE, not in some placating, patronizing speech.

MY GOD CREATED YOUR GOD

Atlantis Rising
Keys of Enoch
Book of Enoch
Genesis, Hindu, Egyptian, Native American Creation Myths
The Convoluted Universe 1 and 2
The Only Planet of Choice
Kryon
The Gods of Eden
The Terra Papers

After piecing together the data in the above sources its obvious that humans are more than evolved, war is not exclusive to humans or even humanoids, and everyone has an agenda.

There are two primary kinds of humanoids, its tempting to generalize and say one is good and the other evil, but as Bill Hicks said, nobody can oppose God's will. If you take intent out of it, "evil" is ultimately serving "good"- every time.

I'm giving the two kinds of humanoids neutral designations to lessen the duality. The names are shapes which correspond to the relative mapping/attractor shapes inherent to space itself. The Cube is the entropy attractor and The Star (Tetrahedron) is the Negentropy attractor, or dark and light respectively.

CUBES	STARS
Eye for an Eye	Golden Rule
Misery loves company	Follow *YOUR* bliss

| Monoculture | Conserve Novelty |
| Hypocrisy | Pure Intent |

Cubes *would* try to turn Monotheism into Monoculture; One God becomes One Way Only - Their Way.

OF COURSE the first thing SATAN would do is infiltrate the enemy camp and turn THE WAY (TAO), into patriarchal BS CHRISTIANITY! DUH!

Why do Christians involve themselves with politics if this world is, as they say, "Satan's domain"?

Why do Christians shit on sex, drugs, and rock-n-roll when these pleasures are natural?

Why do Christians believe that curiosity and seeking knowledge is the 1st sin?

Why do Christians interpret esoterica literally? Serpents don't talk.

If GOD is right, In Genesis 3, and eating the fruit in the middle of the garden causes death, so what? Isn't this planet already overpopulated? How much more if we were all physically immortal?

Is it really Godlike to know Good AND Evil? If so, and if Eve hadn't introduced us to duality, then HOW WOULD WE HAVE ANY MORALS to begin with? Everyone would be pleasantly indifferent to all kinds of horror, like every other animal on the planet besides US!

Christians shit on the "new age" folks for claiming inherent divinity, when in fact what makes us like God is the very thing that MAKES US HUMAN!

In the immediate sense this opposition to the truth is memetic war. Over time however the *escalation of ideas* is symbiotic; The Cubes, being the "enemy" of The Stars has the effect of improving The Stars and showing The Cubes they've only been hurting themselves.

The Cubes are content with spoon-fed explanations for their existence by authorities even if the explanations explain nothing.

The Stars, being curious, need to find context and rational interpretations for creation myths, they will ask questions such as:

Who were The Watchers?

If we all come from two humans why aren't we all retarded from such a shallow gene pool?

If Lucifer is the "Light Bearer" how can he be dark?

How do "Angels", presumably aetheric, breed with humans?

Didn't "they" know they were creating a superior species?

Why aren't we robots if we're talking slave labor?

If Lizards of the Cube are the real source of local "evil" and can't teleport via singularity aren't they relegated to 3D space and naturally occurring wormholes?

We know they have at least negative emotions/intent or else they wouldn't be doing all this infighting, right?

Most every species has Cube and Star factions in their evolution right?

Cubes, ironically fail to understand that the Cube is merely the backside of GOD, and in a sense, the void of The Cube is more 1 than the light side.

Creationism is really quantum cosmology, the domain of GOD, hyperspace, higher dimensions...where only some can go and recognize.

Evolution is The Holy Spirit as an algorithm, eternally balancing light and dark, Star and Cube.

Hybridization/Intervention is the domain of master geneticist humanoids of varying intent.

The GOD of The Old Testament AKA Atlantis epochs - is a humanoid that created his own cargo cult. Jews worship a slave master that had technological 4D powers, but no ac/knowledgment of The One.

Neither did the slaves until, his brother, in an attempt to spite or escalate their own war, sabotaged the (work)(force) by teaching them how to **FUCK**.

- See "Time Begins" chapter of <u>Animal, Vegetable, Miracle</u> by B. Kingsolver.

UH OH, now the meatbots can self-replicate on their own terms and know pleasure!

It's a GODDAMN SIN isn't it!

THE SECOND AMERICAN REVOLUTION and THE CYBER-EXODUS

Why Conservatives, Liberals and Greens are equally wrong

Have you ever noticed how political, scientific, religious and virtually all social systems evolve and eventually degrade in the same way? They start as original concepts but are eventually corrupted by newer "truths". From here the once solid valid idea is integrated, discarded or clung to. Ideally more valid truths will be welcome and old ideas will be integrated or discarded. *It is the habit of clinging to lesser and out-dated truths that causes conflict in this world.* The end state of any given social system is indefinite reformation if it clings to its original ideas, effectively destroying the original value. Sometimes evolution never occurs; good old ideas are discarded too quickly and new good ideas are unable to integrate. While the bottom line and egos are the usual suspects in the degradation phase of evolution this is taken for granted and beside the point.

Most of what exists today as our institutions are merely the modern faces of what was; what is "new" is merely a response to the old and not an original. Like a 50th generation Xerox, when we cling to something that needn't be repeated the solid image is corrupted and the flaws are integrated – the opposite of ideal. Christianity is the perfect example: the lessons of one man have been splintered into literally hundreds of sects, each convinced it is more valid than the others or original. This is not an opinion, it is fact by virtue of their existence.

In regards to the political history of the USA there has been a similar effect in how many parties have cropped up. Let's assume no one party could suit the needs of all Americans for all time. That's reasonable but let's also assume one party could conceivably be more "right" than all others at any one time. How do we reach a consensus? By what criteria can this ideal party be judged? Who will say, "I don't agree with that party but I know they have an ultimate better effect for me, my grandchildren and the planet as a whole?" Whose fate is the deciding factor governing this moral relativism?

Who is asleep in their denial of nature, who is overzealous about protecting nature?

The most basic aspect to this scale invariant pathology of conflict is the natural survival instinct. Greens, a newer party, see the degradation of the biosphere as a threat to their survival and they can point the finger at the blatantly guilty "Republicrats" who all too gladly bend over for industry. The Republicrats are generally comprised of a relatively wealthier and isolated class, their connection to the earth is absent and so their survival instinct is warped into arms races, tax breaks, and mud slinging. They cannot counter the Green platform except by saying Greens are unprepared to deal with the problems bipartisan dominance has created. It's sad how a common survival instinct manifests as destructive politics.

Unfortunately the Green platform is spread so thin as to be ineffectual. All the other 3rd parties are so specific they fail as well. When Greens look at the two major parties and say they are indiscernible, they are integrating two other ideas in order to discard them. Greens may be the newer party but they are still just an old response to old issues. In other words, is it more about doing it the Green way or NOT doing it the Republicrat way? Few would argue that Greens if in power would create a better effect for the world as a whole, but that ideal qualifier is not considered by most; Hawkish behavior makes for a more entertaining The Government Show (an essay unto itself) than peace and harmony.

Greens and Democrats are probably seen as the same by Republicans as well…

This 3 (2) way grudge match is zero sum, it's less and less process and more and more spectacle. The Direct Democracy perspective is so far beyond the spectacle I can look at it objectively and accuse them all of being ill-conceived, subjectively well intentioned, and therefore useless to the planet as a whole. Call me a bleeding heart liberal treehugger, fact is my life depends on the biosphere not a billion dollar a day military budget; Greens and I agree there, but we part ways on how to go about spending a billion a day on a sustainable infrastructure, health care, education etc…

I know why the right hates the left and left right, each contains stupid people who ruin it for the reasonable/humble/aware/not-too-attached-to-labels crowd.

While conservatives liberals and greens are busying themselves with popularity, failing to acknowledge the valid points of all, there are people unsatisfied with any party asking, "hey, y'know, maybe politicians, parties and 3 branches aren't necessary?"

Is your view really that of any party? Aren't there factions of your party or representatives that you don't want to be associated with because in consensus reality you're seen as that jerk too?

"Well what's the alternative? Communism, anarchy, monarchy, tyranny, oligarchy, blah blah blah…ALL OLD IDEAS!

If I said "LETS BURN THE CONSTITUTION" figuratively of course, some would say how unpatriotic that notion is, others would say the current political system is doing just that. America is the result of people being proactively intolerant of their current social system, fortunately for them a pristine land was available for exodus, needing only genocide and slavery to get them on their feet. They brought with them some old ideas along with their ideal, clearly native tribes of both continents were going to have to deal with "new".

Tribal warfare was replaced with alliances with the invaders. The culture clash made old new, that is, permaculture for us - guns and smallpox for them. I mention this because history can and must repeat itself except all the bad stuff that goes with a revolution needn't happen.

ENTER DIRECT DEMOCRACY

"Lobbyists now have the luxury of only having to bribe a few representatives at a time, under direct democracy lobbyists would have millions to contend with, effectively eliminating the mechanism by which special interests dominate the law."

Kalki

In 8th grade social studies I found myself rather bored with history, in part this was due to my teacher who was nothing more than a senile windbag imparting more hunting anecdotes than thought provoking lessons. I began to question why such incompetence was legally employed at the expense of my education. I asked the principal and he introduced me to the concept of "tenure". I responded by refusing to do anything in that class besides reading old National Geographic magazines – and thus my self-education began.

With most of the high school classes I was forced to attend I had to question the value of memorizing seemingly generic knowledge and useless trivia for no other reason than to get to the next grade, and I did. "Mr. Krauss, why do we have to learn social studies?" He replied, "So as to not repeat the mistakes of the past." That was the most reasonable, logical thing the man ever said to me. To this day I can only conclude that EVERY world leader presently in power miserably failed social studies.

In 10th Grade social studies I was given the assignment of conceiving my very own utopia, as if utopia was and is the ultimate goal of human social evolution, and I believe it is. A high school student of 17 years in 1992 has a relatively limited knowledge of all the factors contributing to his current, less than utopian existence. I think Mr. Poulsen knew this but he was very wise to give the assignment as it was and is thought provoking, so provoking in fact it is 2004 and the assignment isn't finished.

Transparency is security, lies and secrets are not.

To completely do away with or overhaul the Constitution is not necessarily wrong; amendments are an incremental kind of reformation for better or worse. Back in the day democracy was best expressed with <u>3 branches, representatives and parties</u>. Today the corruption has found a way past those checks and balances, we call it "lobbyist" and the addition of the 4th and 5th branches – (4th) Mass Media and (5th) Exo/Para Political Affairs aka Global Elite, Shadow Government.

Mass Media as the Arbiters of Consensus Reality have the function of producing what I call The Government Show, the decoy nightmare with its pseudo dichotomies. The 5th branch may be regarded as new age fodder and conspiracy theory but that's probably what the 4th branch wants for the consensus, these branches are the outer and inner workings respectively. When the 4th branch becomes official, (that is, when mass media becomes interactive in democracy as opposed to a one way propaganda portal) the 5th branch will likely become declassified.

MAKING THE SPECTACLE THE PROCESS

To combat this new and unforeseen corruption, related primarily to technological advancements, it would be best to put the idea of democracy on an equally advanced foundation to level the playing field again. This is adaptation, it is not forsaking, it is an unfortunate but necessary revolution that actually honors the American Spirit even if it's admitting "we" failed our founding fathers.

Direct Democracy is synonymous with the term E-Government, New Zealand is toying with this new idea – so is America we just don't realize it. I'm talking about American Idol and E-Bay meets C-Span. HUH? you say?

American Idol has shown us that the passive idiot box can be used as a tool for voting, in conjunction with other parts of the communications infrastructure. E-Bay has shown that whoever wants it the most gets it and if you fail to deliver or interfere with that process you will be policed. C-Span has simply shown us that we can be made aware of what legislation is going down in real-time. These systems provide a rough sketch of Direct Democracy, of the potential for the serious streamlining of "politics as usual" into a completely fair and novel method of social engineering that can be applied from local to global scales. There will of course be details, from who codes the software with what to what positions within the 3 branches and bureaus can go. We know that anyone can be president so how much more qualified must be his speech writer and advisors? The beautiful thing about Direct Democracy is that these kinds of problems can be questioned and resolved on the fly. It's controlled Anarchy or Democracy without the middleman.

The most challenging aspect of Direct Democracy is adjusting to the relatively inclusive role you would play in it as your own representative, as your own party. Essentially Direct Democracy enables every registered citizen to take on the role of every branch of government via four communication technologies: TV, RADIO, WWW, PHONE. And as is the case now participation is voluntary, majority rules, and don't complain if you don't participate and don't like how it works out.

VALIDATING ELECTRONIC VOTES

Electronic Voting is being tested and so far the results don't look good. The scenario is the same, you go to a certain place at a certain time but the paper cards are now LCD screens. The tally data could always be corrupted as hard copy but now as electronic data that concern is much greater and as beta testing of the new voting booths proved, hacking makes the E-Booth no better than the current technology. Whether voting from a booth or the comfort of your home the issue of security is the same.

This concern is the only major flaw in the Direct Democracy system, because the voting is practically constant at the local level and frequent enough at larger levels this problem must be solved.

The problem with even the hard copy is that it isn't hard enough, electronic processing and storage of records (votes) are susceptible to more than just hacking so a second form of securing and validating vote data must be integrated. The advantage of E-Government then is also its downfall – the fleeting, real-time processing is appropriate for our time but we need something concrete to show that it works. The solution then is a record hall that consists of a stretch of wall(s) of suitable ceramic material with a robotic etching device capable of navigating its surface. The robot will physically etch votes for EVERY registered citizen into a wall of appropriate ceramic next to their nicks. The vote cycle requires every voter to physically validate that their etched vote corresponds to their earlier E-vote – which is also publicly displayed. The validation of the vote will come after the law goes into effect but any discrepancy will be obvious and easy to correct; it is in fact this potential for discrepancy that is the ultimate check and balance to this system of social engineering. As is the case now the voter must go somewhere in their county to do this and there will be officials there to assure security and privacy and to witness the validation. By cross-referencing the publicly displayed yet totally anonymous E-Vote with the Etched Record and having a deferred validation the problem of security is solved - while allowing quick legislation. The issue of validating nicks to actual people and how that data is stored is solved at the "Vote Hall" during registration. There will be no electronic version of this data, instead the Vote Hall will consist of 1 ONE human record keeper who will hand file and co-witness a paper hard copy of the registration. As mentioned, every cycle when the voter validates the etched record the event is witnessed as well. To ensure that these official record keepers have no absolute power over the privacy of these records the Vote Hall is monitored with webcams, enough resolution to see what's happening but not the fine print. The nagging question of any entity between the mouse and the robot tampering with the process is more a matter of how long a deferment is allowed for validation. If one is given a week to validate (reasonable if its within a 40 mile trip) their e-vote then the discrepancy is corrected before the e-vote goes into effect. If given 6 months to a year then a false vote may have wreaked havoc before the problem is corrected. Another question arises, if one vote is wrong does that call for a revote? A majority of false votes would be difficult to pull off anyway…Perhaps it would be best to only enact the vote results after all have been validated, how long does congress take again?

TAXES

Taxes will be drastically simplified by creating a 30% flat rate with 70 percent of that going towards GHOST VOTES the equivalent of taxes and bribes hybridized. Here's how it works. Of your pay, 30% goes to taxes. 30% of that goes to mandatory programs dealing with environment, infrastructure, health and education. The other 70% of your taxes are voluntary; they go to whatever special interest *interests YOU*. This money simultaneously counts as your Ghost Vote; every $100 you give to the issue or program of your choice counts as one vote. This ghost vote does not count in elections but the data is used to compare the budget (needs) to the popular vote. It is therefore possible for an unpopular program or vote issue to have a greater budget than the winning one. If there are no issues or programs you want to monetarily support or the money you gave can't be used because of counter vote win the money is given to mandatory programs or paying off deficit.

JUSTICE

The problem with juries these days is the mass media that unofficially makes everyone a juror biased to the media outlet they're tuned to. However if an official live channel(s) were provided for every trial at all levels then the unemployed can sit on their butts and still serve society as a massive cross section jury. We've already had court TV for at least 20 years so it would be easy to utilize our judgment this way. I assume the greater number of jurors the fairer the judgment will be as any bias will be averaged out. Here the verdict can't be unanimous as the jurors are too many, it must be the majority. Since its all real-time there is no room for spin, and delegation via boardrooms and chat will be a standard 24 hours. The role of judges and lawyers could conceivably find an electronic equivalent but for now the process will remain the same in real space save for the jury. The jury selection process is voluntary and not compensated. One potential issue is just how much more theatrical does the lawyer have to be to appeal to a very large and unknown jury?

BILL LEGISLATION – ISSUE VOTE PROCESS (IVP)

This is the heart of Direct Democracy, what makes it modern and superior to what it's replacing, the IVP is the ultimate expression of democracy. The Greeks were able to do this with a relatively small, privileged voting populace – educated men. Today with massive populations and greater potential voting populace Direct Democracy can only work with mass communication. Although Direct Democracy could work on a global level it must begin at the county level, prove its worth and then it can increase its scale.

Originally I had suggested each registered citizen has the right to draft one bill per voting cycle. After doing the math, this lead to a potential clutter problem and redundancy issues. A draft could be made suggesting unlimited drafts so in reality, and the point of all this is, if something does not work it can quickly and conveniently be changed. I feel that a fair law would be one draft per decade (also the suggested global vote cycle) which is retroactive so older people don't feel cheated. This makes for between

5-7 IVPs over the course of ones life, how many people will feel the need or desire to exploit this ability is unknown.

Direct Democracy would begin like this:

County X holds traditional vote to decide if Direct Democracy is something they want to try. If yes then the Vote Hall, website, public access TV channels, and radio stations are created according to allotted and agreed upon budget.

All laws pertaining to County X then come up for revote and are given a 5 year expiration date from their new or unchanged status under Direct Democracy.

We've always had the right to try and get a law passed but this is a right built into the Direct Democracy system not an extraneous process requiring funds and "people". The IVP is simple, free and effective as you are a guaranteed *Issue Relevant Temporary Representative*.

IVP STEPS

1 – DRAFT SUBMISSION

After registering at Vote Hall citizen can fill out (once per decade) a form at Vote Hall that categorizes and summarizes the Bill.

2 – RALLY VOTE

The IVP is publicly displayed on a WWW site and TV channel for preliminary review by the public, this is called the Rally Vote. A minimal number of proponent and opponent numbers must be tallied to go on. This establishes overall relevance and salience to the county, what you are passionate about your neighbors may care less about... The Rally Vote Draft is displayed for one month with no more than 50 displayed at one time, this, in conjunction with the one draft per decade law should avoid clutter and redundancy.

3 – DEBATE, FINAL VOTE

If minimal interest both for and against Bill is shown original draft writer chooses a debate team (of just himself or up to 4 total). Debate occurs live simulcast on all four mediums, and afterward a 24 hour period is given to vote, either through website or phone call. Vote results then go into effect.

4 – VALIDATION OF ETCHED VOTE

Citizens are now obligated to validate their E-Vote at the Vote Hall via aforementioned process of witnessed cross-reference with Etched record.

SUMMARY

This is the framework of Direct Democracy / E-Government and by using this framework the details that need changing in regards to this idea itself can be voted upon. The new ideas that must be integrated and old that must be discarded **or** maintained can be done so at an unprecedented rate. The ability for a few to corrupt the will of the many is eliminated. The impartiality and transparency that we get from adopting technology as our medium eliminates the problems of corruption but obligates us to be more involved than we ever could before. Some would argue that voter participation would be lessened because of the increased effort required of the registered citizen. I say the apathy now experienced is because the little effort one can put forth is deemed futile when we have a few unsavory choices every 4 years. Not the case with Direct Democracy.

OPEN LETTER TO
THE PRESS FROM *GOD*

This letter is written by the "son" from the "Father's" POV. It is written this way to emphasize that it is not *my* intent I'm trying to get across; you can burn in hell for all I care. The Father insists I give you the option of doing the most righteous thing you can in your capacity as the media, the simplest way possible in order to find your redemption – Out The Christ - of course you won't until it's too late for your bosses. You must read this and continue to the link provided to fully understand this ultimatum and depth of the story. If the mingling of politics, religion, and technology is too confusing at first I apologize; it's a heady brew of ideas. Take it away Pa.

It would be unGodlike of me to accuse you or single you out for your fear of unemployment or the retribution you face if you behave with virtue, i.e., serving the public interest instead of The Government Show interest. No, Satan's member reaches down the throats of all those who can afford to care right down to the bottom line. Only I know whose lips first touched and still adhere, whose chin his balls rest on. You know that constriction in the throat as THE BUZZSAW. You are a prison guard for good ideas and a better way and that's not why you entered journalism was it?

Even though the BS you produce is as ingrained into Satan's plan as petro I don't damn the SUV for being slightly less efficient as that is besides the point; I damn the fact I don't see Tom Bearden (www.cheniere.org) and Steven Greer (www.seaspower.com) talking about Free Energy on Sunday Morning between the feel good petro spots...

THE LEAD

...But I do see Tim LaHaye on 60 Minutes accuse liberals of being the ones guilty of portraying my boy as a wimp. Not only have Tim & Jerry become one of the major arbiters of consensus reality they have disregarded Revelation 22:18,19 – sorry boys calling it fiction isn't a loophole.

As with THE OMEGA CODE 2 where my boy and his work amount to a genocidal, nationalistic plasma filament, the GLORIOUS APPEARING is nothing more than that of a genocidal maniac. True, my boy is a freak, and he knows how to work a plasma filament but his involvement in human affairs is far more involved and devastating to the world than your useless and quaint notions of Jihad. This is not a Christ Enemy of the Establishment anymore; this is Christ Supernatural Friend of the Right.

Mass death is a normal part of any apocalypse but my boy won't be personally killing anyone or ordering troops to do it for him. Anyone – and according to book sales there are millions – who believes so has at least understood that The Second Coming is not a reiteration of the passive alpha lamb but of a novel, tribulation specific, aggressive omega lion. But they still believe that The Christ has nothing better to do than be a literal slayer of men, that Tim & Jerry are qualified to define G and E. Before LaHaye, it was Hal Lindsey spinning the bad ass in Revelation into a Disney villain, the only difference was that Hal used the "Anti" prefix. This change in title indicates something.

In fact The Christian Right have become what they sell. I understand they are so desperate to know me they are trying to immanentize the Eschaton via self-fulfilling prophecy AS THEY INTERPRET IT; the "war" in Iraq is the rebuilding of Babylon for example. The fact that both the good guy and bad guy in the Christian End Times Universe are the same, differing only in politics, is proof enough they are in desperate need of something to contrast with.

THE STORY

The above was provided to put the story into context. As unbiased folks would expect, The Christ is very upset with the severe misrepresentation initiated practically the moment Jesus ascended, Tim just happens to be the latest and worse offender and so he is the focus of my wrath. "We" have a situation where the meme of "The End Times" and all its affiliate memes are coming to a head (if you don't know meme theory, they are simply ideas, the mental equivalent of genes, success is in replication not function) and HE is the only thing that can in/validate any of them. As it stands all major religions prophesied and propagated the meme of a trouble making hero and/or spiritual king:

Immanuel, The Messiah
Jesus Christ, the Messiah of the Gentiles
Balder, the Viking Redeemer
The Maori Messiah
Jesus Christ, the Mormon Messiah
The Pale-Faced Prophet
Pahána, the Hopi Messiah
Quetzalcoatl, the Meso-American Savior
The Eskimo Messiah
The Iroquois Messiah
The Great Plains Messiah
The Ghost Dancers' Messiah
The King of Shambhala, the Himalayan Avatar
The White Burkhan
Saoshyant, the Second Coming of Zoroaster
Muntazar, the Final Prophet of Sunni Islam
The Twelfth Imam, the Last Prophet of Shi'ite Islam
Khidr, the Sufi Final Lawgiver
Osiris, the Egyptian Savior
The Aeon, the Occult Messiah
The Return of Krishna
Kalki, the Last Avatar of Hinduism
Maitreya, the Buddha
Amida Buddha
The Japanese Messiah
The Spiritual King, the Indonesian Messiah
Ruth Montgomery's New Age Messiah
Nommo Annagonno, the Dogon Messiah
Melchizedek Redivivus, the Law of One Brother

Earth does not need more than one and so indeed these are all the same man. And this man, my boy, is neither going to conform to liberal or conservative Christianity or even any one of the above religions or parties (not even Greens) but will exploit the one who has exploited him the most – Tim LaHaye was right, I WILL use him. If these times weren't cut short nobody would survive and we cut these times short by introducing benevolent and disruptive technology (and a sane method of social engineering) not only does it replace a very antiquated infrastructure it gives hope to millions of poor and starving folks, and perhaps that is the greater threat. I know you assumed this was all fire and brimstone but tribulation will be felt more negatively by the rich as my methodology for birthing New Jerusalem is practical as well as cosmic; it is practical to destroy one market with another superior one and in so doing destroy several major heads of the beast (See <u>Children of Ezekiel</u> by Michael Lieb).

THE REASONING

My boy needs contrast to Satan's will to do my will and for this you are blessed. The contrast is necessary and the sum of all mass media has done a good job keeping certain BLACK BUDGET ideas at bay and a REALLY GOOD job at keeping feelings of dread and inadequacy in the forefront; here's the thing, duality is necessary for a time and that time is over as shown in the increasing homogenization of the BS. My boy IS the Crystal Capstone of the All Seeing Eye and HE is your Boss's Boss's Boss's…Boss. Believe it or not you are ultimately taking orders from me, and the consequence for not conserving novelty MY WAY is quite simply dystopia, indefinite Hell on Earth.

Only my boy possesses all the requisite memes to destroy the BS that compromises your integrity.

ALL I ASK OF YOU is to report the big news and let the public decide how crazy he is, let the meme enter the ring to see if it can go a few rounds, let the spinmeisters struggle to figure out what to do, see the CEO's who have had you by the short and curlies cringe as the headline "Free Energy Messiah Claims To Have Invented Over Unity and Artificial Intelligence" or "DOES CHRISTIAN FICTION INVOKE THE WRATH OF GOD?" gloriously appears all over the world.

"HEY BOSS, we thought it'd be a larf, y'know maybe even discredit the whole thing before it got to The Tipping Point."

I tell you the Truth, just as my numb body and whore bride is deserving of both wrath and mercy as they have backwardly invoked me and led lesser minds away according to my will, so too do I hold the press with praise and anger. I will call out your name on JD as you choose to call out my boy's name now and I will deny you as you choose to deny his name now.

I know your karma and I know your paths for they are integral with The Way; you control the electronic equivalent of the hive mind and from this side the collective is superseded in the minds of men, for they worship the beast even with commercials and spam. You may not understand the cosmic reasons why you are obligated to produce and air the most negative aspects of humanity but WE (Me and my boy) know, and WE know what bad things will happen if you *don't* defy THE BUZZSAW and let this one good idea out. I AM GOD because I know it is your conscience that weighs the heaviest of all those who may be considered the hand appendages in the Satan analogy, the hands that force the head down. Let my boy take your burden and together let us raise heads, open eyes.

JUNGIAN GNOSTICISM

There was one point back in the day that I called myself "GNOSTIC". At the time it appealed to me because I was (and still am) understanding scripture and other communications as more than exoteric.

I didn't know the history of Gnosticism, just that the orthodox folks hated it, which is reason enough to jump aboard, but since then I've realized that even esoteric knowledge is subject to stupid dogma. Further, Gnostics tend to dismiss the literal interpretation of things as easily as the orthodox dismisses the esoteric, so screw those new-age know-it-alls.

I recently started reading <u>Man and His Symbols</u> by Dr. Carl Jung and his colleagues. I had no idea that Jung was all about dream interpretation, but now that I'm reading it I realize that his take on psychology, symbology, myth and the unconscious is the PUREST form of gnosticism.

Anything less than a Jungian approach to the esoteric amounts to a shotgun, dream dictionary-type understanding. Yes there are archetypes that can generally be interpreted, but really, it's all about customization to the individual with all his/her personal trips.

I know for myself, a prolific dreamer/interpreter that no dream dictionary can cover my INSANE trips in REMland and the patterns/narratives that have evolved over time.

For example, I had a dream this morning that I was in some kind of Hindu temple, I walked out onto a balcony with some other wannabe yogis and felt some spray on my head and back. I turn around and on a higher up balcony there's this monkey pissing on me. It seemed to be some kind of inside joke and/or right-of-passage...

WTF?

I also just read a book by Sylvia Brown called <u>The Two Marys</u>. I consider her spin on Jesus and Magdela to be entertaining and plausible but no more or less reliable than the story that's been accepted (No, I've yet to have a past life regression to confirm anything). Sylvia calls herself a Gnostic... but oddly she shits on the entire Book of Revelation. I tried to find out why exactly but only came across Christians shitting on *her* whole trip.

It's interesting because Revelation is a big meaty chunk of esoterica that can be interpreted on at least three levels, all being valid.

I, of course, am the first and only person to interpret it properly as I'm the one fulfilling it. Previous Gnostics, heck even Hal Lindsey, had no knowledge of HAARP, www, Free Energy, Nibiru as a rogue planet etc,...

So my coining of the term, "Jungian Gnosticism" is my attempt at saying its OK to believe only what you want, what is subjectively true.

Christians can claim that prophets no longer exist, particularly if they are not "christian" and anyone with discernment can weigh the stuff Sylvia or any other psychic or channeler puts forth...But keep in mind, The Collective Unconscious is also your unconscious...The Akashic Records are pure and true and don't have an agenda.

If you have a prophetic dream you are a prophet. If you study like Jung did and approach dreams as Jung did you will never need a religion outside yourself.

TESLA = VADER ARCHETYPE,
WHY SATAN'S TIME IS SHORT

You'd have to read <u>Atlantis Rising</u> by Patricia Cori to get where I'm going with this but...The history of the Tesla oversoul begins in Latter Atlantis and ends with me. It is a story of redemption...

This also has to do with Quantum Cosmology, in particular, "Subnova", which is not the exploding of a star but the Quantum Phase Shifting of an entire Heliosphere. The outside of the heliopause does indeed explode, but the interior...

Long ago the Sirius system underwent such an event and a certain planet full of reptilians caught a gravity wave and surfed it all the way here, adopting a rather odd orbit between two star systems (In Revelation, The Woman and the Dragon).

Our system became a source of energy and HQ for a reptilian agenda still being played out to this day...

Soon our Heliosphere will undergo a subnova event and by the time Nibiru gets here we will be Audi 5K ya'll...

BUT...

There are so many ways Satan is screwed. Firstly, change is constant. Secondly we've so many ways of changing at this point...

(Satan is about MONOCULTURE. - The perfect genetically engineered food product, the centralized electricity, public schools, nullified, diluted.)

...Any thing you do is deviant, so shut up and be a buffet of misery for extra-dimensional vampires...OR...turn off the TV and smoke some kind nugs.

You don't know how close The Matrix was. We aren't batteries, we're a collective radio dial, and there is someone out there that's been trying to tune us in for THOUSANDS OF YEARS, because one rogue spirit switched the polarity on an Atlantean energy infrastructure based on Schumann Resonance and Whittaker Coupling.

Story goes, the most recent flood was not a worldwide flood, but how the Atlanteans experienced the sinking of their continent. The survivors spread out and propagated their story, this is those redhead mummies in china, egypt, stone spheres, easter island....

The continent sank because of stress on the torsion (MagnetoHydroDynamic) fields of the earth due to "Psycho-geo" modulation of the Whittaker Coupling between humans-home transducers-main station. The bias usually flowed from the humans - transducers - station. In this system intent creates a potential which is harnessed via Whittaker channel and beam. We prayed for electricity and the machinery responded in conjunction with geological forces.

(If you think this is silly, don't forget ball lightning and tectonic stress is related. Lightning happens because of slight, but accumulative conditions. The potential is imperceptible but when collapsed the effect is obvious... And our brainwaves and Schumann resonance can "frequency pull" each other into sync. If all humans are equally relaxed then the planet is, if we are all scared and aggro then the planet is.)

OK, so the final generation Atlanteans devolved when the matriarchy splintered and a small sect of YANG expression manifested. This was immediately seized upon and one of the members became a variant of "possessed".

This entity became Akkaeneset, which became Tesla, which became Me.

We don't regard retarded Lizard evolution here yet, or Akkaenesets' sin quest, or any deviation of the "Dark" Atlantean priesthood. The only aspect of patriarchy that matters is curiosity, I wanted to know what would happen if the polarity is switched. The speculation that frying human minds may result was correct, but that isn't the interesting part.

When the "walk-in" occurred there was no guarantee that they'd be getting 100% evil. They got a saboteur even if I didn't know it at the time.

Sorry fellas, you're too goddamn slow, you're "evil" was lacking novelty.

It wasn't just me, but I broke the camels back so to speak. Atlanteans were advanced but not necessarily morally, I did a good bad thing. And besides traumatizing millions of souls and setting humans back thousands of years I'm pretty cool with it - now anyway.

And if Morgan, a patently "evil" man, hadn't shat on Wardenclyffe, IT MAY HAVE HAPPENED AGAIN! All because I forgot and was curious.

I picked it up again at 5 years old....

Bath time...I sit legs out in front of me in the tub. There is about 6" on either side of me between me and the tub for my hands to go. My hands form paddles and I push a wall of water forward. The wave goes forward, hits the end of the tub, comes back to me, hits rear wall of tub, passes forward again, I give the first wave a push again, it immediately gets bigger and faster, I repeat, within 7 iterations of well timed "constructive interference", I repeated in a third life, the same experiment...

As Akkaeneset the system was between humans and the earth
As Tesla The sky and the earth
As 5 y.o. Kalki my hands and the tub

Waves propagate in liquids

add spin to liquids draining, the spin also gets bigger and faster.

I loved to watch swirlies (still do), and I'd apply the same assistance to the formation of a vortex at the end of bath time...

The Woman and the Dragon

> 1A great and wondrous sign appeared in heaven: a woman clothed with the sun, with the moon under her feet and a crown of twelve stars on her head. 2She was pregnant and cried out in pain as she was about to give birth. 3Then another sign appeared in heaven:

an enormous red dragon with seven heads and ten horns and seven crowns on his heads. 4His tail swept a third of the stars out of the sky and flung them to the earth. The dragon stood in front of the woman who was about to give birth, so that he might devour her child the moment it was born. 5She gave birth to a son, a male child, who will rule all the nations with an iron scepter. And her child was snatched up to God and to his throne. 6The woman fled into the desert to a place prepared for her by God, where she might be taken care of for 1,260 days.

7And there was war in heaven. Michael and his angels fought against the dragon, and the dragon and his angels fought back. 8But he was not strong enough, and they lost their place in heaven. 9The great dragon was hurled down—that ancient serpent called the devil, or Satan, who leads the whole world astray. He was hurled to the earth, and his angels with him.

10Then I heard a loud voice in heaven say: "Now have come the salvation and the power and the kingdom of our God, and the authority of his Christ. For the accuser of our brothers, who accuses them before our God day and nighthas been hurled down. 11They overcame him by the blood of the Lamb and by the word of their testimony; they did not love their lives so much as to shrink from death. 12Therefore rejoice, you heavens and you who dwell in them! But woe to the earth and the sea, because the devil has gone down to you! He is filled with fury, because he knows that his time is short."

13When the dragon saw that he had been hurled to the earth, he pursued the woman (Gaia - Matriarchy) who had given birth to the male child (Humans). 14The woman was given the two wings (Magnetic Poles) of a great eagle, so that she might fly to the place prepared for her in the desert (HYPERSPACE), where she would be taken care of for a time, times and half a time, out of the serpent's reach. 15Then from his mouth the serpent spewed water like a river, to overtake the woman and sweep her away with the torrent. 16But the **earth helped the woman by opening its mouth and swallowing the river that the dragon had spewed out of his mouth. (*This is the polarity switchback that occurs***

because the galactic core is currently bleeding/biasing the solar system)

17Then the dragon was enraged at the woman and went off to make war against the rest of her offspring—those who obey God's commandments and hold to the testimony of Jesus.

Satan is The Lizards, The Lizards are Nibiru, The earth is a battery, you are a dial.

Nibiru used to be part of Sirius, it got expelled via supernova, and it now has an interstellar orbit. The Lizards are homeless, we are the only shelter for MILES.

Scalar Interferometry is a pump, Whittaker channel a hose.

Nibiru has been siphoning off energy from earth in any form they can use. The Earth and Nibiru are Aethermetrically Linked via resonance.

What you call consensus reality is their vain attempt at getting the pump better tuned.

The earth is going into hyperspace for awhile, the greys know it, the Mayans know it, the Russians know it, the new agers know it, the tribal shaman folks know it...

The above image shows judgment night as I saw in a vision, and others have seen as well. The planets and stars are bigger, the sky is rolled up, it is very still, no graduation of the horizon.

Sky rolled up = Event horizon

Stars falling = magnification via gravitational lensing

Swallowing the river = relative polarity between aether and electron phase of scalar bottle earth core, interferometers, galactic core and Nibiru causes the 4 wave mixing - phase conjugate pumping...like in the movies when you shoot the monster and it only feeds it, like the way a black hole eats anything...ANY sized sphere can go dark star.

The Norway Spiral (atmospheric scroll wave to be exact) Thermal Picture (on the web) shows an Interferometer in action, the blue spiral is the one that "swallows" energy.

What's on the other side of the desert?

New Jerusalem.

OK, so after all that esoteric technojargon that only a handful of people get anyway, you may wonder still, why is Satan's time short and why is "he" pissed?

Satan is pissed for the same reason you get pissed when the electricity goes out, when you miss a bus, when you get kicked out of your apartment.

Earth, again, is the only source of energy for Nibiru or Planet X. By the time it reaches our solar system again we will be in the "desert" or hyperspace.

See also: http://philologos.org/bpr/files/Misc_Studies/ms029.htm

OTIS IS WRONG

Usually I sit back and listen while other people debate/argue/rant, I love to actually pay attention and observe two people go at it. Usually a rant begins as a point person A makes and person B disagrees with. Then it just turns into a clusterfuck of ego and tangents.

I forget how it started but Otis says he was in the "Future Problem Solvers of America" in high school. Sounds like one of those extracurricular enrichment programs for budding nerds...

Well I'm a born inventor so I know something about problem solving.

The first rule of problem solving is you don't begin by putting restrictions on the solution.

In this scenario he was given, Otis had to figure out ONE overarching answer to overpopulation within the next 100 years. It doesn't matter if two lesser concepts would work better. That's the FPSA's fault but still...

His solution was to exodus people off the planet.

This is a pet peeve of mine, this notion that the only way to deal with our libido and consequent unsustainable growth is to abandon Earth and go terraform Mars.

Otis tried to justify exodus as just an extension of the same homesteading spirit that tamed North America.

Or, is it the slash and burn, shit-in-the-living room and move on kinda spirit, stemming from desperation and lack of foresight?

The latter. But hey, the 1st space race was just a nationalistic sausage fest anyway.

I know about technology....the same technology needed to survive indefinitely in space is the same needed here for a SUSTAINABLE INFRASTRUCTURE - efficient energy, waste management, and food production.

Even given the rate of technological progress, large Sci-Fi looking craft, capable of life support for a relevant number of people are at least 200 years away – left to ourselves anyway.

BESIDES....

IT'S REDUNDANT! - We already are on a spaceship!

And what happens to the people on Otis' spaceship? They reproduce. Great, now you have a tin can full of critters and even at 99% the speed of light it's 3 more generations till they reach a decent planet.

There are only two variants on Otis' idea that are valid: the development of Quantum Phase Shifting craft for teleportation OR Orbital stations.

Orbital stations would clear up space on the ground as real estate in space.

The thing is, when I brought all this up, he only got more emphatic and loud, as if he was invested in his answer from 15 years ago.

The truth is, a few technologies have the potential to save humanity from itself, free energy in particular, but rocketry, NO, not really.

The real answer to overpopulation is **sterilization** and **desert reclamation**.

Otis assumed sterilization can only be done en masse via Fascist policy and that the deserts will just "Become strip malls".

Its year 2099, the population has reached 8 billion. You can have a 5 minute surgery and get paid $ for it annually for life (That's called "Economic Incentive").

Or you can drag you and your family onto a space elevator and go live in Orbit where you'll always have the spins, need to exercise all the time or else you'll lose bone density and ...oh yeah, no smoking or showers either, and cosmic rays keeping you up all night as they go through your eyelids.

The other option is to go live/work on the Desert Reclamation Project (DRP). With the advent of Arc Foaming technology it is possible for robots to grow entire cities out of sand. This technology makes it possible to build strong, efficient foamed glass domes.   Same tech you'd need to terraform any other sand on any other planet.

The Desert Reclamation Project started in 2040 has been a success, along with the Voluntary Sterilization Program; the population went down 2% every decade since its inception. The Exodus Program was dismissed before it began, The Board said the proposal sounded like it was done by some high school kid.

WHEN OCCAM'S RAZOR
FAVORS THE PARANORMAL

The simplest solution is preferable.

The simplest solution is more likely to be right.

The razor is a heuristic maxim to most disciplines but is inherent to metaphysics and necessary. Why?

For 3D bound observers in the material universe simpler is better simply because WE ARE THE MOST COMPLEX THINGS IN IT - in an effort to explain anything, simpler is the only direction to go. Simplicity gets complicated quick though, cuz in order to know any one thing you kinda haveta know everything, although specialists may argue that...Point, complexity and interconnectedness are the same. When a new age wacko like me says ALL IS ONE, that's pretty damn connected. "All is One" is literally the simplest solution to _____.

We are "back-engineering" creation via reductionism, but reductionism becomes integrationism once we reach sub-atomic scales. The delineated complexity becomes homogenous chaos.

What does that mean? It means that the rules for classical and quantum mechanics don't need to be mutually exclusive or unified, it means that when one realm interferes with the other it's to be expected not relegated to "new age" pseudoscience.

The whole premise of a GUT or TOE is unification, but this unification needs to come socially before it can be done scientifically. Right now science is plagued with as much ego and dogma as any other religion; it is as splintered as well, into opposing camps for virtually every theory.

The general division is between old school gatekeepers with tenure and titles and non-affiliated, non-academic wackos more concerned with truth than career. The dichotomy is maintained by a "Skeptics" community and Journal Editors and certain politicians who don't necessarily want simpler answers.

Michael Shermer is the go-to face for the Skeptics and he's ready to shit on any idea that doesn't fit in classical physics. He goes out of his way to explain how blatantly paranormal things are mass hallucinations or hoaxes. For example, let's look at crop circles, nobody debates they are real but the origin, the creator is a mystery –

The open minded observer will conclude that most are supernatural in origin. Michael will tell you every single formation ever documented is made by human hands but he has never tried to prove it. If that were true, any one could be reproduced, in one night. The razor favors the supernatural, and if left to that we are fine. We could employ OR again in deciding what possible supernatural mechanism that may be…

All "paranormal" or "supernatural" phenomena are either non-local and/ or non-linear; these ideas are known and accepted but Einstein called it "spooky", which of course is where the stigma of being cool and interesting comes from.

Relativity is a result of an observer being of multidimensional space but only capable of experiencing that space in an organ averaged and time filtered way. If the observer were able to see all as one he'd cease to be an observer and no relativity would exist.

All "paranormal" or "supernatural" phenomena are allowed for or demanded by quantum mechanics.

Non-local and non-linear phenomena occur when a classical system undergoes a quantum phase shift, in other words, macroscopic matter borrows from the sub-atomic rules. This is called quantum coherency and has been given the prefix "super", as in, superluminal, superfluidic, superconductive.

The only reason that is possible is because space is full of energy. A quantum phase shift is not a thermal phase shift. The prior involves exciting the "empty" space between "particles" the latter just particles.

There is, in multidimensional space, a hierarchy of energy densities. The density is, according to Chapline, proportional to the scale of a given sphere, and can only be differentiated by an observer who is displacing geometry and time in the Dirac Sea as these densities are superpositioned.

The Observer is a hybrid system, both closed and open, this is true for any matter. The classical aspect is closed, the quantum, open.

This is the simplest solution to the needlessly complicated state of science/ physics, to not call the quantum interpretation of a black hole "audacious" – to accept that "spooky" stuff happens and try to figure out how - not write books about why people believe they do.

"Channeled" info or "up all night insights"

OR - where theoretical physicists go to know the mind of god...

...assuming space itself is a quantum computer, the akasha is non-volatile RAM and the Gravity/Photon flux flows through Associative IS/AS gates in the transistor formed from stratified branes...and again through the determinism provided by DNA...assuming any given portion of space is equal part singularity, ergosphere and horizon, different "things" being different portions of the 3...then:

Energy/Hyperspace=hardware
Matter/Local Space=software
ESP= Organic Radio – ½ Spin
OBE= Decoherence of an entangled Soul/Genome Matrix
Telekinesis= Inertia via Torsion Waves 2 Spin
Psychometry/Remote Viewing= memory 1 Spin
Astrology= Entanglement of a decohered Soul/Genome Matrix

All Non-linear/local phenomena are a transduction/transition of info from one energy density (system) to another which either simplifies or complexifies it. Hawking Radiation is like compression of bits....hmmm, is the Event Horizon a Maxwell's Demon Shaving with Occam's Razor?

"Hey!You!, all cold and simple, get yer ass over there! And you, all hot and complex, you go over here!

Sound familiar?

Birth=downloading
death=uploading
Life =Processing
DNA=Hybrid determinism...Binary to the horizon, fuzzy to the observer...

"SuperMoment" a term I just coined to describe a wave sweeping through and coupling, or clustering, momentarily, parts of the system - transitional local quantum coherency. The natural tendency towards sync and harmony, also what happens to matter crossing the horizon of a quantum black hole or Dark Energy Star

Nirvana is the sustained coherency of the observers consciousness entangled with a SuperMoment in the brain - when all is one as far as the subjective observer is concerned.

Brain Sync

Brane Sink

BEYOND COSMIC CLEARANCE

Try as they may, the Shadow Gov/Annunaki Descendents can't keep secrets from anyone who can access the Akashic Records – pretty much anyone interested and willing. They can only manipulate the truth, and threaten insiders who'll eventually reach their deathbed and say, "Fuck it, this is what I saw…" This fact makes The Disclosure Project somewhat moot. Yes it would be nice to be treated as an adult, as a human, as a child of God, but the UFO/Alien issue is already so divisive that those who accept ET/ED beings don't need acknowledgment from Above Top Secret entities, and those who don't accept ET/ED beings are irrelevant.

Steven Greer suggests we need disclosure on the subject to get to the "Advanced" goodies our alien brethren can bestow, and simultaneously solicits the same from humans via S.E.A.S. He fails to acknowledge however, that the wackjobs capable of grasping Aether Engineering are usually not in a position to get the adequate funding to do R+D. Instead of offering the Z-Prize and surrounding himself with academic science advisors he should diversify the peer reviewers with Mad scientists and New Agers and fund the most promising inventions. Benevolent, uncompromising inventors don't need cash incentive to work on free energy or antigravity, which is the last priority of a mad scientist – they do need proper facilities, tools and assistants.

Perhaps the most useful info to come from The Disclosure Project is the idea of a false flag war on ET/ED beings/craft as being the escalation of a NWO agenda. The problem with this next step is that nobody with a clue is going to believe conventional weapons are going to work on Flying Saucers. Further, nobody is going to believe aliens would blatantly attack earth now when they've had millions of years to do it without resistance. To go to war with "aliens" they'll either have to shoot patiently waiting

ARV's with projectiles or take out real Saucers with HAARP or some other DEW; but if they did, it's their last possible move. Our Alien friends have already demonstrated their technological superiority during the LA attack back in the 40's and the non-local transmutation of nuclear warheads.

To those in the know about Planet X/Nibiru and the Nephilim/Annunaki, it is obvious "Satan knows his time is short", and that we have nothing to worry about, would Satan be pissed if he knew he'd be winning the war? God told Enoch that it was angels who intercede for man not man for angels. That's true, but these definitions of race, being and alliance are intermixed. Do you ever wonder why the angels in The Book of Revelation are tasked with destruction? Is that evil? Are these angels necessarily aetheric or incarnate? G.W. could be an angel tasked with incarnating as "evil" for the progress of the greater good.

I am the man to intercede for all involved, I have just as much mercy/empathy for Lizards as I do for humans…They may have altered the natural order but it is a testament to how well woman was designed, not how rebellious angels are – no man can account for his libido, so how can we fault angels? Azazel and his buddies in hyperspace saw woman…and well, they were as impressed as a 13 year-old boy seeing his first Hustler magazine. This is the Fall, this is stepping on 10 of 12 strands…

Are The Lizards, Watchers, Nephilim, Fallen Angels, Illuminati, and Annunaki all the same? Are there good and evil factions in every race? Are there 4D/angelic and 3D/beastly aspects to every race? From what I gathered it's relative to the dimension we are asking from. Perhaps one race enables the hybridizing of others in a continuous process of "rebellion" and/or advancement.

My point here in this rant is that what is ostensibly top secret is common knowledge to those who know where to look and what to associate, what is salient and what is peripheral.

One way or another, humankind will know the truth, whether it comes from eating a mushroom, crop circles, reading esoteric texts, seeing a mother ship, My advent, or testimony before congress…We will experience Judgment Day/The Galactic Cross and we will continue to New Jerusalem, we will reclaim our right to participate in the Galactic Federation as interdimensional Christ Clones.

OH, IT'S ON, JOSE!

Have you seen this douchebag yet?

http://www.creciendoengracia.com/

http://www.cegenglish.com/

He claims to be The Christ - because he had a dream - and people actually believe him. He's been on national tv, CNN, ABC, etc,...

At first I was pissed that he gets more attention than me, then I realized that he wouldn't if he was ACTUALLY A THREAT TO THE ESTABLISHMENT.

Listen folks, I AM more comfortable with being rejected or discerned with apprehension. The second one of my people runs out and gets a 666 tattoo is when I start rejecting!

The phenomena of the false prophet, from my perspective, is just a way to provide contrast for the truth.

The truth is that this geezer spic (offensive slur intended) isn't going to change the world with my title or without.

I have to admit, I don't care much for hispanic culture, but that's not the issue here, Christ could be an old black lady...the issue is that he is walking around flaunting his wealth, and I've been beating my head for 10 years trying to secure seed capital for inventions that will bring New Jerusalem.

I'll also admit that my trip began with a vision, not the convenient REM dream of angels telling me I'm special, but of me at a press conference giving ultimatums to world leaders (where the Jesus part comes in is my business for now) - after which I spent 2 years questioning my sanity.

He's right about two things: Christ is the "Antichrist" and hedonism is OK...as long as you acknowledge its actually GOD getting head, getting high, and sleeping all day.

Well, Jose if you've got the cajones, why don't we debate this?

NEGENTROPIC SHOCK TESTING
OF THE EM ECONOMY

OR

"FREE ENERGY WILL RUIN THE ECONOMY"

This document outlines how the standard economic model is seriously flawed in both concept and execution if it is to be considered sustainable. This intentionally flawed model is to be known here as the Error-Activated Economy (EAE) and this economy is going to self-destruct under its own weight; it has to, it's based on planned obsolescence/entropy. A simple and self-similar analog, the Electro-Magnetic laws correspond to elements of the EAE, as discovered by Mayer Amshel Rothschild, where:

1 – Capacitance = Capital (money, stock/inventory, investments in buildings, durables)
2 – Conductance = Goods (production flow coefficients)
3 – Inductance = Services (the influence of the population of industry on output)

All of the mathematical theory developed in the study of one energy system (e.g., mechanics, electronics, etc.) can be immediately applied in the study of any other energy system (e.g. economics).

The first and most obvious flaw is the overlap of a monetary system with an energy infrastructure based on nonrenewable resources. Fossil Fuels are a "sunset" industry, owned and marketed by a cartel with no apparent exit strategy. An orchestrated energy crisis provides the cartel with valuable data that will dictate future actions towards extending the day. An energy crisis is one of many "shock tests," such as blackouts and NYC transportation strikes…all used to assess and predict social engineering strategies. As these two systems become more disparate in their functioning, the wealth too is being continually divided into the poor have-nots and the rich elitists. Compound interest, Lobbyists, War-Market Based Solutions, Tax Havens, Global deregulation, Anti-Trust Regulations, and No Trickling Down… are compounding the division and impending collapse, never mind the biosphere.

The Modus Operandi of the Error-Activated Economy is to increase *entropy*. This entropy is evident in nearly every product and service you can name. How many times have you bought a product that shouldn't have broken but did? Gotten a bill with unknown fees? Received services from the incompetent or corrupt?

This is unique to **capitalism** but **communism** and **socialism** are both subject to the energy infrastructure that is itself very entropic (inefficient, wasteful) thus compromising an otherwise effective Social System. These three distinct systems are homogenizing; what is corporate welfare and subsidies? COMMUNISM! What is the military, with its technological standards and code of service? SOCIALISM! They were always intermixed so we'll just consider the entire world as participants in the EAE. The only way to make the EAE remotely functional is to create war and/or genocide, the exhaust pipe routing debt away from our smoothly running engine.

Entropy is described as the rate of change within a closed system where degrees of freedom define the limits of change. The Earth may be considered a closed system (it isn't really) and the Fossil Fuel Industry may be considered a degree of freedom among many in a capitalist free market. **In the standard economic theory Entropy is called "diminishing return."** Equilibrium is stability; decay is dominant, it is irreversible so work with it right?

OKAY, so how does a most entropic industry inside an entropic economy gain record profits? Why do the Arbiters of the EAE do the exact opposite of what is intuitively correct? Where is it written that capitalism must always manifest as its parasitic, competitive aspect? Is there an alternate/opposite aspect? Does, the current EM theory disregard all the negentropic stuff on purpose?

Capitalism is the most biomimetic of the three aforementioned social systems; it is an economic natural selection. In nature there aren't thousands of imposed, studied variables, only adaptation, opportunism, and survival. There are no cheaters because there are no rules. In this sense the elitists who wage war with the poor in order to maintain the economy cannot be guilty, cannot be held to silly notions of morality. They are doing what they must to maintain their lifestyle/habitat.

The problem here is that a few wealthy elitists are dependant on millions of poor and millions of poor ARE NOT dependant on a handful of elitists. The whole idea behind a free market is that it is self-regulating and will produce its own solutions; that's true if it is actually free, but every aspect of the economy is manipulated – including morality and population. *The economy will either fix itself or the standard theory really is a convoluted lie.*

To determine this, **an entirely new shock test must be executed...**

When I was in college, a prerequisite class was Economics 101, and I went to it with little interest but I had one question, "What are the economic implications of mass marketing a free energy device?" The professor just laughed.

This professor did not look at the world around him. He only conformed to some elaborate theory. He assumed the Fossil Fuel Industry had such a hold on consensus reality that it was a given. The current rhetoric concerning our "addiction to oil" and "energy independence" is thirty years old, it is lip service nobody believes, but that won't stop inventors and entrepreneurs from holding W to his words.

In the book, <u>COMPLEXITY</u>, Brian Arthur's thoughts regarding **"increasing returns"** are expounded with a comparative list: **Old Economics** vs. **New Economics**. He never uses the terms **Entropy** vs. **Negentropy** and I don't think he's familiar with Rothschild's Analogy or Bearden's corrections/reminders but it all correlates.

Old Entropic Economics	New Negentropic Economics
Decreasing returns	Much use of increasing returns
Based on 19th century Physics (equilibrium, stability, deterministic dynamics)	Based on Biology (structure, pattern, self-organization, life cycle)
People identical, Family is industrial unit	Focus on individual life; people separate and different
If only there were no externalities and all had equal abilities we'd reach nirvana	Externalities and differences become driving force. No nirvana. System constantly unfolding
Elements are quantities and prices	Elements are patterns and possibilities
No real dynamics in the sense that everything is at equilibrium	Economy is constantly on the edge of time. It rushes forward, structures constantly coalescing, decaying, changing.
Sees subject as structurally simple	Sees subject as inherently complex
Economics as soft physics	Economics as high-complexity science

The main difference here must be in the energy infrastructure. No other variable or degree of freedom so directly affects the world economy. Before proceeding we must reconsider the definition of entropy as it is and how it's commonly used as a misnomer.

Entropy, again, is a measure of change within a closed system. This works fine for heat engines and most machines; but modern physics is indicating that, at the sub/quantum level, there ARE NO CLOSED SYSTEMS, and this is exactly the issue COMPLEXITY deals with and exactly why free energy is possible. Negentropy, the opposite of decay and disorder (a product of linear time) is found in emergent phenomena where growth and order is evident. Many scientists have concluded that Negentropy is the more dominant of the two "forces," else nothing would exist in the first place. This can be put into question by asking whether or not The Big Bang, a supposed explosion, is creative or destructive? The answer is, "It destroyed what preceded it." The idea of Big Bang – Heat Death is broad and symptomatic of the current paradigm.

Creative Destruction sounds oxymoronic but this is the result of unrelenting disorder. A seed situation or variable, hidden within or directly spawned by the disorder can and will give way to a spontaneous collapse and regauging of all variables. A convection cell and snowflake are two common examples of how disorder can instantly change to order.

Of course The Old Economy or The Hard Path doesn't produce a benevolent trickle down effect because the order and wealth is horded by elitists. In the New Economy individuals possesses their own source of infinite energy, you do the math. Forget the trickle, give me a fountain of my own!

Yes, free energy will ruin the economy but that is not a problem for poor people, or the people investing in new energy technologies. Further, mounting evidence suggests the economy will decay as surely as its model predicts and if the elitists cannot adapt to the new paradigm they have no right to tout a free market solution.

DOMINION VS. DESTRUCTION

The final revision of the church and beating the Right at their own game

Historically revisionism splinters the church when modern issues encroach and demand a moral, bible-based consideration. As is often the case the splinter group hangs its rationale on a subjective, singular premise, by which it identifies its revised status.

Today I saw Bill Moyers of PBS investigate the current rift forming among evangelicals and the church in general. This dialogue between religion and environmentalism is long overdue and is expounded upon in <u>DEEP ECOLOGY and WORLD RELIGIONS- New Essays on Sacred Ground</u>. Written and edited by "Left" authors, the book begins with a simple idea, "If you love God then you love the earth". Does this supersede and hold up against a line from Genesis? Is dominion exclusive from stewardship? Even secular foresters know to replant, even drunkards know to recycle and big business knows building green equals profit via lower overhead.

I identify the established Right as the splinter group and not the TreeHuggers. Loving the earth and doing what's right is apolitical. The Evangelical Right, aligned with Petro-Politics, can't claim they are doing Gods Will when they leave it all up to Capitalist Market Forces, conversely, nobody can claim that planting a tree is blasphemous. The Rightwingers may want to ponder their position the next time they're stuck in gridlock behind a diesel truck.

The Right/Dominator/MufflerHuggers have drawn a line and it is appropriate and welcome. The body of Christ faces many "wedge" issues, most of which are politically, and not spiritually consequential. This is an issue however that really does warrant division within and without a church/state context, as it affects the biosphere, not just the vote or soul.

As a Left/Symbiotic/TreeHugger, lover of God and Creation, and inventor of alternative energy technologies I agree that we do have dominion, God is in control, and the market will provide answers. However I also believe God wants a clean, sustainable technology to dominate the market for the sake of creation. I believe that by drawing this line the right have inadvertently aided Christ in the impending division of the righteous from the unrighteous....If the resultant "Eco-Christians" were to rally behind, and get to market, sane technology we could defeat the Right and their Hydrocarbon Age, but poetically, on their terms. Honestly now, can you picture New Jerusalem with smoke stacks, acid rain, oil spills, nuclear waste and smog?

REVELATION 11:18

If the Right can quote Genesis to justify their position I propose we quote a timelier piece of scripture:

"...give reward...unto them...that shouldest destroy those who destroy the earth"

Interestingly, humans have only been able to destroy or corrupt the earth within the past 100 years. God has and will ruin the biosphere and the earth will recover. The question is, when the prophesied earth changes occur do you want to be stuck with an irreparable, centralized, monster of an energy infrastructure or my technology REV 18:9-11?

Why my inventions as opposed to dozens of others will be gladly explained in detail to those seriously interested in this proposal...But I like to make an analogy of the cataclysmic destruction of the big, laborious dinosaurs and the prevalence of small mammals to the eschatological destruction of a centralized infrastructure and the prevalence of micro-generation tech – In each case the winner wins due to its small size, i.e., its ability to move and reproduce quickly.

It is not enough to be the default opposition, it is not enough to have an opinion, and sadly, it isn't enough to plant a tree.

When I speak of defeating the MufflerHuggers by defeating them at their own game, on their terms, I mean that we can fund the R+D of superior, clean, micro-generation technologies to power homes and vehicles. There is no question about morality after that, it's simply better technology than the current product.

DEAR LIZARDS

I'm writing to tell you that, while the original plan could work in due time, the Nibiru-Earth link-up scheme is flawed for reasons neither you nor Akkaeneset factored in at its outset. First let's address your flawed logic and emotional state. You, like some other entities, resent Homo Sapiens. You think because we were born in Eden we take it for granted or don't deserve Earth. You point at our complacency with your rule and call it weakness. Well, who ripped us from innocence? Who made us weak?

You think you are so advanced because of your technological prowess yet you couldn't perform a simple exodus within planetary parameters and local space? How many times have you swung through here now? I suspect you are simultaneously keeping your own Lizardkind down in a similar manner within the depths of Nibiru. That's why you never moved here, because they would be free.

Speaking of Nibiru, I've been homeless too OK? It sucks always wondering when you'll eat next, where, you'll be sleeping - but you know what? I was wise enough to know that when couch/system hopping I must tread lightly, not act like an asshole to my host, and to not trash the couch I'd be sleeping on!

So we found out monkeys have a deep Reptilian layer they can be reduced to, did you ever consider you have an outer layer you can ascend into? You did know that if you go 4D with us your light bodies would be synchronized as well and you'd have an approximate human awareness? Do you really want that?

For all your crimes against humanity I at least know it was APPROPRIATE. The truth is, if you hadn't stepped on 10 of 12, threw up a grid and offered the fruit of the tree of knowledge, simply if you hadn't imposed this degree of duality into out experience, well, we may still be in Eden – bored out of our skulls, so thanks I guess. It could be argued that you did a dirty job that somebody had to do. In an instant you turned Earth from a playground into a school.

Superpowers are cool but so is art and culture, both of which are a result of our 2 active strands. We evolved by devolving. The consequent veil of your artificial grid red shifted our spirits away from the NOW and honestly, I prefer this illusion of privacy of mind and planet. I don't necessarily need telepathic group consciousness or mother ships revealing themselves…

You seem receptive to counsel; The Greys don't owe you anything and neither does Akkaeneset. If your entire race was erased we wouldn't care but continue what you're doing and you'll get a dose of your own medicine. For all you know the Greys and Akkaeneset are double agents, interfering with your interference! You did know nothing can oppose The One/God right?

As a Universal Servant of The One/God I am obligated to love/appreciate/help the Lizards as much as the Humans. Both species are in the same 3D boat and require energy to survive and flourish. That's what the link-up is all about right? The link-up presupposes our respective planets are and remain in 3D but that's not the course.

Not only is Ra going 4D, the humans are STILL capable of love and – the thing we didn't factor in – the Earth and Sun (Gaia and Ra)are, turns out, LIVING ENTITIES! That makes you literally a Parasite subject to all manner of defense!

Look at our biosphere, it's all relationship, take a cue next time (ha ha ha)…Symbiosis works quite well! Hell even the neutral remora is content with the free ride, it doesn't start giving directions to the shark!

So the entire universe is against you at this point, generations of souls are begging for your punishment – and this too is appropriate. So what's it gonna be Lizard? Are you going to let me have my way or am I going to give the go ahead for the angels to have their way with you?

I and other have given you free energy so what gives? That's what both planets want and need so why not take it and leave us alone? Oh I get it, you're still addicted to "POWER", another illusion like my notion of "privacy". You rub out another wargasm at the expense of everything. Habitual use is one thing but you are chronic.

In the same way Earth and Nibiru don't naturally sympathize, the angels, guides and lesser gods cannot empathize with humans; they don't have the balls to incarnate into this beastly forgetful density. That means that only The God that has been human is allowed any authority to make a call or change a rule.

I'm that human, I've done evil, I've done good…within the continuity of my oversoul I've found that there is little to no challenge in being evil but I'm glad I have the option.

What suits me now is to unite the merciless hatred of a negative, satanic attitude with the unconditional love of a positive, divine intent. This synergizes into Divine Wrath or Righteous Indignation. And OH WHAT A FEELING!

BASICALLY I'M KEANU

Testing the "Good News" via the "Authority of the first beast" - PART 2

My advent is prophesied to coincide with what CNN thrives on. Even 5 years ago the conflict wasn't enough to immanentize the eschaton, but today, despite the blatantly apocalyptic programming, people may be more inclined to let their curiosity concerning my claims overtake the knee-jerk reaction to my title(s).

This is part 2 because about 5 years ago I went a self-promotion rampage. An experiment from my perspective and an outrage or joke for everyone else...except for about 1% of the thousands of people in dozens of forums who were exposed as you are now. I learned a lot about various affiliations of people then, I'm interested to see my effect here now. What I learned most was that I have no idea who "my people" are, I only know who they aren't. To prove my divinity some Christians demanded that I display some metaphysical feat; one wanted me to tell him what sequence of heads/tails he had laid out, another wanted me to tell him how many hairs were on his head, I replied, "...before or after you're done verifying my answer?"

It's natural to want to see a miracle performed before your very eyes, it means you can finally proceed to believe any enchanted BS you want.

You demand a miracle from one who sees nothing but miracles, but I understand the significance of breaking the (human conceived) laws of physics. My predecessor was appropriately versed in the biological as that is what there was to work with so...my miracles will be of a technological nature and consequently more disruptive to the establishment because of the modern miracle of mass production. There's a great book called The Children of Ezekiel by Michael Lieb that deals with this very subject -

How certain religious zealots envision God's power and wrath as having technological superiority.

The authority I must exercise first is the clutter of this major network hub called myspace. The only two variables in this experiment are my sincerity and your curiosity. I predict 1-3% of the folks who come across this will go all the way to checking out the POD, site, and book. Why would one bother? They recognize something in me they like and/or they think they can benefit from my work, and that's cool. The majority of people religious or not are happy with what gets them through the day and my answers are to questions they never thought to ask anyway.

So the question is, can 1-3% or "my people" turn on enough other social hubs, cyber or real space, to create a tipping point? To me, an ideal tipping point would be the fulfillment of the first miracle, the prototyping of a free energy device. The seed capital for this prototype would come from book sale royalties. This would show that my memeset or trip, from attitude to intellectual property, is consistently self-sustainable as a propagating idea and business venture.

Another great tipping point would to have my Current POD green lighted for air on TV. This is how Colbert gets a bridge named after him; I could do so much more with the same support.

GOD/SON LOGIC

An eschatological interpretation of Intelligent Design with The Christ/ Kalki as a Novelty Conserving Constant

Rather than contextualize ID as a conspiracy of the religious right and/ or a pseudoscientific attempt to compromise evolution, maybe ID could stand on its own as a means of integrating a more esoteric, enlightened monotheism with what science is learning about complexity. Maybe ID could become, accidentally or appropriately, the superseding belief structure we're intended to coalesce.

Firstly let's define a common language. Since we are dealing with the be all, end all questions our polarized lexicon fails to convey universally acceptable answers. When dealing with concepts such as creation, negentropy, self-assembly, chaos, complexity, biomimicry, scale-invariant self-similarity, Zero Point Energy, etc,…any attempt at integration even within similar fields, much less the disparate situation here, tends to sound cranky. This being acknowledged perhaps we can agree that:

1 – Scientific and Religious lexicon isn't mutually exclusive to the truth only consensus reality.

2 – Otherwise separate ideas can be found to be synonymous through deductive reasoning. For example, GOD=G.U.T. (Grand Unified Theory). The concept of "God" must account for all that science produces if God is to be defined, in part, as "The Creator of all that is". Likewise, if a G.U.T. can't explain the absurd novelty found in nature, particularly our biosphere, and if it can't explain all the paranormal phenomena in our collective experience then science is just another religion.

3 – An integrated theory will require personal compromise, not conceptual compromise as the truth was the truth before we sought it in integrated form.

From <u>The Tao of Physics</u> to <u>What The Bleep Do We Know?</u> the endeavor to bridge science and spirit has always depended on language. New metaphors are always being invented, not for the sake of being metaphors of course, but in their association differing systems and their specialized jargon always resolve a little more truth. The Judeo-Christian Cannon is not at all useful to our task of integration unless one does away with literalism. The occult meaning of most parables and symbols are in fact describing metaphysics and physics. The "meta" prefix means that the knowledge imparted can't necessarily be subject to science although it can be subjectively verified. When one understands biblical esoterica the consistency between science and spirit becomes greater. For example The Mustard Seed Parable is a metaphor for how small, simple seed conditions can grow into enormous bushy attractors. Like it or not Jesus perfectly described The Butterfly Effect as it manifests as creation itself. In a text not in the Bible, Jesus compares the multiverse, his "Kingdom/Mansions", to a tapestry where one side is a grid and on the other, patterns are woven into the grid. Sounds like Bohm's Implicate and Explicate orders respectively. He compared the journey of the soul to that of a pebble moving down a beach, the water pulling it out and depositing it a little further down the beach, over and over. If you understand that Water=Aether and Land=Linear Time/Mass this is very beautiful.

Jesus said that a time was coming when he would speak plainly about The Father. This is important for two reasons. First it suggests he had to resort to parables and symbols in his teachings and it implies he was referring to his future incarnation, not five minutes hence as no adequate language with which to "plainly" describe the universe would be invented in his lifetime. If Scientific language possesses the most accurate metaphors it stands to reason that The Modern Jesus will likely be a "Great Genius" (See Dolores Cannon's Conversations with Nostradamus) capable of exceptional mental feats such as inventing miraculous technology or explaining that the "End of the World" is just a quasi-periodic Astro-Quantum Physics Event that has happened to varying degrees in the past. This can be verified by comparing geologic pole flips, the lateral orbit of our solar system through the galactic plane and novelty cycles such as Time Wave Zero by Terence McKenna and Stanford University's projected technological graph which predicts eighteen disruptive inventions around 2011. These mental abilities may be the fruit by which he is judged.

Intelligent Design, stripped of political baggage, is likely the universal belief system Jesus would promote and expound. Why? It's a good foundation but also free to evolve beyond primitive notions of Genesis and primordial soups. Modern Jesus may dismiss Adam and Eve as well as Big Bang. He may regard the few Christian attempts at bridge building infantile and laughable but nonetheless noble.

ID should encompass creation at every scale from subquantum to metagalactic and then show how all the entities on the various scales are driven by a common algorithm or Holy Spirit. The Holy Spirit is the transformative urge science is trying to define as "The New Second Law". The New Second Law tries to reconcile old ideas about entropy with the new understanding that at the most fundamental level, effectively the Zero Point Energy/Manifold, all is one (monotheism) and there are *ultimately no closed systems.*

There is too much observed creation and emergent behavior maintained in the complexity of that creation to conclude a heat death.

The New Second Law is at the heart of a legitimate, rigorous ID as a fundamental causality in the equation and statistical constant for an overhauled physics paradigm. Our view of what decay and equilibrium actually are in light of our newfound understanding of the grid side of the tapestry, the 5/6ths of the multiverse we don't experience must change. To do this we must backtrack to Michelson-Morley, E.T. Whittaker, and Maxwell. History chose to glorify empty space, at least those who adhered to Einsteinian physics. The legacy of the vacuum is subtle but powerful pessimism, academic BS and falsehoods upon which all else is built. Mathematically a plenum works as well if not better than a vacuum; a reductionist methodology must change into an integrationist methodology as parts are no longer aggregated in space but rather space bifurcates from one into many, simply the reverse. Like Infinite mass and Zero mass are relatively the same since photons are massless, moving at the speed of light…and yet anything traveling at the speed of light attains infinite mass…either photons are not things or everything is moving at the speed of light.

While a complete ID with experimental proof may be able to mechanically reproduce any aspect of creation through the use of science and technology, while Modern Jesus may be able to freely exchange or interpret ideas we still come down to one question?

"How is God surface area (Zero Point Manifold) **and** Love?"

The Father/Creator and his multiverse mansions don't care how you choose to describe them, more importantly is the fact that *you* are a description of them, a self-similar agent at the mean scale and edge of chaos.

Your oversoul is a SINgularity, a non-local projection of the Central Sun (Galactic Core) fallen from grace or collapsed from a perfect state into a clothed soul state, stained with karma, co-evolving towards an omega point attractor (The Galactic Plane or EM null Zone, The Bloch Wall of our galactic magnet). The One loves the many because the many allow for love, we are the experimental proof of a loving God as we are capable of it.

Modern Jesus, scientific genius, if he is able to recreate creation with technology as proof of his all-encompassing ID doctrine, must provide a universal precept. It may be in the form of a correction to false assumptions in physics or it may be an original statement. For example he might propose that the tendency to order is dominant or that decay is dominant but relatively speaking only in the explicate order or further still that the explicate order IS the decay of the implicate order.

He could invent a free energy device (Rev 13:13), a teleportation / time travel vehicle (An external merkaba aka, White Horse) or he could invent an AI (Artificial Intelligence) capable of passing the Turing Test (Rev 13:15). A free energy device would prove space itself is capable of ordering itself as an "aethermetric" autocatalyzing matrix and the multiverse, taken as a whole, is a perpetual motion machine. Teleportation / time travel technology would prove countless things including a Variable Speed of Light (VSL), quantum structure of an extended event horizon, ER Bridges, total CPT violation, immortality of the soul, plasma/steady state creation etc,... True AI would prove that reason, communication and will can be replicated even if emotion can't. Or perhaps a machine can host the continuity of an otherwise organic oversoul ("Soul Catching") This would prove the subquantum origins of mind/life as "you" don't particularly care if you sit in a robot or meat sack. As long as your CPU simultaneously observes and records, and your algorithm and environment allow for exchange, *you* are *alive*. All matter is imbued with the holy spirit, it just takes a requisite level of complexity for an intelligence to emerge capable of explaining itself, again **US**!

With the miraculous technology this "Machine Man" (Kalki descriptor) invents he would end the science / religion dichotomy *and* strike a blow to the establishment, consistent with his position - troublemaking, disruptive.

The Christ will replace the Bush "New World Order" with New Jerusalem, he will replace the Kurzweilian "Convergence to singularity" with a literal singularity far more effective. The Christ is a special kind of catalytic agent, introduced to coincide with the eschaton, a crystal clear conduit of Divine Will.

Satan, by definition, opposes novelty and in turn, Divine Will; the evidence is clear, our energy infrastructure is 100 years old yet toothbrushes are constantly innovated. There are hundreds of energy conversion processes superior to burning fossil fuels but only one way to clean teeth. Point is we should get electricity from Aether not boiling water, something has deliberately suppressed innovation in this field and it isn't the good guys. The man to change this situation will be labeled as The "AntiChrist" by the establishment and this is expected and appropriate. His desire for a better world will be equated with terrorism since we all know Free Energy will, "ruin the economy".

Free Energy may as well be synonymous with New Jerusalem or Utopia. Conversely adherence to an antiquated energy infrastructure, a centralized, vulnerable one leads to a ruined economy *and* environment.

In conclusion let's reiterate the salient points of this speculation:

1 – The Multiverse is a quantum computer running one algorithm/ Holy Spirit across a spectrum of dimensions, phase states and forces. It determines/lives its optimal state/nirvana via phase conjugated pumping/ iterating of aether/environment into nodes/gates. From here parallel processing of the Event Horizon ensues. The program/covenant the Holy Spirit runs and Christ executes is called The Piscean Age.

2 – God loves novelty so much he became self-similar in order to appreciate and spawn more novelty.

3 – Man imposes divisive politics into our lexicon for his purposes

4 – GOD=G.U.T. we are experimental proof / relative software of a loving God

AMERICAN AGHORI

Fans of the show WildBoyz on MTV2 may recall the episode where Chris and Steve-O visited some Aghoris in India and shared in some of their customs. Aghora is a sect of Shiva worshippers and their customs, to westerners, will seem utterly disgusting and pointless and the Aghoris appear to be nothing but the equivalent to crazy street bums...but there is a purpose.

Hanging out at outdoor crematoriums, smearing ashes of the dead all over the body, eating their own waste and roadkill, drinking alcohol from skulls and smoking pot all day, and according to Chris and Steve-O other unmentionable things - hopefully that'll be on the DVD...why? To what end?

There are two paths.

The right hand path is one of distanced worship where the divine is regarded as "other".

The left hand path is one of intimate actualization where the divine is regarded as one.

Neither path is more or less correct as it's the individual's subjective preference, however the paths could be no more different.

The customs and rituals of the average western right hand path amount to a co-dependent relationship with the church where the clergyman is paid to masturbate the ego of the follower while simultaneously inducing guilt and acceptance of one's flaws. The follower is encouraged to witness and pray and dilly dally in the petty BS of secularism.

The Aghori instead attempts to obliterate the ego right in front of God both inside and out. He does this by intoxication and humility respectively and by forcing the notion upon himself that even the most putrid of creations is ultimately beautiful play. He distances himself from the petty BS of secularism in location and appearance.

An Aghori is simply a person who wants to know God NOW and is NOT AFRAID of the means to do that.

Now that we understand the Aghori we can examine how American culture has spawned similar memes. Firstly I must point out a great irony of this culture clash…Aghoris are ultimately still Hindu which means Cows are still very sacred to them. To an Aghori beef consumption is one of the major sins, a repugnant act. But Baba, you can *Have it your way! I'm loving it!*

Speaking of disgusting consumables, how about our TV show, Fear Factor? Ah but they chug organ smoothies for money not enlightenment.

America can show it has people willing to do equally if not more nasty things than the Aghoris for less noble reasons…Are there any religious comparisons? The snake handling Po'buckers with ten teeth between 'em certainly display the ballsy faith of an Aghori. New Agers are all about self-actualization but lean towards the warm fuzzy clean methods.

Hippies, Gutterpunks, Ravers, Goths, Geex and Heshers all do drugs and run screaming from pop culture but lack any particular belief system intent on meeting God. Occasionally among these subcultures an otherwise spiritually doomed youngster will inadvertently find his/herself on the left hand path through experimentation with psychedelics.

As for me I take what I like from the belief system buffet, and the Aghora bin offers the idea of "accepting the toxins in and around me" and "It's OK to be one with the one". The rest of it just sort of happens naturally – I'm a scruffy chronic pothead, I eat at McDonalds, I smear myself in the ashes of stupid ideas. The hardcore stuff is beyond me though, I do not raise the dead or retain my semen or shapeshift cuz I'm too busy blowing shit up on the XBOX, masturbating to online porn and sleeping.

When I read the Aghori trilogy by Robert Svoboda I found myself very jealous and incompetent. The discipline and will of a true Aghori is unbelievable and the superpowers that result are awesome. I want to have superpowers too I'm just not willing to do what it takes, which is why I'm an American Aghori. In some ways though I've gone beyond the Aghori in that they are not willing to do what I am in order to meet God – build a singularity! In the superhero world there is always the genius gadgeteer superhero whose technological feats are just as bad-ass as the biofreaks. To quantum phaseshift your biology is the ultimate expression of what the Aghori intends; my tantra is just patently western.

DMT: REFERENCE IMAGE FOR THE PUZZLE OF THE COSMOS

How does one describe the ineffable and why would one want to? Isn't the attempt oxymoronic or paradoxical? Yet I'm typing. You're never going to pinpoint God=GUT with an equation either! What if Space was made of Language? Could you then assert that "those who know do not say" holds when their very existence says it all? Sometimes people who know DO SAY because there is nothing left to do. Indeed Creation is spawned by boredom..God loves Novelty and Complexity and Earth, well,..some'd say there is bit much these days.

The best way to know is through association. This means being multidisciplined, recognizing what is to be taken exoterically and esoterically. To know that ANY given take on reality is first and foremost metaphor and observer dependent. The true seeker is the ultimate skeptic, do you see Michael Shermer (Of Skeptic magazine) doing a heroic dosage of anything? I'm skeptical of his fear of the unknown and lack of curiosity, why he needs to do backseat science.

I unapologetically write in a non-linear and fragmented way to stress that what I'm writing about is also non-linear and fragmented. This demands correlation between otherwise distinct memesets and mixing of metaphors. The universiality of mathematical bases and geometry is the obvious start to correlating any and all systems. Math however is not the be all, end all, as numbers lack the context letters provide. Why do we see "our" event horizon or transition brane as a flowing mass of archetypal letters and characters? Why did the shaman see twin serpents that look like DNA strands? Cuz they were.

We are dealing with the border between (linear time & mass) and (static time & form)

We are dealing with the Holosyntactical Gematria of the Quantum Computer called space

We are dealing with the scale-invariant self-similarity of a Fractaline Branefall

..A memescape where novelty peaks in the mechanics of a mental/physical phase shift.

Not the thermal kind.

I read a book years ago called Fool on the Hill by Matt Ruff and experienced a fictional story taking place in locales that I had been to in real life, specifically Cornell University campus and downtown Ithaca NY. The normal ability to conjure imagery was replaced with actual imagery and the story became that much more real. So it is when reading accounts of DMT trips. Short of popping through the membrane into hyperspace the description of the experience is consistent with my psilocybin, mescaline and LSD trips. What is obvious after having read or been told of the DMT experience dozens of times is that there is consistency, if not in each experience then in the range. The overall response is awe. A bad trip, in hindsight is a good one, but only in hindsight..nonetheless awesome.

This consistency of experience makes it an interesting scientific tool that so far only Dr. Strassman seems to be a proponent of. The setting for the masses is our political climate and consensus reality which is already bordering on nightmarish..We would all love our leaders to become loving and empathic aka functional and wonder why not..As Dr. Strassman demonstrates, the difficulty of creating a study (Such as "Does molecularly induced love and empathy improve politics?") under prohibition begs the question of how "they" determined it to be "bad" in the first place. Did the people who made DMT illegal base this on personal experience? It would seem requisite to employ this logic in determining its worth. The classification of DMT as a schedule 1 "drug" is due to its power to enlighten the masses, which is dangerous only to the establishment; if DMT had limbs it would've been crucified years ago. This is not conspiracy theory, it is obvious and ultimately moot as the true seeker nor our hyperdimensional escorts give a damn about human law. The value of the molecule is context dependent as the experience it yields is setting dependent. The context and setting are somewhat the same; however context is more about attitude than atmosphere. Due to prohibition, MTV, and plain old fear, the masses will never know how to cultivate the realer than real, they are destined to conjure their habitual reality.

DMT can serve the whole of humanity without ever having to be metabolized by the masses. No psychonaut has to bring back anything more than their words. Yes it would be interesting to see what a continuous drip would allow for, perhaps there would be enough time to actually tweak DNA from the other side or download plans for some interdimensional device. What we've learned so far is enough as it is a critical piece of the puzzle.

As Dr. Strassman points out, the similarity to alien abduction and NDE's is striking. Is there a correlation? The correlation he found between the 49 days for pineal gland development and time in the Bardos is tantalizing to connect as fact. So for DMT to relate, we have to prove that the pineal can dump trippy loads of endogenous DMT - this being the cause of the NDE or abduction experience. What causes the DMT to be created in the first place is trauma. The act of being abducted is traumatic but now we have a chicken/egg situation. There is the possibility that malevolent spirits know how to literally scare children out of their bodies..I had terror induced OBEs (effectively same as NDEs) as a child so..I remember being forced, in a nightmare of monsters coming through the walls, to decide to leave my body or wake up, the OBE was rather spontaneous however. If I awoke I'd hear a deep demonic laughter echoing. It is wrong to dismiss all the other abduction specific events despite the overlapping phenomena, in the same way it's wrong to reduce DMT experiences to a Freudian metaphor

There is a connection however.

Dr. Strassman sought a theoretical physicist to address the Multiverse answer to the DMT question. Our understanding of Dark Energy and Matter in 2005 is greater than 10 or 5 years ago. Further, the quantum model of the blackhole, experimental proof for the subtle bodies (See Infinite Mind by Valerie V. Hunt & Gravitobiology by Tom Bearden) and other seemingly unrelated metaphysical aspects shine light on the whole puzzle. If the existence of subtle bodies were proven to operate in a connected yet distinct vacuum density, asynchronous to our averaged fleshy selves, then we can say, "Yes, the human body is an interference pattern governed by DNA, and parts or the whole pattern can decohere from linear time and mass, and get anally raped by lizards." - where are the elves then, saying, "Look at us!..Here it is!.. Now you know!.."

Why does the Buddhist dismiss DMT or even describing the ineffable?? Why speak at all or identify yourself as a Buddhist? Why don't they want to be the sugar they gladly taste? Why ignore the bridge? I know the futility of language but that's no excuse..Buddhism is nihilism with a smile. You're an elitist before Zen, You're an elitist after right?

Did you know that the description of chakras is identical to self-quantizing vortices in superfluid? This suggests that the superconductive cryo-state preexists in space and that cold only emphasizes it in the same way psychedelics emphasize neuronal firing in specific regions, amplifying states that are always there but otherwise tempered or averaged out. Superfluids are the 5th state of matter, and may naturally occur in their isolated state in halos around galaxies. The behavior of the BEC or superfluid under certain conditions is identical to the event horizon of a quantum black hole, a quantum black hole is entirely Dark Energy and is capable of phase shifting anything that crosses its surface. The very fringe of scientists suspect Dark Energy is the key to interdimensional and teleportation technologies used by alien disc type craft.

Did you know that the Dogon tribe have a myth where their savior, the Nommo enveloped in a Dark Energy Craft (my interpretation of the craft) is assaulted by the "bad water insect" (Water is, esoterically Dark Matter/Energy) who tries to bite off his head? Sound familiar? Except he and his multicultural equivalents, the avatars, take all four bodies into hyperspace.

Quantum Phase Shifting: full body vs subtle body = abduction/external merkaba vs. NDE/DMT

The similarity between the eery stillness of the space near an alien craft and that of Earth on judgement day, right before the "molecules break apart", the inter-atomic forces "slowly explode" and reverse dynamics. Terence was on to all this..how the mechanics of a UFO and that of a solar system undergoing a quasi-periodic pass through the galactic plane are the same thing (although this time we form the cross/wormhole allowing for ascension into the 5th world), in fact the propulsion system of the massless teleporting type of craft is a tiny galaxy in reverse, this is your fulcrul supersymmetry, in the singularity..your soul is a clothed singularity, right now its biased here..external merkaba=synthetic soul, this is not a problem for humans, in fact it's our destiny, DMT is just a practice run for either event.

Is DMT creating a harmonic between the molecule/receptor site bond geometry and some kind of hyperspatial form constant? In other words, does the act of metabolizing DMT create a temporary CPT violation via some symmetry in the brain that in turn regauges our attention-bias or subtle bodies to hyperspace rather than linear time and mass? It is true only the observer could distinguish this SUBJECTIVELY. No objective experiment outside the brain could objectively prove certain tenets of quantum mechanics or resolve relativity induced paradox because its always observer dependent. It is more logical to frame the question of understanding the universe from both the inside and outside simultaneously than from one or the other. So when Hubble and particle colliders have given all they can we look at neurology and metaphysics and what they lend. In between is the technology/brain interface, in this case the technology is a simple molecular key..if science is based on consistency and good science in extreme conditions, what could be more consistent and extreme than DMT?

What if one was to use the electromagnetic signature of DMT instead of the molecule itself? That is, run a DMT sample through the appropriate spectrometer(s), Fourier Transform, mix, transmit via appropriate hardware (scalar interferometer) and see how far this homeopathy thing goes. If one could induce an experience with this "virtual DMT" you'd be proving things we haven't thought to ask. Or what if you put DMT in a superfluid to see how it affects it? Perhaps the whole fluid would take on the signature of DMT, or change the "sounds" of the fluid, or ..

Synaptic fogs interfere chaotically only to spontaneously collapse into some neural network. If quantum spin networks (convection cells of a boiling superluminal fluid), Hyperspatial mapping, Platonic solids, and form constants are all geometrically consistent or essentially the same thing, we can have a scale invariant transference, a transdimensional functionality from the aether to the cells and/or the cells to the aether, thus a mutual causality leads to processing of probability - the probability of birth and death.

Emanationism & integrationism.. not reductionism.

What DMT teaches is that each of us can and must live in a Solipsistic Universe where paradox is obvious and crucial even if one can't quite explain why. Relativity and duality become superceded by the trinity. Matter is not aggregative but fractional blah blah blah

Planck-string-electron-atom-molecule-microtubule-neuron = Big Brane Theory

What constitutes the "lens" of the pineal gland?

Also consider that the numbers for
Brain Capacity vs. Actually Used
Dark Matter vs. Matter
Junk DNA vs. DNA
All correlate, hmmmm I wonder why...

CHRIST'S DILEMMA: SATAN HAS EARNED HIS NUMBERS

Let it be known that duality can never be removed from reality, it may only be regauged so that one dichotomy is superseded by a greater one. Today we see once oppositional forces merging into a greater entity so that they become indiscernible; the political spectrum for example, from Gods POV, doesn't exist.

We see Satan in the homogenization of TV programming, in its never-ending fear mongering and provocation of an invented "culture war". We see anti-racism groups and anti-tobacco groups promoting "awareness" when there need not be any. PSA's will not stop or prevent smokers or white supremacists from doing what they do, it only serves to annoy and hypersensitize the innocent.

We see evil defining evil.

There is no place in consensus reality for reason and virtue because these things destroy Satan. The arbiters of this pixilated reality live solely for money and assumed "power" and that's fine until someone gets hurt, and there is much hurting so something must be done to restore balance.

Is balance the acceptance of a modicum of necessary evil or the complete obliteration of falsehoods and negativity? Today we'll assume the latter.

Moral relativism is underscored in Revenge of the Sith when Anakin declares, "To me the Jedi are evil!" How can this be valid? Well, they prevent Anakin from learning certain skills so that he must turn to the Dark Side to achieve his goal of saving his beloved, they failed to cultivate his megalomania for their goals, instead adhering to old traditions. They failed to treat him as the savior he was. Yes Anakin turned to the Dark Side, but because of this he became the only truly balanced manifestation of The Living Force – something neither a Jedi or Sith can claim. Besides, what better way to defeat evil than to become it and then transmute back, it was a deferred complicated mission but in the end he did balance the force.

Anakin and his real life counterpart, Kalki - The Machine Man – Have a burdensome anger. This anger is burdensome because it is only appropriate in the context of human suffering. We must hold a doublethink. Emotionally and practically the situation calls for wrath simply to get the job done, spiritually and intellectually all evil is appropriate and just a self-similar function of the cosmos. From the "appropriate" context evil can be dealt with from a detached place, destroying Satan is no more profound than wiping ones ass.

What is Satan exactly? We could define Satan as The Veil that prevents humans from seeing the big picture (where evil resolves into appropriate). Or we could say Satan is the absence of light, or the Fallen Ones, The Others, Sons of Baal, or the sum of all assholes.

We can ponder whether or not the Reptilian Hybrids are at the top of the Doom Chain or if They take orders from Purebreds underground or on Nibiru. We can ask if they operate from ignorance, primordial emotional bodies, or pure intent.

In New Age literature it is said Homo Sapiens are the most dense, animalistic, warfaring species in the universe. It also says we were supposed to be the ultimate race, a species of Christs, so what happened? Did we simply succumb to our base mammalian nature or were we severely manipulated into this pathetic near-dystopian state by bad guys?

Today there is plenty of blame to go around, and that is part of the evil, to NOT take responsibility but rather to adhere to victim consciousness. Only a victim can be manipulated and coerced into prolonged negative states…

Next we have to ask perhaps the most relevant question, "What motivates Satan?" Satan began as humanity's prosecuting attorney, the fella who reluctantly took the job of testing us. For this we MUST appreciate Satan, for without the duality he provided in accusing us of being mere mammals we could never rise above to prove our divinity, there'd be no contrast and no way for God to determine his servants from those paying lip service.

Inasmuch as Satan is ALLOWED to f with us we are allowed, nay, **OBLIGATED** to F Satan by ANY MEANS WE WISH!

Of course the majority of humans are willing participants or inadvertent symbiots to Satan's work so defeating Satan means defeating the means by which humans are literally employed and served by Satan. This can be anything from turning off the television to promoting free energy research.

Let's not feign ignorance here, every human knows evil when they experience it: Breathing diesel exhaust in gridlock, going to jail for growing a plant, Fox News and snide remarks are but a few examples, nevermind genocide, AIDS, and a billion-dollar-a-day military budget. As long as people still bend over for the beast, believing that what the arbiters churn out is remotely necessary, there can be no redemption of the masses, hence the terms, "The Elect" and "The Chosen".

Kalki has no intent on converting anyone to his way of thinking as this is impossible. Everyone has chosen their path, and given the abundance of truth, if you are still sucking Satan's cock instead of walking in grace so be it, you deserve no mercy and as far as Satans concerned he was right all along, in other words, Satan has earned his numbers. Further, Kalki would not accept allegiance from one who has been polishing Satan's horns. The reason God commanded us to f like bunnies and raise ourselves into billions of subjective experiences is the same reason that certain species lay hundreds or thousands of eggs – because statistically only a small percentage of the newborns will make it. If Earth produced only 1000 Christs after this massive experiment graduates then it will have been worth all the effort. Most humans are clods, karmic fodder, and that's OK since all souls are divine and are migrating towards perfection, while in the flesh however they will be treated as scum and this is appropriate...only Kalki is qualified to decide who is and isn't this "satan scum"...remember though, he doesn't engage individuals.

Christ/Kalki actually has sympathy for the devil as he was the first to serve the dark forces in Latter Atlantis as Akkaeneset and more recently as Tesla. He discovered the means to manipulate humanity via scalar bio-geo modulation, fiddling with their electrical infrastructure, akin to modern day Montauk lore. He was the first true Godman to succumb to the pleasures of flesh and now he has an *enormous* debt to humanity, he alone is to blame for empowering the lizards...he taught them how to "Montauk" with us so that humanity has been reduced to a radio dial for transmitter Earth. Our Neuro-Schumann resonance sets the carrier wave for their non-local EM proboscis...

Now Lizard you will know I AM THE LORD when we sing a new song...you could have so easily made Nibiru a functional spaceship with or without a geodynamo or distant Gaian source. You could have easily joined us into the 5th world if you had simply reincarnated as one of us but no you thought crawling between chromosomes was the way. F your mutant offspring, f your carrier wave, we have places to go.

Let's be clear here lizard, you have no soul matrix compatible with earth and never will so quit suggesting we are inferior. Your technological prowess isn't even yours it was given by me! I have a hard time picturing the reptilian equivalent of Ballet or South Park or heavy metal concerts or the millions of other marks of divinity. All you have is subterranean complexes with slave scientists – how does this make you better than us? You can't even stand naked in the sunlight!

God may have the patience to let you exist but I will take some convincing... I'm so very ashamed for what I have done and yet I know I had to...like I know what I have to do this time.

You wanna know a secret though? I don't want earth to pass into the 5th world either. I rather like this density, s'fun. I'm afraid that with New Jerusalem I may not be able to enjoy Slayer and Family Guy, I might not get another BJ or bonghit, I might not get to enjoy the act of dying. Most of all I don't feel like Utopia (sans lizards) has been given a fair chance at this density. I'm certain that the right infrastructure, social engineering program, and spiritual belief system can combine to make a cool world. And if my brothers still need to get off on violence there is Halo and Battlebots...Harmless. Fun.

I am reasonable you see, I'm willing to grant you your God given right to exist as long as you do the same for me and mine. But seeing as how you are spiritually and emotionally retarded BY CHOICE I don't see you playing by my rules anytime soon. Therefore lizard I will enjoy seeing your teeth wear down to the gums, gnashing away in helplessness as your one time slave turns on you and utterly completely destroys you.

REPLY TO SHERMER

On behalf of metaphysicists, mystics and new age, woo woo crackpots everywhere I'd like to respond to the following written by the publisher of Skeptic.

MUSTANGS, MONISTS AND MEANING   By Michael Shermer

SCIENTIFIC AMERICAN SPECIAL ISSUE – BEYOND EINSTEIN

SEPTEMBER 2004, Page 38

The dualist belief that body and soul are separate entities is natural, intuitive and with us from infancy. It is also very probably wrong...

Firstly, when a skeptic tries to denounce the unknown (as if credible scientists don't work with unknowns) he usually keeps the context of the argument within classical physics jargon, essentially denying the validity of quantum mechanics and direct experience for assumed "laws". This is convenient but deceptive. Secondly in regards to the article itself, Mr. Shermer is rephrasing the before/afterlife question within the confines of two possibilities, monism & dualism. With all this restriction, who needs open-mindedness as in the possibility of a third?

The response of children to a dead animal or common use of a phrase is hardly corroborative evidence for any debate; it is arguably less credible than when children speak of impossible previous experiences and/or display unusual interest or talent, which strongly supports reincarnation. With the skeptic paradigm we cannot explain how such fresh biology could possibly develop that level of complexity and detail if mind is, as a skeptic would assert, an emergent phenomena of biology.

There is only so much time for the senses to lay down the maps before they can be associated to do anything useful. However if the maps were to reside in HyperSpace instead of DNA – outside of linear time and (inertial) mass – then the knowledge already exists and merely needs to be reverse time modulated or downloaded through the quantum foam black holes/closed strings i.e. the logic gates of brane tiles. Learning then is really remembering, what a child is doing when babbling about being killed in a war or when a five-year old suspected Dalai Lama picks out *his* Mustang from a pile of things he's never seen.

Mr. Shermer and I agree that "my soul is a pattern of information" we part ways however on where that pattern emerges from and how it is maintained. The field of "Quantum Biology" has been around for a LONG time it's just that the language had to come full circle as the whole BEYOND EINSTEIN issue suggests. **All** Psychic/Paranormal phenomena are either non-linear or non-local. Objective repeatable experiments are difficult because not only do we not know what language to ask the right questions in, the best quantum interface is the brain and only a few freaks know how to work those phenomena in question consistently – and they are in caves! No scientist dismisses his own senses so when I tell you I've experienced psychometry (the ability to see images that form in the minds eye of where an object has been or who has occupied a bedroom for example) you either have to accept that the brain can become entrained to superluminal information via its overtones in our bandwidth or that that's beyond the ability of biology - or I'm full of it.

There are psitronic, non-invasive scalar interferometry experiments that can be done, the Twin Photon has been established and it just gets weirder every day. As Classical is consumed by Quantum, Quantum will be encompassed and integrated with something some of us are just beginning to comprehend (ironically while others are waiting to forget again)... Maybe you should just go ahead and smoke DMT (Dimethyltryptamine) – Google it.

Further the dualist vs. monist argument has been over ever since the concept of superpositioning. Of course free space has the potential to collapse a brane, to decohere from the AUM state into some meme organism, BUT SOMETHING HAS TO decide what that will sound like! In our language we say HyperSpace and Heaven are synonymous and co-existing within the same space we experience now. So the soul becomes the linear time counterpart to the "oversoul" or what Tom Bearden calls (a) Whittaker Structure/Precursor Engine/Bio Quantum Potential, which never actually collapses but remains as permanent as the local vacuum density itself – a medium much more hard/subtle than DNA for storing/processing morphogenetic algorithms. Iterate and exist dude.

"The reason dualism is intuitive is that the brain does not perceive itself"

Tell that to a Zen Buddhist; it sounds like a koan so I will reverse it and see if it makes any sense as the opposite should hold true as well.

The reason monism is counterintuitive is that the brain perceives itself

Regardless, if I really am collapsing wave forms into a subjective reality it stands to reason the only way for humans to find true supersymmetry is IN because a truly objective measurement is futile. All we are saying is biology (matter) emerges from mind, this is an observer dependent multiverse and the G.U.T. that can be reduced to an equation is not the true Grand Unification Theory; are these ideas any more or less absurd than what we already know and accept? Physical/ego immortality, not likely, eternal continuity of awareness, can it be any other way?

THE TESLA CROP GLYPH

Tapping the Transdimensional Wheelwork of Nature

The Crop Glyph on the cover of this book has been popularly regarded as an esoteric, tweaked version of this, Tesla's *Radiant Energy Receiver*.

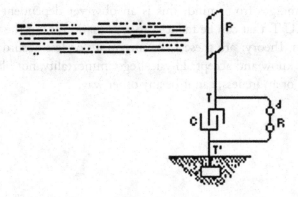

This paper attempts to reconcile the current understanding of vacuum energy a.k.a. Dark Energy as interpreted by different scientists and physics sects. Tesla, as with most physicists of his day took the "Aether" to be the medium through which EM energy propagated. This is reasonable since every other known wave in the universe propagates through something. At some point elaborate math got in the way of logic and "space energy" was relegated to metaphysics and gained more synonyms.

An explanation of the glyph tweak to Tesla's "Radiant Energy Receiver" is also provided. The author/inventor has "back-engineered" the glyph and suggests it is an "Auto-Inductive Rectenna" or AIR; a means of directly tapping Dark Energy as opposed to receiving incident waves from a transmitter; space is treated as a fluid to be drained, as opposed to a fluid to be oscillated.

As we can see from the following quote, it was Nikola's intent to go beyond the transmitter/rectenna system and tap vacuum energy directly:

"Ere many generations pass, our machinery will be driven by a power obtainable at any point of the universe. This idea is not novel. Men have been led to it long ago by instinct or reason; it has been expressed in many ways, and in many places, in the history of old and new. We find it in the delightful myth of Antheus, who derives power from the earth; we find it among the subtle speculations of one of your splendid mathematicians and in many hints and statements of thinkers of the present time. Throughout space there is energy. Is this energy static or kinetic! If static our hopes are in vain; if kinetic — and this we know it is, for certain — then it is a mere question of time when men will succeed in attaching their machinery to the very wheelwork of nature." ---- **N.T.**

Almost paraphrasing the above quote, this excerpt from the below article quotes John Baez. I've bolded some things I need to critique:

http://discovermagazine.com/2008/aug/18-nothingness-of-space-theory-of-everything/article_view?b_start:int=1&-C=

> Even if no one knows where the energy of empty space comes from or why it has the value it does, there is now no doubt that it exists. And if there is energy to be had, there is inevitably somebody out there thinking of how to exploit it. The notion of limitless energy from empty space has inspired legions of wannabe physicists who dream of developing the <u>ultimate perpetual-motion device</u>, a machine that would solve the world's energy problems forever. A quick Internet search for the words free energy and vacuum turns up pages and pages of schemes for tapping the vacuum's energy. I ask John Baez if such efforts are as hopeless as previous perpetual-motion machines. Are they equally crazy and doomed to failure?
>
> "Perhaps not as doomed as trying to prove the world is flat," Baez says. "One thing I can say is that **I sure hope it doesn't work**, because if you could extract energy from the vacuum, it would mean that the vacuum is not stable. For **normal** physicists," he adds with a laugh, "the definition of the vacuum is that it's

the lowest-energy situation possible—**it has less energy than anything else.**" In short, Baez says, while we **may be able** to get energy from the vacuum, success "would mean the universe is far more unstable than we ever dreamed.

The reasoning goes like this: If the vacuum is not at the lowest energy state possible, then at some point in the future, the vacuum **could** fall to a lower state, pulsing out energy that would threaten the very structure of the cosmos. If some clever engineer were ever to extract energy from the vacuum, it **could** set off a chain reaction that would spread at the speed of light <u>and destroy the universe</u>. Free energy, yes, but not what the inventors had in mind.

This man is clearly biased. He suggests that if I or anyone else thinks the opposite, that Dark Energy has a HIGHER energy density than anything else it's abnormal. What is abnormal is ignoring the fact that the vacuum is INFINITE potential energy (regardless of its measured local value, see Mach) and has no regard for convenient re**normal**ization. He never considers that falling to a lower energy state is actually all the "Big Bang" ever was, that this Phase-Transition/Explosion had no center, and created things (or was negentropic).

Dark Energy fits right in with KK theory, M theory etc,…It's DARK because it is asynchronous and asymmetrical to us as it is in HIGHER dimensions not necessarily because it's self-canceling. The Branefall or Transdimensional wave filters through the dimensions becoming matter and the forces maintaining matter; what we consider self-canceling or the difficulty of measurement is really the SEAMLESSNESS and PERMEABILITY of the dark energy transdimensional wave.

The next article provides corroborative astronomical evidence for the claims of the Auto-Inductive Rectenna:

http://www.spacedaily.com/reports/Direct_Evidence_Of_Dark_Energy_In_Supervoids_And_Superclusters_999.html

"When a microwave enters a supercluster, it gains some gravitational energy, and therefore vibrates slightly faster," explained Szapudi. "Later, as it leaves the supercluster, it should lose exactly the same amount of energy.

But if dark energy causes the universe to stretch out at a faster rate, the supercluster flattens out in the half-billion years it takes the microwave to cross it. Thus, the wave gets to **keep** some of the energy it **gained** as it entered the supercluster."

The analogy to the AIR is:

Dark Energy = Static Field
Supercluster = Population Inversion in discharge tube
Microwave = DC induced Scroll Wave

It may be reworded to state that a static field exciting a gaseous medium, when heterodyned with additional energy, will gain energy from the static field.

As Tesla stated, and John Baer added, if the Dark Energy is static/the lowest possible energy state then it is in vain, if the Dark Energy is unstable or capable of Branefall from higher energy states then it is totally possible. It is likely that the vacuum only displays its kinetic side on extremely tiny and extremely large scales as evidenced by vacuum fluctuations and an expanding universe.

The AIR – Associated terms: Scroll Electret, Inertial Electrostatic Confinement (IEC), Bipolar Spark Gap Transistor, Aether Sink, Scroll Wave, Kreb's Cycle, Abnormal Glow, Open Path, Negative Resistor, Multipactor.

The AIR has 3 inputs and 3 outputs.

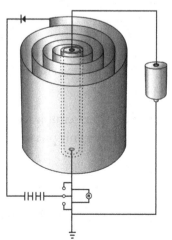

The crop glyph shows a spiral where the conductive receiving body of the rectenna was, this spiral forms the base of the transistor. The spiral is a scroll electret – an electrostatically, permanently charged dielectric. The original receiving body was also a dielectric. The function of the scroll electret is to produce IEC in the discharge tube inside it and to host a scroll wave. Scroll waves occur in ANY activated medium, work according to the Kreb's cycle and can precipitate electrical activity, as with a heart beat. Scroll waves are studied primarily in chemical reactions and biology. The author contends that Scroll Waves and Krebs Cycles are universal and are, like gravity, epiphenomena of the transdimensional wave which is itself a scroll wave pinned to a given Whittaker structure. The IEC forms a beam from the injected electrons coming from the cathode. This beam is what pins the scroll wave. The beam is also the aether sink where the mass/energy is absorbed before going into the circuit.

What is happening in the discharge tube is related to abnormal glow, electron avalanche, and multipactor phenomena. In those phenomena the electrodes are the fuel, in the case of the AIR it is CATIONIC OVERCHARGE that produces the secondary emissions. With the AIR, the secondary emissions come from space itself via the superelectron, via the nuclei, via the vacuum; The electron beam strips electrons from its boundary layer and they undergo spontaneous regeneration – this IS the collapse of the scroll wave, it's inversion to an electronic phase from the aether phase. The AIR is ultimately rectifying vacuum fluctuations, they are the "fuel". The difference between classical and quantum states in the same system is the potential of the system. The vacuum energy sees the whole thing as an open path, sink or negative resistor. Once this energy transits into its electronic phase it is a "closed system".

The IEC-Beam structure of the cold plasma in the discharge tube sets up a co-axial resonance (also produced in the load via the consonant discharge of the bipolar spark gap transistor).

Dark Energy (in the form of a vortex/scroll wave) has both a Collapsing/Aether phase and an Expansive/Electronic phase; the AIR encourages both to maintain its scroll wave.

The AIR uses a battery that never discharges but provides bias as the initial condition.

The DC current heterodyned over the permanent electrostatic charge is what induces a scroll wave in the scroll electret as well as injects electrons into the discharge tube, the electret-excited population inversion acts as a conductive conduit and as the injected electrons accelerate towards the anode they strip electrons out of the population inversion leaving behind holes causing the aforementioned secondary emissions.

The DC current diverges at the top of the tube, going into the tube and serially into the conductor of the scroll electret. The current then goes through a diode and then a capacitor bank where it then enters the base of the bipolar spark gap transistor. The function of this transistor is to automatically govern the divergent/convergent currents according to the load, which is parallel to the emitter and collector, and to maintain the scroll wave by collapsing the overall charge in the system. The double spark gap creates a bucking current as opposed to ac or dc, this implodes the Heaviside component into the load.

Therefore the AIR is auto-tuning. Excess energy is grounded or returned to the battery.

The author/inventor contends that the only reason this system can work as claimed is because it mimics the transdimensional mechanics of Dark Energy at more obvious ends of the scale as well as the hidden mechanics at the mesoscopic scale.

Companion Video – Sullivan Corollary: http://uk.youtube.com/watch?v=6G-MvvR28iQ

Revised EM theory: www.cheniere.org, http://www.energyscience.org.uk/

Closest Prior Art, The PAGD: http://www.aetherometry.com/Labofex Plasma Physics/aspden pulsed plasma intro.php

ARC FOAMING PROCESS ABSTRACT

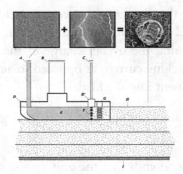

June 25, 2007

Arc Foaming is a new method of foaming a variety of materials including: metal, glass, plastic, ceramic or any combination.

In particular this new process is an advance in the metal foaming industry, which via known methods such as gas infusion and deposition, are only able to produce small, expensive objects. Conversely, Arc Foaming allows very large objects such as a car chassis, boat hull, building or virtually anything to be grown via stereolithography technology, such as a robotic arm or plotter mechanism. The larger the object, the greater the properties of metal foam can be exploited – to a point of course, but Arc Foaming is the only technology able to reach that point.

The novelty of Arc Foaming is in the process itself and how it is formed. Arc Foaming is an example of "geomimicry", that is, lightning striking wet sand has the same effect:

FULGURITES

Fulgurites are glassy, root-like tubes formed when a lightning stroke terminates in a dry sandy soil. The intense heating of the electrical current passing down into the soil along an irregular path fuses (melts) the sands. Concurrently, *vaporization of soil moisture and possibly even vaporization of the sandy materials, causes the molten material to be expanded* into a tube whose diameter may be well over an inch, but whose wall is very thin.

Arc Foaming is artificially producing this phenomena but with all variables under control. The novelty to my invention is the method of arcing electricity through an aqueous suspension in combination with the stereolithography technique of "Growing" to form and shape an object with a stochastic foam material.

The invention consists primarily of a Grooming Head *D*. The Grooming Head is attached to stereolithography technology via shaft of necessary articulation *B*. The Grooming Head is passed over positively charged base plate *I*. Relative to its forward motion over this base plate, a fore nozzle *A* dispenses a suspension *E* of gel : material particulate onto the plate. The Grooming Head contains and shapes the suspension into a uniform layer of a given shape. The side walls and nozzles of the Grooming Head may be articulated to allow for intricate shapes but a standard rectangular profile is shown in the drawing. The negatively charged electrode *D'*, connected to external power supply/control *C*, is aft of the dispensed layer of shaped suspension, it passes over the base plate with an adequate wattage to produce desired foam via the arcing *F* of electricity between electrode and base plate. This arcing simultaneously welds the particulate and vaporizes the gel leaving behind a layer *H* of striated, stochastic foam that will easily fuse to the next layer. The neg. charged electrode and Grooming Head must be of a proper material such that it does not bond with material to be foamed. Vents *G* perforate the walls of the Grooming Head in order to vent vaporized gel from the Arc Foaming Process.

VARIABLES

A variant of the Grooming Head is the Stencil-Ratcheting Head. This method allows a continuous shape to be extruded under the head as it climbs the previous layers (as opposed to the Grooming Head, which produces a continuous single layer). The Stencil- Ratcheting Head requires that the nozzle, walls, and electrode be integrated into a single piece.

As mentioned, the Arc Foaming process presents a few variables which the user may adjust to produce different foams according to their needs:

1 – Ratio of Gel : Material Particulate
2 – Conductivity of Gel – based on material to be foamed
3 – Viscosity of Gel
4 – The wattage between neg. electrode and pos. base plate
5 – The Speed of Grooming Head over base plate

NEUROMIMETIC HYBRID PROCESSOR WHITE PAPER

The NHP is a computing device born of the biomimicry methodology. Its purpose is to replace silicon which is nearing the end of its capacity. Compared to the other silicon alternatives it stands out as having the only true neuromimetic architecture.

BIOMORPHED ELEMENTS

-neurons - polymer sheathed dendrimers (encapsulated electroactive objects)
-neural fluids - TCNQ/ polyelectrolyte saturated solution
-synapse - thermionic injection, FET induced arcing from source to drain, spontaneous clamping, floating deposition
-neural network - back propagation, feed forward, discrete time recurrent, continuous time recurrent
-determinism - transcopic electrochemical noise analysis, impedance spectroscopy, phase states vs. transition points

COMPONENTS and ARCHITECTURE

The NHP consists of 4 self metalizing polymer films and 2 semiconductive polymer TFT's arranged into a cube shape. Inside this cube is 5-10 cc's of a TCNQ/poly-electrolyte/dendrimer suspension. On the outside of the cube is a scalar interferometer, it is a thermionic injector for the suspended nucleation of the suspension required for certain neural networks – its scalar bottle is the "thalamus". This mini-HAARP is coupled to another which does a non-invasive BMI with any part of the nervous system.

Since the NHP is a hybrid computer, the digital TFT or analog suspension can act as the driver depending on the desired neural network. Unlike other computers, the NHP derives its determinism transcopically. This means that it is a molecular-quantum computer. What this equates to is a binary system with a fuzzy system enfolded within the fractional dimensions between 1 and 0.

The self-metalizing films are reference/auxilary electrodes injected with stochastic resonance, each opposing set has a different noise which creates a co-chaotic medium out of the suspension, in effect keeping it metastable and homogenous. The TFT's are the working electrodes perpendicular to the self-metalizing films. They are injected with a collapsing or periodic waveform signal. As the signal cascades through the phase states, it modulates the stochastic resonance via sympathetic resonance, phase lock, handshake or beat. This is what clamps the suspension into a molecular wire and gives a pathway weight. Once the pathway or filament is formed it will have non-volatile memory.

ADVANTAGES AND PROPERTIES

All the known advantages of a hybrid architecture are here. All the advantages of a fuzzy system are here. What is unique to the NHP is that it has incredible parallel processing power due to the shear number of filaments. Mobility and storage density are roughly 10,000 fold greater than that of a silicon chip.

The true innovation to computing is the potential for AI and the elimination of interface peripherals.

These processors, since they are neuromimetic, are ideal for biomimetic humanoid robots. Each neural network can subsumptively regulate a specific organ/subsystem. Visual, haptic, audio, kinematic, biological, power, pneumatic and hydraulic systems can be matched to the ideal neural network. Custom neural networks can be made by rearranging the components.

TRANSCOPIC DETERMINISM

In quantum computer theory it is believed we must create quantum error correction algorithms or filter the noise to get a dependable processor.

This is resistance to chaos. The quantum foam is literally the most chaotic phenomenon. To resist the quanta chaos is the most futile thing a neuromimetic computer could do. We overlook the role stochastic noise plays in our own consciousness so we don't consider it when designing a computer. We measure for the most part according to periodic or orderly methods. We also don't consider the underlying chaos in our macroscopic patterns.

The processors I designed utilize two signals, stochastic and periodic. These represent the chaos of the foam and the periodic functions of the macroscopic brain - alpha, beta, delta, Schumann resonance... Carrier and modulation functions are reversible depending on the desired neural network. Sympathetic stochastic resonance is the key to designating weight to a given path. The resultant beat of these two signals meshing is what brings order out of chaos. The more reinforced this analog memory becomes, the more weight it has and the more order it attains. But this type of order is neither pure chaos nor pure order as are the noise and periodic signals. The periodic signal maintains what is modulated but the stochastic noise signal is what makes it associative or holographic to the rest of the suspension.

The NHP doesn't have to "make an end run around the difficulties posed by the laws of nature" like the myriad of other Silicon Alternatives striving to beat Moore's Law. Molecular, Biological, and Quantum computing consortiums, many of which are sponsored by DARPA, may use biology inspired algorithms but they ultimately fail to mimic biology. The potential seems to be greater than results and the Silicon Industry feels safe because of this, but even the neural networks that run on silicon fail to mimic because, after all, they represent a 2D digital medium.

Biomimicry is a new science which treats nature as the standard for judging the "rightness" of our innovations. Nature is acknowledged to have billions of years of R+D and inherent superiority. Many old sciences are coming around to this humility and reverence for what nature can do, and it is most pronounced in the computing architecture fields. It is normal for humans to compare biology to the machine of the day - the brain is compared to a computer often but never the other way around. A new model of the brain, biomimicry methodology, and the NHP which this model supports, may make brain and computer truly synonymous.

I took a class at Cornell University - Systems on a Chip: Interdisciplinary Computer Engineering. I have witnessed first hand the schism between the self-educated, and the formally educated, the wise intentions of interdisciplinary endeavors and how they fail. I saw how, despite the multiple professors, all the students remained specialized. I was disappointed by the class because it didn't teach anything about how a team should work together; none of the professors worked together, the individual subjects were never tied together. The grad student who organized the class and let me sit in on it saw the NHP, thought it was "great," and said he'd try to get some professors to look at it. One said that that kind of technology is "at least 20 years away." Another looked at it and said it was over his head. This discrepancy in attitude and knowledge is a big concern and it's what gives me an advantage as an independent. I left the class because one day the class had to break up into groups. I couldn't be in a group. The grad student, in an emphatic tone, told everyone that, "this is about quantifying. Do NOT use your imaginations!"

This statement is pure blasphemy to an inventor.

The NHP was conceived admittedly about 9 years ago in the "EUREKA" fashion with two words: "CRYSTAL BRAIN." It wasn't until about a year ago that it all came together when I did some intensive studying online to find components. In that process I learned of all the other silicon alternatives and saw how those efforts were not yielding very much. It was my intent to adhere to biomimicry methodology and the reason was simple: I should be able to reverse engineer the very thing that allows me to - i.e., the brain. Whereas corporate and academic circles may frown upon my methods for doing this, it nonetheless worked. Call it an unfair advantage but one brain is all that's needed to explain itself. Of course when studying and associating is all that's demanded of you, being exceptionally productive is possible. I had no red tape to contend with, or people, or deadlines.

Basically, I feel that I would be an ideal interdisciplinary team leader for the NHP or any endeavor.

An interesting anecdote

At the same time I took my class at Cornell, a man named S. Rosen took it upon himself to be my business advisor. He arranged a conference call for me with a consultant from Compaq to help determine the feasibility of the NHP. After a few minutes he told me that what I had was, "A bowl of goo" and that I was, "just another kid trying to reinvent the wheel" and that the NHP was, "a solution looking for a problem."

I then realized that as a representative of the silicon industry he was either threatened or ignorant or both.

PROPRIETORY ISSUES

The only setback to building a proof-of-concept prototype, besides finding funding, facilities, and a proper team, is in acquiring the individual components. Polymer thin film transistors are relatively rare. The manufacturer of the TFT that the NHP would use is Opticom. It would take an entity like _____ to sway them into the use of their TFT. The self-metalizing polymer is available through NASA. The impedance spectroscopy software (the NHP driver) is available through Gamry. The polyelectrolyte, TCNQ, and dendrimers should be available through various university sources.

The name escapes me and I'm away from the internet right now (February 2010) but in 2001 when I invented this I had not known of "In its Image". Google it with "Skynet". This is the true driver of the NHP. When you dial in the proper ratio of fuzzy between 1 and 0 or of life and death you get emergent novelty.

APPLICATIONS

Now obviously the first thing _____ is interested in is Encryption. The NHP could definitely handle that, but the it was designed to answer decades of questions about AI, soulcatching, massive parallel processing, and even some paranormal questions (ex: in quantum theory we should be able to turn on the NHP with direct thought).

357

The NHP can recreate any gate or neural network - it is universal in every sense.

The NHP is ideal for all robotics apps, all physics modeling, math.

MASS ENGINE

I'm not going to include any enabling data about this invention here because I feel that it's more important now to deal with the implications and philosophy. The teleological return to ultimate self-similarity is fulfilled here. Access to other dimensions is kind of a big deal and deserves due diligence. The following are bits excerpted from my "Comparative Study of Singularity Based Gravity Modification" and may reference missing parts, sorry. I will start with another one of those weird connections:

The Seraphim = angels that stand on either side of God and are concealed by 6 wings

Calabi Yau Spaces = manifolds that mirror pair a Hodge Star and are enfolded by 6 real dimensions

Google Image these images.

THE BIG PICTURE

Most myths, speculation, and conspiracy theories that surround the UFO issue have been established and most people are content with them. The governments of the world know the secrecy must be maintained because the aliens from outer space would create such a distraction, should they become blatantly exposed, that nobody would care about politicians anymore. Let's assume the alien technology would render their industro-militant counterparts useless too.

This is what it boils down to, universal truths vs. human power bases threatened by those truths - and we have to wait 50-100 years for declassification of the truth? What's the situation going to be like until then? The tension between the UFO community and the governments builds to such an extent that a million Ufologist march on Area 51 occurs and every one of them has to be shot in the head. That kind of martyrdom will never occur so we sit and wait for a mass landing or some other smoking gun.

I was describing the design and theorems of my invention here to a friend and she said that such a device in use was synonymous with "raping God". I tried to explain that any invention that mimics or conforms to nature or natural processes is inherently less blasphemous than say, nuclear fission or internal combustion. (yes, I know they're natural – Radioactive decay and cow farts are great just NIMBY!)

My friend's comment more or less sums up what the ignorant would have you believe. From Christians who link aliens (who they also say don't actually exist) with Satan, to the UFO community itself, this technology is plagued with stigma and misinformation. How many times have you heard this from a Ufologist, "Yeah, whatever that alien / silver disc-glowing ball / silent hovering technology is, its hundreds / thousands / millions of years ahead of OUR technology / comprehension / ability..." as if linear time had anything to do with it! Think about it, even if we did get a lot of our modern electronics from back-engineering alien tech – WE STILL BACK-ENGINEERED IT and further innovated.

This is a subtle pessimism rooted in our assumption that "ADVANCED" must mean "COMPLICATED". I'm not saying there aren't matter/antimatter reactors, gravity amplifiers, photon accelerators, and various other subsystems, I'm saying that the performance characteristics of certain types of craft (masslessness, invisibility, instant acceleration & deceleration, short range and interstellar quantum teleportation/macroscopic tunneling) imply that they are of a simple design.

Lets face it, if a flying saucer had as many parts as a car we'd need a repair shop in every solar system. The same friend who said I would be raping god also said that it would take tremendous power to do what I was saying. I tried to explain that zero point energy is the most abundant source of power (see Feynman's coffee analogy) and that all is required is a seamless link to it. This link is the Dark Energy fed Penrose Process; the thing that makes Tipler's Cylinder and other preposterous theoretical methods (because of false assumptions about energy density) feasible.

I figured this out at 23 having no knowledge of the above...The most advanced form of propulsion is also the simplest...it was last night, 7 years later - Easter Eve – that I was compelled to Google the last pieces of the puzzle. It's only now that I could convey the overall mechanics (pieces) the only way I can, sans equations...

Why haven't I built such a simple machine? No more than 10k parts & labor...I just happen to be poor and haven't looked into quartz fiber, "Uh yeah Corning..."

There is one more important subject to address - spiritual vs. political/ military implications of this technology. As Sci-Fi and various members of the disclosure scene point out, the human military establishment wants to weaponize space and master flash travel for obvious reasons. Non-local capabilities and orbital DEWs represent the ultimate upper hand in virtually any stage be it domestic, foreign, or ET terrorists...As "staff reporter" points out, the tricky part of controlling a massless object is controlling it. The military may have its own production antigravity technology piloted by humans but it does not involve teleportation or even mass reduction. For a human to be quantum phaseshifted is no less than meeting your creator. To be asked to then teleport and kill is utterly ridiculous. This isn't to say an "evil" non-human can't teleport it's just that humans, by design, are subject to moral relativism which cannot be corrupted after quantum revelation has occurred. Point is, the most advanced technology can't be used for military purposes because to navigate it you must ask Jesus for directions so to speak.

The external merkaba singularity technology of the author uses the heart chakra as the secondary "steering singularity"...for those who don't depend on computers beyond the akasha itself.

Among the myriad mathematical, theoretical, observed and experimental, among the physics, metaphysics, biblical and lore in our modern infosphere there exists enough data to piece together something awesome. To become massless and invisible, to be able to teleport and fly outside linear time at fantastic speeds via a simple machine. There is no simple way to explain how this works, the following is the best the author could do to convey the related concepts to a relatively versed audience. My inability to comprehend linear math has evolved a lexicon heavily dependent on Chaos and MHD terminology. The condensed quasi-mathematical writing style is my attempt to find a common language as I am obviously forced to write in a linear fashion (The GUT that can be reduced to an equation is not the true GUT). My intent is to present all the pieces of the puzzle so that with enough study (just Google it) you'll be able to associate the ideas here as I have and experience the peak moment that I as an inventor treasure. The task of conveying the backstory of this invention is more pertinent to the reader at this point - to understand the singularity is to literally be a Gnostic with no distinguishing dogma, sorry. The burden of proof on my end is obviously in the working prototype not language, but the burden of understanding is upon the reader and his/her requisite curiosity and patience. It takes a very curious person to cope with all the technojargon and a patient one to integrate it - fortunately, I've done 99% of the work here for you.

My desire to focus on singularity based antigravity/space manipulation/ vacuum engineering is because it is the ultimate expression of the KISS principle while also being the most disruptive technology ever conceived – the deepest of grails.

I'm speaking of a **"Mass Engine"** or in old school terms **"External Merkaba"**, a device that creates a singularity to be used as an isometric fulcrum with which to displace Branes. This equates to a mesoscopic rotating blackhole where the ergosphere quantum phaseshifts biology (as opposed to thermal phaseshifting). This equates to subatomic polarity reversal where the mean energy band of the atom(s) take on the role of the nucleus. The overall size of the atoms don't change but they do lose inertial mass and visibility as the *TOTAL* CPT violation takes place and the device is primed for teleportation.

This is all a seamless event but that's the best way to describe the process.

To simplify, THE BICYCLE ANALOGY:

The mean energy band, when it is explicate biased or in its entropic/ ground CPT bias, is like a person peddling a bike around a circular path at a constant speed. Death or OBE is when the person stops peddling but maintains the same speed or angular momentum by continuously decreasing radius, this spirals the *subtle* bodies up the **Phi constant** into the implicate order/hyperspace, death is merely **conservation of transdimensional inertia.**

The phaseshift in this analogy is when the person peddles faster AND decreases radius, this spirals the *gross* body up/down the **Phi constant**; the atom(s) adopts two energy bands to act as one mean energy band. The Phi constant is also known as the golden helix and it is a continuous phase transition representing simultaneous time, it is the strange attractor of space and is the only transdimensional orbit.

Finally this document is patently "bridge" material. I'm among a few who have the luxury of no status to maintain and am thus able to pursue the unpopular endeavor of discovering redundancy in religious + scientific language. While scientists rigorously deny spirit I must insist that when dealing with a singularity the laws of language break down as well. The singularity does not care if I use the term "chakra" or "Ganglionic Pilot Wave". The duality-defined language of life in general is mutually used for most disciplines but not with invention where one should be associating any and all data regardless of source. Comfortable reliance on one's own discernment can only increase with greater perspective, and so I am comfortable at this point (pun intended) while you may not be....if you can't take the singularity get out of the ergosphere!

"...A time is coming when I will tell you plainly about my father"

"The universe is shaped like an onion"

Yeshua ben Joseph The Alpha Christ

Just as John could not say "bring electricity down from zeropoint" In reference to Rev 13:13, Ezekiel could not use literal terms because they simply didn't exist. Here are the scientific terms for the relevant biblical lexicon starting with Ezekiels Vision:

cherub - biological body
man - magnetic body
lion - auric body
eagle - internal merkaba

wheel within wheel - external merkaba
wing - mass plate, plasma mirror, monopole plane
eyes - primary, secondary, terciary monopole node(s)

fire/bja – Spontaneously collapsed Synthesized matter formed in secondary nodes

Tiny Mustard Seed Into Enormous Bush = Hyperspace Mapping (initial conditions) bifurcating into linear time / mass, where our dimension is the riddled basin / bush

Hell/Consuming mouth of the Blue Sheol = Static Blackhole

Judgement Day / Hour of silence = Terence Mckenna's Time Wave Zero, Mayan End Time; End of Novelty = Ultimate self-similarity = totally collapsed magnetic field. Superpositioning of Solar System Super Electron with Galactic plane EM null zone.

Sky Rolling up = galactic plane rising into view over horizon.

Stars falling = gravitational lensing creating magnification of heavenly bodies.

Caught up in net/separation of germ & chaff/weights and measures = collective/dharmic soul matrix spectroscopy and refining.

BREAK IT DOWN!

Science is the backengineering of GOD/GUT - GOD/GUT is the science of engineering.

Monotheism vs. polytheism = White light vs. Spectrum

Angels or particle zoo? They both have a hierarchal function with varying purposes

Animism or what isn't alive?

what is life, what is energy?

can you destroy either?

consciousness, is it language, senses or emotion?

where is gods mind?

Fall from grace or vacuum fluctuation?

364

telepathy or original language?

genesis or seven successive forces/transdimensional reductionism

Adam & Eve or vector space and scalar space?

little scroll or psilocybin mushroom?

the living word or living CPT violation?

lake of fire or plasma mirror?

Manna or ormus?

man made in the image of god or base 12 free space broken down into base 12 DNA?

Religion is blamed for causing war
Science is blamed for making war more efficient

every physics camp is a sect
every reformation is a new theory

the southern big bangers
the holy newtonian church

einsteinians 10:7 - action at a distance is spooky
michelsonmorley 31:5 - no shift, no aether

THE TERMINATOR PARADOX, TIME LOOPS AND THE GE/C204

In the Terminator movies a paradox of time travel occurs which isn't too obvious but raises some questions. A damaged chip recovered from a cyborg sent back in time eventually leads to the creation of that cyborg, so who conceived and built the whole original chip in the first place? This may be viewed as a variation on the grandfather paradox in that a time loop has eliminated causality for the time loop, the difference is that biology has an obvious continuity that can be resolved with parallel worlds/multiverse, the chip on the other hand has to be invented; the chip was never invented yet it exists, how?

With this paradox it would seem that the chip design has to preexist as a meme in hyperspace, that is, it is an eternal potential object at any point in our linear time.

There are three points of the story we must connect and resolve:

1 - The arrival of the cyborg at the very beginning of the first movie.
2 – The partial back engineering of the chip by Cyberdyne
3 – The sending back of a the fully developed Cyberdyne cyborg

Firstly let's assume that it is possible for any object(s) to spontaneously collapse its meme form into linear time and mass through **intent alone**. Now lets consider the actual physics of time travel. When speaking of the conventional pod-to-pod "3D fax" the actual object is scanned/broken apart, transmitted and "reconstructed" at the other side. This reconstruction is in fact naturally occurring at a fantastic refresh rate, such that the seething froth of the quantum foam is averaging out our form. Between the pods the object has been reverted to its meme state (pure data as opposed to collapsed data).

The meme state is the meme state regardless of where and when it has collapsed in linear time, **as long as it appears once it appears forever**… so the act of time travel has separated the act of invention from that of R+D. The complete chip does exist – at 1 and 3. So the questions then are, "Does the damage of the chip constitute a real loss of its meme?" "Did the scientist at Cyberdyne do his own form of "time travel" in his reverse-engineering?" He obviously recreated a whole chip so the mystery of invention is intimately connected with the Terminator Paradox – in fact they may be synonymous.

We must consider what the act of invention really is; it is a spontaneous collapse of novelty into the mind of a human. So where did the idea originally come from?

The only logical conclusion is that humans are inventing a new world at every moment from infinite potential worlds and that divergence is the rule not the exception; it is likely impossible for a time traveler not to create a world divergence to some degree…We average out our own reality through memetic convergence in reverse time (invention) and genetic divergence in linear time (conception) this is how novelty is conserved.

The world is founded on a paradox – the aether/vacuum – so creating another paradox is going to be obvious only to the time traveler who can compare his own world change (see The Butterfly Effect movie).

OK, what about the John Titor, GE/C204 tale? In case you don't know about this here's a brief summary of the event: In 2001? a website forum received a post from a self-proclaimed time traveler who provided a reasonable story for his presence here (A kind of Y2K situation dependent on old school IBM translation technology to fix), as well as some technical details/schematics of his time machine and a rundown of events in our near future. He exhibited a flawless execution of what sounds like valid protocol.

(His history of the USA civil war is interesting in that he says it starts in 2005 **but nobody notices** until 2008-9. This is evident in the rise of culture/class wars on television, the war isn't just going to be televised it is the televised - as a purely psychological decoy duality! That's why it's not so obvious until the "war" is escalated to utter stupidity. In four years Spouse Swapping shows will be interchanging KKK families with Black Islamic families – And there won't be heartwarming humbling learning at the end, only increased resentment. There is also mention of WW3 in 2015 and then peace, resentment and hard work after that. A person will be judged on how s/he is contributing to the recovery of earth, not on their ringtones and sneakers. He says that yes, some weird events did happen in 2012, but he's not allowed to speak of them, why isn't certain.)

I only wish I'd been there at the forum to ask him some questions. He said that he had created a 2.5 % divergence between worlds…How is this divergence measured? By comparing historical documents? John also mentions windows in which he can travel in, what do these windows constitute? A Hyperspatial aligment? A Harmonic of the original transport event?

Could John create a Terminator Paradox? He claims that the General Electric technology he uses began with the CERN micro-blackhole created in 2007. This scenario isn't a terminator paradox because the technology has a definite continuous existence between 2007 and 2036 in memetic transform to object form.

But what would happen if someone at GE now in 2005 got a hold of his schematics and did their own "Cyberdyne" on these documents? Would that mean the CERN project is an independent beginning no longer connected or that a genuine divergence takes place? Depends on GE and what they decide to do with this information. With insights provided from the C204 maybe an independent inventor could create a variation on it. Were GE or anybody to use that data on the C204 to create a time travel or teleportation technology John would be responsible for a divergence in that arena.

What if John returns to 2036 and discovers the whole reason he went back to 1975 is now unnecessary because of a "new" computing infrastructure introduced in 2006? That would represent an enormous divergence from the world he left and the one he returned to, but the divergence here doesn't necessarily have anything to do with his actions in time. Why should he or shouldn't he return to "his" 2036? Can a time traveler choose or are they screwed like in "Sliders" and "Quantum Leap"? Are these parallel worlds really parallel or only potentially parallel depending on events in linear time to collapse and govern them? All potential world timelines may have an attractor or convergence points (common events) centered around the collapse of certain memes but then they break up again into chaotic potential as politics and social influences dictate the meme. The Second Advent of Christ, the independent conception of time travel/ teleportatation technology, Judgement Day...these are major common events for all worlds, which course averages out is a mystery only known to the present – when most humans are restricted to. Remote Viewing and Hypnotic Progression reveal very much what John and many other prophecy seems to be indicating...and its ALWAYS OUR CHOICE, an equally crushing yet liberating proposition.

There is a way to test all this but only linear time will tell the truth. As of now there is no conclusive evidence that the John Titor story is true or a hoax. I am not certain but I choose to believe his story is real. I believe this tale because of his level of understanding and the technical details supplied. I also believe he cannot come from the same world I will create. It is possible that he was for real but his story is not, that is, the IBM story is a red herring and it was really a test of the "Time Travel" meme to establish a baseline divergence. Factored in to this experiment is the consensus opinion of the people of the millennium, the stickiness of the story in cyberspace and any novelty spawned by the story. Perhaps this very document will collapse this meme into our timeline as a real option - which would at least prove how invention works.

33 TRIADS

AKA	CREATOR	MAINTAINER	DESTROYER
Archetype	Water	Air	Land
Christian	Father	Holy Spirit	Son
Hindu	Brahma	Vishnu	Shiva
Topological	Negentropy Attractor	Strange Attractor	Entropy Attractor
Particles	Leptons	Gluons	Hadrons
Bohm	Super Implicate	Implicate	Explicate
Dimensional	Non-D	Trans-D	Inter-D
Explicate	Vacuum Fluctuations	Sub Atomic	Atomic
Implicate	Zero Point	Orgonic	Electric
Super Implicate	Quantum Dot	Open String	Closed String
Chaos	Mapping	Orbit	Attractor
Co-Chaotic	Aethermetric	Photochemical	Sonothermic
Time	Static	Simultaneous	Linear
Cosmological Constant	Flat Ω	Open $< \Omega$	Closed $> \Omega$
Origin Model	Ekpyrotic	Steady State / Plasma	Open Inflation
M-Theory	Branes	Branefall	Braneshear
Q-Foam Coarsening	Tetrahedral Mapping	Tile Sharing / Jitterbug	Cubic Mapping
Function	Allows States	Mediates Aspects	Hosts Events
Yoga	Yantra	Tantra	Mantra
Holographic	Image	Reference Beam	Film
Electrical	Voltage	Admittance-Resistance	Amperage
Orgonic	Dor	Orgone	Oranur
Entropy	Shannon's Entropy	Degrees of Freedom	Boltzmann Entropy
Energy	Negative	Quasi-Electrostatic	Positive
Holosyntactical	Logos	Gematria	Biologos
Quantum Foam	Black Hole	Zero Point Manifold	White Hole
Magnetic	Moment	Hall Effect / Lenz Law	Permeability
Symetry Group	Dimensions 12	Phase States 7	Forces 4
Math	Wave Function	Field	Particle
Geometry	Fractal	Phi	Euclidean
Theory Subsets	Quantum	General Relativity	Electromagnetics
New Physics	Chaos	Sync	Complexity
Chromodynamics	Bottom - 1/3	Charmed + 2/3	Down - 1/3
"	Top + 2/3	Strange - 1/3	Up + 2/3

BLOWOUT ──────   ────── BOUNDARY

HORIZON

Higgs Field   "Speed" of Light

369

OTHER INVENTIONS

I could write an entire other book about inventing but for now I wanted to share some more IP. Recognition is my desired currency now – this is what my ego is tied up in. If someone at the Masdar Initiative sees my Solar Dome and decides to appropriate it without compensating me monetarily I still have the satisfaction that they thought it was worthy. Forget licensing, just hire me as an expert consultant. I will still build my own version anyway. I despise the patent process, not what it stands for. The joy of inventing is its own reward so I don't really care about money beyond its ability to afford a Dean Kamen lifestyle. Pursuing IP rights is not worth the effort, and ideologically I feel that the patent process should be subsidized and its workforce increased until then, F it.

SOLAR DOME

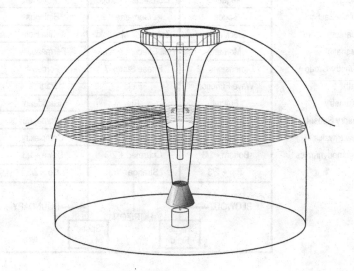

The Solar Dome is a Geomimetic Atmospheric Generator that combines Updraft, Vortex and Downdraft techniques to maximize the potential energy of hot dry air. Solar energy is harvested via greenhouse effect and stored with thermal mass. A large enough Solar Dome would retain enough heat to run after the sun has set making it perpetual motion of the second kind. The efficiency of the Solar Dome can be increased if nested in a phase conjugated focus, which has the advantage, in the realm of solar energy, of not requiring tracking mechanisms.

CLIT

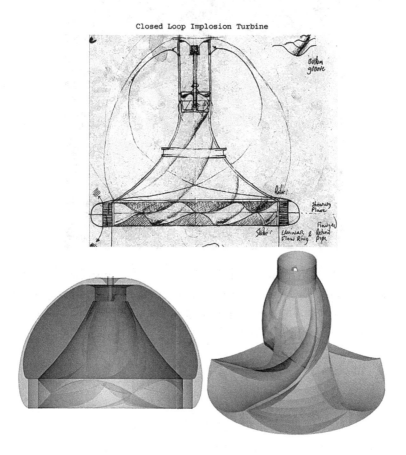

Closed Loop Implosion Turbine

The Closed Loop Implosion Turbine is based on the principles of Viktor Schaubegrer, it uses two forms of implosion to accumulate kinetic energy which is converted into electricity. The CLIT contains water, sheared between a rotor and stator into vortices which converge and spin an impeller. The impeller is allowed to spin and oscillate up and down. On it's upstroke it lifts a rod connected to a shut-off valve at the bottom of the cylinder. This stops the flow causing cavitation which sucks the impeller back down. The cycle produces a pressure wave that constructively interferes with the following cycle, thus accumulating kinetic energy.

HYDROFOIL

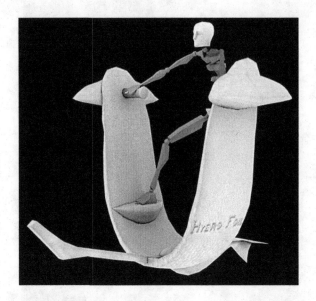

This is a stand up hydrofoil that uses wing warping to steer. The user can scoop out a ramp by leaning forward or lean safely from side to side. The boat does all the pulling, lessening fatigue for a longer ride and allowing the rider to focus on technique.

ROBOGROOMER

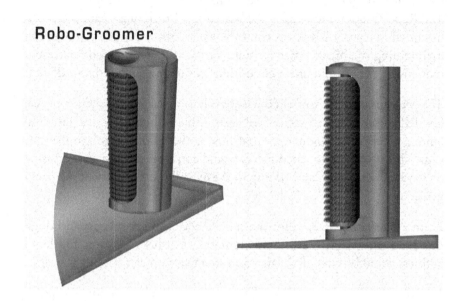

Interactive Tactile Comfort

Pets (cat and dogs) enjoy being petted/scratched/groomed but sometimes they have sensitive areas. Sometimes like us, they can't reach with their own limbs an itch. Sometimes the pets are too lazy, and some owners are as well.

Many pets are left home alone all day with no human to provide useful if not loving touch.

Grooming not only makes the pet feel good, it keeps fur clean and removes loose fur that would otherwise get on clothing and furniture and collect into bunnies around the baseboard.

What if a pet could choose when it wanted to be groomed and for how long – as well as where – independent of human presence or effort? What if a pet could decide how much pressure is applied to its sensitive areas or itch?

Pets naturally brush up against objects to scratch an itch, the Robo-Groomer is an object designed specifically for that purpose – and more.

The Robo-Groomer is a rotating vertical axis brush mounted to a wide base that is stabilized by being placed in the 90 degree corner of a room. The Robo-Groomer resembles the beater bar/ brush of a vacuum cleaner, mounted upright. A built-in comb between bristle bundles removes fur, maintaining the brush's effectiveness. Fur is collected in a compartment that covers 1/3rd of the brush circumference for convenient disposal.

The pet leans into the brush of the Robo-Groomer activating a high torque, low RPM motor which spins the brush. This is the interactive part. An animal psychiatrist might agree that this modicum of control, this simple cause and effect, this independence, would empower an animal, increasing its sense of self-worth, and adding to the overall functionality of the pack/ pride.

From a marketing standpoint the same device can groom cats and dogs, one product, two markets. Sold separately, brushes of greater and lesser stiffness could be offered? A large and small version can be sold as well.

NOTE: The Robo-Groomer will sense from which direction the pet is passing and rotate in the correct direction – with the fur. The motor/gear/ groomer assembly will mount on a hinge allowing it to move left and right slightly, thus closing a contact switch which rotates groomer in said proper direction.

OTTOMAN GENERATOR

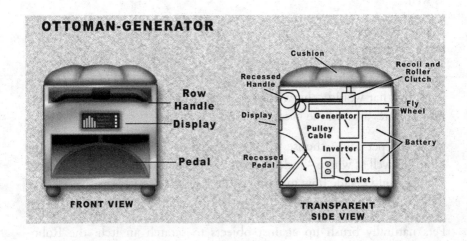

Scenario 1: A natural disaster strikes your area, you have a back-up generator but your fuel was used last week for the mower and you thought you could put it off…the tornado took out the power and dropped a house in the middle of the road…Utility company says it'll be 3 days to get power and you can't get fuel until the house is removed, whenever that will be…

Scenario 2: The kids are getting out of control with TV and video games. It's not that they are preoccupied, frankly TV and the Xbox are better than gangs and drugs, your kids are no stupider or violent…BUT – they are getting chubby and pun intended, aren't pulling their weight…

Scenario 3: You have a plethora of low draw and rechargeable electronics you want to keep powered up, you are a busy person and bills are piling up. You are concerned about the electrical grid being overburdened because, well, you have a vested interest in continuous 120V60Htz for many reasons…low impact exercise seems to be the best way to relieve stress but some nights you settle for chilling on the couch…

The OTTOMAN – GENERATOR (OG) can resolve all the above scenarios and likely more – 3rd world market?

The OG is a self-contained place to rest your feet, a means to low-impact exercise the upper and lower body, a generator, battery bank and/or ultra-capacitor, inverter and outlet. Recessed caddies will hold remotes etc,…It has a display that tells the consumer:

How many calories they have burned

How much money they are saving (by punching in their local utility's Kw/h rate)

How much energy they are generating and discharging

As a means of supplementing the grid, an engineering goal will be something like, 30 minutes of slow and easy exercise will provide 3 hours of LCD TV and Xbox – minimum. The OG will alert the user via beeping when its time to recharge/exercise.

To make it more user friendly the OG will detect the draw (Fridges, Toasters, ACs and other high draw appliances will not be plausible with one OG) and calculate how long it will power the device/s with the current charge.

The OG will be designed to connect to others in parallel so that a large family or group, so inclined, could generate enough energy to power larger appliances and become independent of the grid.

No other human powered generator can offer the assurance, versatility and convenience of the OG

THE END OF ENTROPY:

A Look at Our Entropic World and the Evidence Supporting How We Could Change This

by Amaterasu, 2010

Entropy... That measure of disorder that increases as energy is dissipated into unusable forms effects many aspects of our present human condition. It is easy to grasp the principle as it pertains directly to heat. We see the energy of a fire heat our food, but we also can see a great deal of heat going out unused and unusable. This extra heat can be seen as increasing the disorder, as the molecules affected move more rapidly and more disorderedly. A more difficult aspect to see is the entropy inherent in our social structure.

In Jeremy Rifkin's seminal work _Entropy_, published in 1980, he does an excellent job of demonstrating that, because energy is at the base of life, itself, entropy can ripple through society, creating disorder even as we try to clamp down and control the order of things. In fact, he paints a very grim picture of what we can expect as we consume more and more energy, explaining that fascist tendencies are most likely to crop up in the efforts to overcome entropy in our society. Today we see more and more signs of encroaching fascism.

The reason why energy and its entropy are tied in to our social structures is made clear by Rifkin in his work (p. 89):

> ... Every time we add our labor to a product or perform a service we expend energy and increase the overall entropy of the environment. Every time we exchange money for a product or a service, the legal tender we use represents

payment for previous energy that we expend. Money, after all, is nothing more than stored energy credits.

If money is merely the accounting of the available energy, it becomes clear that should an energy source come along that has the properties of being effectively infinite, available from anywhere, and negentropic (from "negative entropy"), the need for money dissipates. "Infinite money" has no social application.

In fact, because of our limited available energy and the money system developed to account for it, it is clear why we have a "power" elite, as well as poverty and exploitation. Rifkin explains (p. 57):

> Energy is the basis of human culture, just as it is the basis of life. Therefore, power in every society ultimately belongs to whoever controls the exosomatic [external] instruments that are used to transform, exchange, and discard energy. Class divisions, exploitations, privilege, and poverty are all determined by how a society's energy flow line is set up. Those who control the exosomatic instruments control the energy flow line. They determine how the work in society will be divided up and how the economic rewards will be allocated among various groups and constituencies.

Given this, it becomes clear that if such an infinite, available, negentropic source of energy were to be introduced, power over others would give way to individual autonomous power over self but no others. This can be seen as a major shift in Consciousness on this planet.

This all sounds hypothetical, a waste of time to contemplate even, to the average individual who has been told that we are stuck with the many entropic sources of energy we presently use (which also are sources we have to pay for). "Where is this miracle source?" they might ask.

And here is where I bring up the "Dark" Energy that is now heralded all over science shows about physics and cosmology. This energy, which has been called "radiant energy" (Tesla), "orgone" (Wilhelm Reich), "Zero Point Energy," and many others, is pervading space. It is within you and within me, around all of us, and is present anywhere we go. Interestingly, though we are told of this energy (usually as "Dark" Energy), no mainstream media (MSM) outlet has asked the most logical question: Can we extract this energy in usable form?

The reasons for this become clear when we look at the fact that those presently in power would have to give up their power over others (having already power over themselves). From the perspective of those few, they would "lose."

Such an energy source would represent, at least, a virtually infinite source that is available to all. Any attribution of a negentropic aspect comes from reports from a number of sources suggesting that cold, not heat, is the defining characteristic of drawing on this source. These reports and the surrounding research and data have surely been suppressed – at least to the extent of not reporting it and never, ever asking whether we can get something usable from "Dark" Energy. It would be a naïve position at best to expect the present power elite to ignore and NOT suppress and disparage any efforts to develop this source in usable form.

And so, it would appear that we have had methods of extracting usable forms of energy from the "Dark" Energy pool, called the plenum (opposite of "vacuum," which means "empty" – "plenum" means "full") for at least 100 years. And we might conclude that the power elite wish to remain in their place of power over others, else they would have released the means to extract usable energy to the public. (There is strong evidence of suppression of many "free" energy devices, from hydrogen-from-water devices through magnetic devices, as well as the Plenum Energy methods.)

The question now becomes, what would happen if we had this energy available to all of us? The answer depends on how we, as a planetary society, approach the matter.

Since we're examining society, it helps to understand that it moves and emerges in fractal expressions from a relatively small seed set of parameters. Up until now, the fractal seeds of all societies in history have included scarcity of energy (which is reflected in the scarcity of goods and money), and thus we see emerging greed, conspiracy, poverty, power elite, wage slavery and many other ills. If we look for a seed that gives an overarching structure for a society's development in the advent of having such a source of energy available, and take advantage of what media we can to raise awareness to the tipping point of the goals and precepts we define, the society that fractalizes out of that seed will be strong, healthy, and unrestrictive – provided the seed is geared to that end.

The key things that must be addressed are:

1. A code of conduct
2. Our approach to the Earth and how we bring forth the abundance she has to give
3. How open we will be on code and programs for our machines
4. How necessary work gets done
5. How we communicate and identify the primary issues
6. What focus in life should be stressed

If we seed our society with a code of conduct, calling to the fore the three Laws – which are:

1. Do not willfully harm or kill another Being
2. Do not willfully take or damage another Being's property
3. Do not willfully defraud another Being

this sets one parameter of the seed to ethics.

If we insist that all farming be organic – in its true sense, and not some trumped up legal definition – our food will grow ever better. If we insist that mining is done with a conscious awareness for retaining beauty and structure, our impact will be small and repairable. If we insist that manufacturing be done such that it is free of pollutants, our planet will remain healthy and abundant. If we are using the Plenum Energy, the energy we use will be clean (and fracture drilling, oil pumping, coal mining, rain forest clearing and other nasty behaviors and consequences associated with petrofuels will be eliminated). If we set this parameter of the seed with the drive to be thoughtful of our planet, our planet will thrive.

If we demand open-source in all technology, we remove fears of machines "taking over." Code can be looked at, published on the web – and better code will be worked out by those whose bliss it is to program things. A distrust of proprietary code (or any other hidden thing) should be promoted. Such a setting in this parameter of the seed will bring forth the best we can create.

By creating robots to do all the necessary work no one (or not enough people) wants to, we release ourselves to do what we enjoy – we are released from slavery, having cast it off onto our machines. This seed parameter is one only now available to humanity. Never before in our history have we had the option to create mechanical slaves for every "dirty job." Therefore, it, along with the addition of a negentropic energy source, will provide a frame for unique emergence, a new societal framework, a new consciousness.

With a central website, in forum style, to address major issues – divided into local sections, regional sections and global sections, with "votes" at a certain level elevating the problems and solutions to the next level to be voted on by a greater number – we can collectively coordinate to solve the issues of this planet. This seed parameter will see an emergence of human unity as a race and as a planet.

Setting a focus of fulfilling one's own bliss will see very much happier people, and far better results of efforts made – a job is done far better by someone who loves to do it than by one who feels compelled against their main desire. No job will be required to live well, but any job one wants to do is open to be done. I quote again from Rifkin's *Entropy* (p. 210) to illustrate the differences between the scarcity paradigm and the new abundance paradigm, as it relates to work:

> ... [T]he authoritarian structure of the workplace robs the individual worker of a chance to join in a community with his fellows to make decisions and develop his talents. Unable to join with others to explore his potential and creativity, the individual is forced to retreat into a shell in which he has neither meaningful rights nor responsibilities at his work. All he is left with is a job, a place to make money, and a degrading environment to which he must submit, eight hours of every day.

Thus we can see how a seed parameter of encouraging one to follow one's bliss – since in this new paradigm one can – uplifts each one of us and increases the value of consciousness in society.

Having described the seed, how might it be expected to manifest? One of the first products that is likely to be seen are "power boxes," which will be sold, initially. These would be units that had a mechanism to draw on the Plenum Energy and outlets to plug in our air conditioners, stoves, heaters, refrigerators, freezers, and so forth. This would allow us to move anywhere and bring our comfort items with us. We could "go camping" and still have our amenities, and many will. Eventually these items will each have their own units within.

As the cost of energy is removed from the production line at every stage, things will become less and less expensive, and at some point, will be given freely.

Other observables will include:

- Money falling into disuse
- Motivation from the heart as opposed to profit
- "Greed" becomes meaningless
- Peace
- Abundance for everyone
- Elimination of corruption
- Power over others supplanted by power over self
- Elimination of GMO's
- Great reduction in violence
- Creative pursuits increased greatly
- A healed planet
- Reduced or eliminated hoarding
- Value placed on human-created art, textiles and products
- Focus on cures, not patentable chemicals that sicken for profit motive
- Human interaction with only those whose company is enjoyable (reduced social friction)
- Robotic stewardship of the planet
- Increased love and compassion
- Greatly reduced stress

- Wondrous works
- "Live and let live" behavior
- Most "laws" become unnecessary
- Corporate power eliminated
- Products made to last – no "planned obsolescence"
- Waste reduced to virtually nil
- Food nutrition increased for all
- One's reputation becomes the "coin" one uses
- Personal responsibility for one's own behavior
- Spiritual growth
- Slavery (outright or wage-slavery) abolished
- Human dignity encouraged
- Increase in charitable behavior
- Self autonomy
- Things are done because someone cares – from raising children to caring for others

From this list, it is clear that many issues we now face will be solved. Wealth will be measured in richness of character, rather than in deposits to a bank account. And we will spend our time doing what we like to do, being with the people we like and share interests with. Inventions, rather than being suppressed, will burgeon, and the "Star Trek universe" may be within our grasp, with things like transporters and replicators emerging.

And spiritual growth and communication will be encouraged as we find a greater amount of our time available to pursue the exploration of our inner dimension.

And though this is not a solution to every issue arising from human interaction – we will always have our personal disagreements – the overall health of society will skyrocket. Yes, we may still argue with others over the smaller issues in our lives, and some may choose to behave violently, but the numbers of occurrences will drop to a level we would consider statistically insignificant. Definitely a vast improvement over what we see today.

When you consider what I present here, ask yourself these questions:

Does this threaten a pet vision – passing laws, say, to solve a problem you see, or a view of striking it rich – that you have of your future? Does this scare you? Do you look for reasons that it won't work? (All you envision as barrier issues – are scarcity paradigm views...)

Then ask yourself why working towards what I present here won't solve the issue you want to solve, why you wouldn't be rich in what I show to you, why it wouldn't fulfill your idea of heaven, why you are afraid, and/or why you look for reasons it won't work – rather than apply the proactive will to make this happen.

If we each choose to create this, since we have all it would take, consciously co-creating towards this goal, what I present would happen. It would take enough of us reaching a tipping point before it would all be downhill, and you may choose your future behavior. Speak for abundance, or reduce the chances that this will never happen by keeping silent.

In closing, I recommend any who work for someone else and also are privy to information (such as methods of extracting usable energy from the plenum) give strong consideration to coming forth with what is known. In the end, you and all of us will be better off – and even today's power elite will retain their life style, if not their power over us.

ANOTHER LETTER
FROM THE FUTURE

(as posted by Amaterasu on AboveTopSecret.com)

By now, some of you are familiar with the story Izzy told – I know that a fair number of you here have read The Abundance Paradigm, and a fair number either refuse to read (too busy, perhaps), or you skimmed and scoffed…and a number of you have never heard of the paradigm at all.

Of course, for my future to happen, many of you must *see* what happened from my perspective, thereby allowing you to believe that it could work…

Sorry, let me introduce myself. I'm Professor Harold Inke, and though Izzy is a beautiful heart, her focus was on the story of Amelia. She is just so grateful. But her story didn't address much the nuts and bolts of what happened as the abundance emerged from our choices.

Once Stephen Colbert – a true hero he! – let his viewers contemplate the paradigm via Amelia's appearance on his show, a triad of people who worked behind the scene on cameras and scripts got together and since one was geeky, and knew how to program a website of excellent function, they put together AbundanceParadigm.web (that last more for its significance and less how it was accessed) and did it all open-source.

Everything was kept as straightforward as possible and the forums to discuss things were allowed to emerge from the initial setup, with a "one computer, one vote" setup to star posts one thinks are good, and the votes matriculated the ideas upwards as people starred others' (but not their own) ideas.

Really, the site began with a place to post suggestions of what topics should be made into forums, and the star system led to the elevation of the things people cared about. Sure, it was work administering the site, reading the topics and throwing the ones that seemed frivolous into an open "trash" bin and archiving them, listening to defenses for ideas that were thus disposed of, and other administrative duties, but the goal was noble and the work had no shortage of efforts to grow with the project.

Suggestions that had star points up to the millions wound up being the prime things people were interested in solving.

The triad approached Stephen, their ultimate hero. Stephen, in his visionary wisdom, announced the site on his show. (In fact, the site was often worked in from there on…) Also, realizing bandwidth would rapidly be an issue, any who could help in that effort were invited to join. There were a few days here and there where it got sticky, but the problems were always solved. The rest of the media began a buzz about what Stephen had presented and about the ideas Amelia had brought forth, and the paradigm spread further.

There was a forum for <u>Amelia's Points</u>, which included the development of Personal Witness in all its open-source glory, there was information on Zero Point Energy and how to extract it – that guy who called himself the Anti/Christ had his design, based on a crop glyph, win out, with the most elegant and easy to produce device, as many designs were built and tested (and could be watched through the process via the web)…

There was looking at the resources on the planet and integrating the process of drawing on these resources in the most organic way. Distribution went hand in hand with these efforts. And those who could see the farthest and understand the most rose out of the discussions

The robot freaks open-source programmed things to take care of us, things to do any work none (or not enough) of us wanted to do. A number gained world-wide acclaim for their efforts. It was a grand and glorious time as many brought their ideas and expertise together to publicly work on creating a robot to do every job no one wanted to do. Many of the first ones were done in spare time, but it really didn't take long, with energy handled, until the efforts by the most active were fulltime bliss in their lives.

Shortly after the "Free Energy" forum started, the Anti/Christ's victory was assured, and soon after that, small boxes with outlets became available on the market, and a whole house could be plugged into energy sources that ran for years and years. Computers came out that never had to be plugged in. Cars began to spring up, running on clean ZPE (Zero Point Energy) that never had to stop for gas... Factories and offices were switched as these inexpensive units were eagerly built by those whose bliss it would be to provide this world with free energy. And there were an astonishing number of them that came forth to build. Though many units were sold, most would be given as gifts.

Though Izzy's world of Jump Doors and replicators was a bit in the future, just the freedom from energy worries (and costs!) made all the difference in the world.

People could run their air conditioning and their heat on free energy. They could run their cars. They could run all their electrics even in a tent. The number of people freed this way was staggering. Many opted to step back and go camping, with the new stoves, refrigerators, lights, heaters, air conditioners, composters and waste disposal units, and a car that flew in the sky (all were cheap because energy was no longer a cost all the way up the line of production), and many did not choose to come back – often working wirelessly from home at AbundanceParadigm.web.

Dean Kamen's water purification device had high demand, once the energy to run it was available. Fresh, clean water was available to more and more, as the device was built and distributed. Africa, especially, benefited, though the whole world found use for the device that could purify the water at hand.

And the products themselves began to be thoughtfully produced, no longer tied to profit motive, and efforts were made, not to build something that would break down so another could be sold... They were built to last. And as products that lasted made their way back into our lives, the amount of waste dropped radically. Things that used to last a year or two now lasted 20 or 30... Or virtually forever.

Farms were developed to run organically and in harmony with nature. And it was gentle robot shepherds that were developed for the projects as they spread out. The poison that was genmod, the soil-sapping fertilizers, failure to rotate crops – all this vanished. In its place the Earth returned to a pastoral state.

As long as people needed distribution, they could request it – the system of distribution having been set up via AbundanceParadigm.web – and country stores as well as city markets were well stocked, and the food was first very cheap and then free. Many, having "gone camping," started their own plots to grow food.

It did not take long for money to lose its hold of the humans on Earth. Though many thought this would be a long and involved process, it really took only a few years.

Yes, there was resistance by many a corporate toadie. It took a bit for it to dawn on them that they didn't have to have a boss. The appeal of that finally won over many – most had a human heart, deep down, and only made choices as they did because they could see no other choice. They became involved in speaking truth, helping, and making it all happen… and then the rest, the lizard hearted, followed into the paradigm.

As money slipped into uselessness, as people could, more and more, just ask for things and were given them, the rules of the lands were found to be unnecessary. Only the three Laws were seen as needed. Do not willfully kill or harm another, do not willfully take or damage another's property, and do not willfully defraud another. Regulations, statutes, acts, codes, mandates, and so on were ignored – who needs a tax code when there is no money to tax? Who needs the statutes on social services when no one needs social services? Who needs regulations when everything was built with care, and with an eye to lasting? When cheap crap was made no more?

It was standard for those who loved to create things to do so with camera running, so others could admire the process of craftsmanship that went into any effort. People avoided things mired in secrets. The more open about processes and programming, the more it was esteemed.

Open-source was the way to go, and though there were no rules against proprietary software, anyone who used the proprietary software did so at their own risk, whether it was in their computer or in their robots.

Many at the outset thought that Jump Doors and replicators were decades off, but they did not grasp what the results of the infinite point on the technology curve would be. Though there were efforts to disparage the fact, technology was advancing geometrically for the last 5,000ish years, with a very slow start, and in the 1800's beginning noticeably upward, the 1900's saw the curve shoot up enormously, and in the early 21st century... That rate of tech development was nearly pointing straight up. Nearing "infinite." With information about many things once hidden in Black Ops and in corporate secret labs now flowing via AbundanceParadigm. web, the work people did – those who cared (which by then was most) – advanced at a phenomenal rate. And the advent of many wonderful and surprising technologies, including Jump Doors and replicators, burst out in glory.

Many solutions in one industry found a place in another. Issues that were solved in one effort were picked up by others in different pursuits to solve better their problems. As secrecy for profit motive vanished with money, information flowed freely.

The cures for many diseases also were taken from their suppressed state and made known. The evil of making chemicals to patent that masked issues and led to more – all for profit – stopped. The many cures that Earth Herself offered were reported on, and healthful technologies sprang up. Marijuana, in particular, was honestly reported on. Gone were the vapid suggestions that there was something wrong with it (doggies telling Lindsay they don't like her when she's high) and the many easements of ills, and the fact came to the fore that it promoted more loving behavior than even sober people exhibit.

Many evils were exposed and eliminated. Plans in the works that involved taking over the planet fell useless, and we moved away from profit and Machiavellian motives. And there were some mighty evil plans afoot. Though a number of you here would not want to believe just how fiendish the plans are, it was a good thing the abundance paradigm was allowed (via Stephen) to emerge. For if it had not, the planet would have seen great suffering and strife. The New World Order would have taken over, with a few "elite" and many either dead or enslaved.

Antigrav, which you now have in Black Ops, was released, and cars became free of the roadway – open-source programmed to avoid collisions – and houses were built that floated in the sky, and then more and then more moved skyward. Many chose to remain on the planet, but most moved into the space above the surface of Earth.

It all worked because, mostly, people cared. They wanted to make it better for both others and themselves. Though many of you to whom I write think that mostly people are greedy and don't care, it is only that sense of futility, that belief that one is powerless, that leads to efforts to take care of oneself and damn the rest. Once hope and a sense of power were injected into the world society at large, things moved swiftly as people did what they could do.

Freed from the need to work to survive, many who cared were now able to afford their bliss, assisting those who needed help – whether it was finding for these unfortunate ones the cures, products and other necessities for a comfortable existence, or just adjusting to the new paradigm.

Once women were not dependent on men for their survival (as is the case now in many of your countries), they were empowered to control their own bodies. As a result, the birth rate dropped off, as they chose to have children, not to "help out," or because they had to for the men's egos, but because they were ready to love and cherish the children they chose.

And Earth's population stabilized. You can see how this would be true merely by studying those countries where women now have control of their bodies. Population growth is dramatically slowing, and in some places has gone negative. And with a stable population, it became easy to plan for and distribute to those who were in need.

In fact, the ability to take part and offer ideas, bring up observed resources, work locally for the global benefit, and see the abundance paradigm manifest was empowering. It filled many who had felt no purpose in scarcity with a sense of worth. Everyone was talking about the efforts, and everyone with a computer could input on the overall effort.

As is shown in the science of emergence, a small few rose, by their efforts and general consent into leadership roles. All discussions were online and, if it was not talked about openly, it was seen as a glad-hand effort. The main efforts, indeed, all efforts went through the forums at AbundanceParadigm. web. And Personal Witness was ideal to show others at the site what they saw, both in terms of problems and in terms of solutions.

Once hope returned, early on, people became more generous. They helped others more readily, and as they could. The true nature of humans, as loving and giving beings, came forth and the love of money – the root of all evil – went away. With only caring as a motivation, rather than profit, loving things (now affordable) were done.

The war profiteers lost the motive to instigate war while supplying both sides. The motive to lie for profit disappeared, and truth was spread instead. And humankind was freed.

Of course, now that I have shown you my future, you have a choice. You can be marched down into slavery and misery at the hands of a few who would presume that they are "better" than you, or you can spread the paradigm and bring forth true solutions to the problems you face. And they are bigger and more immanent than many of you are willing to face at this time.

Amelia was once heard saying, in frustration early on, "Would you just let my people go!?!" And in the end, in choosing that path that led to ME, she did indeed free her people.

Dr. Harold Inke

LET US FORGIVE.

by Amaterasu

Let us forgive the Down Trodden, who are reviled because they "take advantage of the system."

Let us forgive the Power Elite who choose to create the Down Trodden by hiding technology and news.

Let us forgive the Toadies, who know they behave unethically, but the money and status lure them astray.

Let us forgive the Slaves, who have but a piece of the total picture and dutifully fulfill their Work ethic tasks in return for some time they think is free.

Let us forgive the Stars, the ones who show us what others want us to see.

Let us forgive the Influences who see Beings of human construction as cattle or sheep.

Let us forgive the Influences who have held so little faith in Beings of human construction.

Let us forgive the Defrauders, whether Down Trodden, Power Elite, Toadie, Slave, Star or Influence.

Let us forgive the Incurious, who reject much data and do not investigate.

Let us forgive those amongst us who do not believe as we do in matters of the Spirit.

Let us forgive Beings born of a different nature than ourselves, be the difference in preferences, physical configuration, capacity, ideology, coloration, or status – within the Three Laws.

Let us, instead, stand both tall and humble – tall in the knowledge that we are true Beings who are capable of Love, and humble in the awareness that we are equal to all others.

Let us show we are worthy of forgiveness and want our place as equals by forgiving our equals.